The Challenges of Transition

The Challenges of Transition

Romania in Transition

by Vladimir Pasti

WITHDRAWN

English Translation by Fraga Cheva Cusin

EAST EUROPEAN MONOGRAPHS, BOULDER
DISTRIBUTED BY COLUMBIA UNIVERSITY PRESS, NEW YORK
1997

EAST EUROPEAN MONOGRAPHS, NO. CDLXXIII

Copyright 1997 by Vladimir Pasti
ISBN 0-88033-370-7
Library of Congress Catalog Card Number 97-60827

Printed in the United States of America

CONTENTS

FOREWORD

Putting this book together was not an easy job. The idea of an analysis that should make the Romanian politics after the December 1989 revolution understandble, by singling out the major economic and social actors, has resulted in a first variant as early as the spring of 1990. Transition was at an embryonic stage at the time, so the book enlarged mainly on the power structures of the former communist society and tried to anticipate their way of reaction to the new environment. It was a "scientific" work, in that it was written in a language not palatable to the common reader and it was stuffed with quantations and bibliographic references that made its reading even more difficult. However, the conclusions regarding the former regime still stand, I believe, and I have included them in the first part of this book. They make the mainstay of the whole book, for one cannot understand what is going on in Romania now, unless one understands the salient features of the former regime.

The analysis proper of the transition was rather technical, once its main actors – technocracy, administration, the private sector and the workers – were identified by their tendencies and characteristics. The Romanian transition has proved remarkable stability in this respect. That same stability made the political analysis too, much easier. The Romanian political parties are unwilling to change, for all alliances, splittings, delimitations and inner dissents. And, above all, in spite of the fact that the reality in which they are so static, is quite the opposite, meaning so very dynamic. The most important consequence of this situation – the gap between politics and reality, which is tantamount to politics' not being involved in the administration of the power, and is manifest especially in a lack of government, is actually the main theme of this first volume. In this respect, the privilege of having been a great deal, on these years of transition, close to and, sometimes, right in the middle of what makes "the power quarters", has helped me get rid of many superstitions and beliefs about the motivation and mechanisms of political decision-making, which a researcher confined to the academic environment is bound to share with public opinion. There are no school-books or bibliograpy to equate such an experience which I hope to be able to communicate to the public through this book. The final image it produces is as disappointing as it probably is disheartening. Romanian culture has credited the political factor with a great deal of national initiative and responsability ever since the Middle Ages, and reality has never ceased to disappoint the Romanians. For all this repeated experience, hopes have been pinned to politicians also after 1989. The Reform – meaning the politically coordinated economic and social change – has focussed, for no justified reason, the attention of all and everyone, both at home and abroad. Consequently, the Romanians have spent almost six years reading and listening to statements and speculating on political "messages".

This book gives but very little attention to the "Reform", because the reform has failed to play a role of consequence within the whole of the changes that have taken place. Instead, it deals far more with the spontaneous transition, meaning the whole of the evolutions of reality that, although having actually occured, have never been included in the political program of any party or politician. Who are the actors of these changes and what makes tick the mechanisms that generate them, these are the questions this first volume is trying to answer in its last part. The result is a history of the transition quite different from the one known and accepted by almost everyone.

No history is complete unless its consequences too, are known. This truth is even more profund for us now, since the analysis of transition is pointless unless it relies on the understanding of the variants of future that lie still within our reach. Therefore, this first volume, dealing with the past and the present, is only a necessary preparation for an approach to the far more difficult problems of the future. It is not only a matter of requirements of the scientific approach. The response of all those who read the manuscript of the first volume was stressfully unisonous: "Well, what next, what's to be done?" The mere analysis seemed perfectly useless to everyone unless it was able to substantiate a future.

Such an approach is a bit too pragmatic for a work which is still meant to be scientific, in spite of the language and of the absence of the traditional annexes. The choice of a future from the possible futures is a matter of applied politics. But, although unable to take the place of politicians as far as the options are concerned, the scientific analysis can single out and describe the probable evolutions. This is the name of the second volume of the book, designed to cover "The Building (Forging) of the Future".

I am indebted to many friends for their generous help with writing this book, the more so as I sometimes had to venture in domains which were less familiar to me. Vasile Secares, Ioan Mircea Pascu and Cornel Codita very patiently explained to me essential aspects of the international background of the events occured prior to and after 1989. But I will take the blame for all possible weak points of the book in this respect. I have learned a lot from Mugur Isarescu about the macro-economy of the transition and I have learned even more from his unique experience as a sociologist applied to one of the most sensitive domains – finance. I would not have been able to properly understand the complex issues of industrial restructuring, had it not been for the support of Dan Dumitru Popescu, Vasile Baltac and academician Constantin Ionete. The understanding of the private economy and of its intricate connections with politics, administration and the public sector of the economy would have been incomplete without the long conversations on the matter with Constantin Iavorski, to whom I am indebted for his ideas and for his help.

I owe much to the debates conducted at the Foundation "A Future for Romania", where I found information, ideas and explanations provided by some of the most lucid-minded connoisseurs of Romanian realities. Gheorghe Onut and Vasile Munteanu criticized with jusitifed severity parts and ideas in this book and helped me improve them, and Hella Bara had the patience to read the manuscript through and come up with useful stylistic suggestions.

A big part of the book was articulated over June-October 1994, when I was in Japan on a scholarship granted by Japan Foundation. The touch with Japanese realities has helped me understand both concepts and essential contents of advanced capitalism, as well as the diversity it can evince. I wish to thank here too, the Japanese experts and businessmen who generously let me share in their knowledge and experience and especially Mr. Kenichi Ito, President of the Japan Forum on International Relation, Inc., who organized the whole study term in Japan.

Last, but not least, this book would have probably remained just a manuscript, like other ones, had it not been for the support of Viorel

Hrebenciuc and the contagious enthusiasm of Valentin Nicolau, owner of the Nemira Publishers– Bucharest and editor of the book, to whom I am indebted and grateful.

Vladimir Pasti ,
September 1995

INTRODUCTION

Any analysis of post-communist transition generally, and of Romania's transition particularly, is bound to start with the understanding of western politics. And that not only because the West acted an important part in triggering the process. But in Romania, just like, in fact, throughout the East-European world, the prevailing idea was that, after the victory over the communist political regimes, the post-communist transition was a job to be accomplished rather by the West than by ourselves. The tremendous popularity enjoyed by the Romanian revolution, shown on Christmas Eve by all television stations around the world, entrenched even more this idea with the Romanians. After Ceausescu's overthrow, the Romanians acted as if they had been victorious and expected their reward from the West. In actual fact, we had lost a war, the cold war and now, instead of waiting for prices, we had to pay the costs of four decades of "straying" on a road which history disproved. However, these things were not clear in the beginning, either in the West or in the East.

1. Adjusment to post-communism

The European communist system exploded in 1989, and advanced capitalism has remained triumphant, to dominate the world and model it to its look and like. Such a future seemed, at least in the first period after the unexpected victory of the anti-communist revolutions, very normal. The prevailing picture both in the East and in the West was very much like the story of the stray son. The communist Eats had returned "home". The peoples had got rid of the communist "heresy", of the small bunch of communist politicians that kept them obedient by using police, special tribunals, camps and, especially with the help of Soviet tanks (which, in the name of communism, were actually serving Russia's imperialism).

The East obviously expected the West to slaughter the fattest calf to honour its comeback. Twenty billion dollars given to Hungary and other forty billion given to Poland to enable them prepare their "liberation" seemed to indicate that the West was ready to pay. The European Union assistance programs (of the PHARE or TACIS type) and the long-term soft credits granted through the IMF and the World Bank and especially the setting up of the European Bank for Reconstruction and Development and the triggering of a speeded-up process of integration of the former communist countries with the West-European structures (from the Council of Europe to NATO), seemed to be as many signals that the West was very serious about its role as the integrator of the newly discovered world.

In the beginning, euphoria and optimism were prevalent also in the West's behavior to the East. Within the balance of forces that had been established between its own camp and Russia, the West was bracing itself to take one more step ahead, by "swallowing", i.e. integrating politically and economically, the medium-sized zone that was called Central Europe (East Germany, Poland, Hungary and Czechoslovakia), the control of which had secured for Russia an important tactical advantage for half a century. Such a policy fitted in the West's traditional policy toward the Soviet Union, namely to get small tactical advantages, by leaning the balance of forces toward it, without however breaking completely the equilibrum forged so painstakingly.

All along the confrontation that followed after the triggering of the cold war, the West wanted and even fought to win small battles, but it was not prepared, either ideologically, politically or economically, to win the war. It did not expect a victory, nor did it know what it could do of it. Even Central and Eastern Europe alone was a bigger bite than what the West was eager to swallow. It had accepted with satisfaction and had even backed the fall of communism in countries like Romania and Bulgaria, just like it had encouraged the defections of the Soviet Union's peripheral republics, like the Baltic republics or Moldova. It assessed the maintenance by the very frontier of the Soviet Union of West-oriented political regimes to be an important tactical advantage. But to have them too, integrated in the newly projected European Community was not only difficult but seemingly impossible. It was not only about a less interesting, more remote zone and, culturally more difficult, especially because of its Orthodox faith. The zone was also economically more backward and, above all, too big. East Germany's integration with West Germany was fairly indicative of the extent of the effort and resources required by a process of integration. Therefore, the European West, mainly Germany which was to act the main part in the region, on the one hand, and had to pay for most of the bill on the other hand, were trying to divide the zone by sub-regions and to phase-out the expansion of the West to the East as much as possible. But, whereas in terms of resources they were giving obvious priority to the immediate zone of integration – the Vishegard group countries -, they did not make any distinction among zones as regarded the manner of approaching the post-communist transition. Ideological approach was prevalent in all cases.

Although articulated in a hurry in the West that was dominated by the late '80s American "Reaganism", it was espoused also in the East. And that not only because the ideological pressure put up by the West was too hard and the political legitimacy offered by it was indispensable for any construction in the East. But anyway, the East did not have an alternative of its own, nor did it have something to build on. "Perestroika", with its variants, had proved to be a failure. Reformist communists had been pushed aside by the winds of change stirred by their own reforms. The new political leaders did not avail of a strategy of transition or of a theory that would have allowed them to try one, but they displayed a lot of geniality, enjoyed sizeable popular support to the accomplishment of such a transition and expected the West to come up with the solution complete with help.

The project of transition was built upon what Galbraith termed "simplist ideology". Some words – and objectives – were more than axiomatic, they were deemed sacred even for the economic change – private property, free enterprise, free market, competition and so on. This situation repeated itself also with politics, where phrases like multi-party system, freedom of expression, free elections, "entering Europe", had – and they still have – the same touch of infallibility as the basic principles of a new religion. Unfortunately, all these concepts and principles, at least in the form they have been promoted both in the West and in the East, have been employed to create some sort of upside-down communist ideology.

In the end, the realistic economic and political actions, relying on bases far sounder than the strictly ideological ones, prevailed. They have crystalized two types of action by the West in the relation with the East, differing but complementary in nature. One is an integration based on the extension of a metropolitan country to the integrated zone. The way how Federal Germany integrated East Germany is the purest example.

Something similar, but at a different scale, is what is happening with the Czech Republic. Actually, this type of integration needs no theory or specific model. It consists of the mere extension of the metropole to a territory and a population that were first "cleared" as much as possible of all historical, cultural and social peculiarities introduced by the half a century of communist regime.

As this cannot be done with the other East-European countries, their integration is far more restrictive in nature, more similar to a colonization. It mainly consists of the taking over by bigger or smaller Western companies of East-European enterprises, or resources, or activities, etc., as an immediate consequence of the processes of privatization and attraction of foreign investments. In this case, the "colonization" only requires that the host country endorse the needed legislation and build the fit logistic, industrial and financial infrastructure for the functioning of such "colonies". But, although the effect is not similar to that of development, the "colonization" leads to the attainment of at least one of the purposes of the East-European revolutions: their economic integration in the world system.

Other effects of the opening of new zones for colonization, at a time when capitalism had adjusted to a final and closed world, are hard to forecast in their entirety, but they are undoubtedly expected to be consequential. Some countries, like Germany, France, Britain seem, here and there, to be reopening the dusty files of their turn-of-the century policies, but now they are starting from the bases of a technological, financial and miltary superiority that is incomparably greater than at that early stage. On the other hand, one more force, more coherent and sometimes more efficient than the governments, come in now: the multinational corporations. Too weak a century ago to have been able to play a really important role, they are now more powerful than many of the governments or states in whose colonization they have started to show an interest. Their behavior is not even. One behaves in one way in the "civilized" markets of the West and in another, quite different way in the world lacking rules and coherence, of the East. Hence, their ever stronger tendency to revert to the questionable ways and ethics of colonization, with all its arsenal of graft, unfair competition, military intervention, encouragement of smuggling and organized crime, fiscal shelter and dishonest financial arrangements. At any rate, this triggers with the "colonized" ones reactions and consequences that bring back to the memory, at least partially, Latin America with its troublesome transition to capitalism.

The East-European problem remains a pending and important problem for the victorious capitalism. It is not only a theory that misses but also its basis, an approach that is, for the settlement of this problem. Never has capitalism been faced with a more important challenge than this one. If, after its triumph over communism decides to turn former socialist into some kind of third world in the middle of Europe, it will mean to it a just as heavy defeat as the one sustained by communism. Having brought communism to its knees means only half a victory to capitalism. It has yet to prove that it can succeed where communism failed, meaning in the economic and social development of East Europe.

For, none of these already tried attitudes and approaches results in the promotion of developed capitalism in the East; quite the opposite, they lead to the building of some sort of European "third world". Sure, it does not have the same features in East Germany, which West Germany is striving at tremendous costs to make avoid precisely this fate, as it has happened in Romania, Bulgaria or Ukraine. The Czech Republic, Hungary, maybe Poland, the more developed countries of the former socialist camp, evince a tendency to blend third-world features with features of the developed West-European world. It depends on which side of the apple you look at. For, what matters in the end is the economic and financial infrastructure and the other, social and cultural infrastructure, on which the former two rest. And the infrastructures are tending to grow, in all these countries, including the former Germany, after a model similar to the one that turned southern Italy into a part of the third world, after the salient features of underdevelopment.

Anyway, the process of integration of East Europe had already started when the Soviet Union too, exploded in 1991. Faced with the disaster of the communist system, the Russian leaders made two extreme decisions, so daring they seemed incredible. First, they decided to give up their own peripheries, the host of technologically, socially and financially backward southern republics the maintenance of which took Russia an effort it was no longer willing to make. All history and experience of the West after World War Two had proved that a zone of economic, financial and military dominance was infinitely cheaper and more efficient than a zone of occupation. And Russia, the last of the world's big colonizers, abruptly decided to give up that obsolete and inefficient structure – the colonial empire, several decades after Great Britain and France.

The other decision, even more consequential, was to give up communism itself. Russia's renunciation of communism seemd surprising, although it was foreseeable years before and had become necessary after the East-European countries had done it, with Russia's blessing. However, the abolition of communism in Russia, took everyone by surprise, even the Russians. The East and the West alike were simply unable to anticipate the next move.

Russia's entering this process has dwarfed and rendered immaterial all the big issues of the small East-European countries. It was for the first time now that the process of passage from communism to capitalism was defined with its true dimensions. The chiefly financial approach the developed West had conveniently made to the post-communist transition has proved to be insufficient. If West Germany's experience with the formerly communist Germany was telling, then it was clear that the whole developed West – including Japan and the developed zone of the Pacific, did not have money enough to "pay" for Russia's development and switch to capitalism. And it was very clear that Russia could not be simply let collapse, an option that seemed to gain ground in the more rebellious cases of the transition: Romania, Bulgaria, Yugoslavia, etc. And, for nobody to have any doubt about it, Russia has been keen on emphasizing over and over again that the alternative to its success would be world disaster instead of a comfortable remaking of the world's balance with an underdeveloped Russia that has given up its status as a big power. But, since 1991 to this day, the West's failures with modelling the transition in the East have never ceased. More than aby other former communist country, Russia was the clear proof that the passage to "capitalism" had reached a blind alley. That was bound to affect not only Russia but the West as well, and all the other former communist countries that were now witnessing powerlessly the changing of priorities to their disadvantage and for the benefit of the two giants now focussing the undivided attention and the bulk of the Western resources – Russia and China. The West's answer to this tremendous complication of the primary problem of the integration is "adjustment to post-communism".

Adjustement to post-communism is actually the way in which both the East and the West are substituting the achievement of genuine and complete integration with an action on the minimal resistance line, meaning to respond gradually to the changes post-communism would bring to national and European realities and to adjust to them. It is a pragmatic attitude resulting first from the absence of a project and, second, from the difficulty of achieving it. To the West, the adjustment to post-communism is the consequence of the failure of the initial enthusiasm (ebullience), full of grand projects for sui generis European constructions. Germany's reunification was their only part that came true. Yogoslavia'a never-ending war, Czechoslovakia's splitting, the chaotic decomposition of the USSR, the Italian crisis and the reactuation of the national minorities' problems are the deplorable debris of other projects.

The Yugoslav war is obviously the best illustration of the problem and of the evolution of the West's attitude to the East. The fact that the West did not want the war but it however made an essential contribution to its ignition, betrays naivety and incoplete appraisal of the real state of things in the East. And its inability to stop it afterwards is the peremptory proof of the West's ineffectual approach to the East-European problems. The major preoccupation of the West now has become to prevent its extension, on the one hand, and to do almost everything to stop it. Whcih proves that the West has given up the big projects and turned to a more realistic, less ambitious and generally rather defensive policy.

Faced with the tremendous complex of new problems and unprecedented situations brought about by the collapse of the East-European communism, the West has found itself in the position of the apprentice wizard. Except that there is no master to get him out of the mess. The solution endorsed in the end is to accept any formula that can allay its worries and press a lid on a zone that is seething with growing problems. When, after the revival of a primitive imperialism in an empoverished Russia confused by the "reform", the US President publicly states that the reforms in East Europe ought maybe to proceed at a slower pace and accept intermediate forms of economy, between the "market economy" and the socialist one, this can only mean that the West proclaims its readiness to accept any solution for East Europe that should reduce the problems instead of aggravating them, while allowing for an approximate integration of the region. This more realistic stand of the West toward its own expectations and requirements addressed to the former communist countries however has also its reverse side. The West is now adopting a new position vis-a-vis the East – the political evolution in Russia and the war in Yugoslavia have counted a lot in its adoption – characterized and legitimated by several towering ideas. One of them is that the problem of the East belong mainly to the East and it has to settle them by itself. The added touch here is that the West will back these efforts, but it does not imply more than a minimal presence, in form or financial aid and, possibly, political-economic assistance of the kind of the Most Favored Nation Status or a gradual, long-term association to the European Union's economic, political and security structures.

The other one refers to the fact that the transition from communism to psot-communism is a complex and long process the acceleration of which is curbed by the stress imposed on the population by the reform measures. This idea, no matter how commonsensical it may seem, means nothing but putting in polite terms the dooming of the formerly socialist world, that should become a third world, maybe of a new type. It entails also the conclusion that the West will pose less radical requirements to the East, but also that it will not consider these countries as "normal" countries for still a long time to come. The third idea is that transition, as a complex process, must still allow the existence of intermediate forms between the two types of societies, both at an economic and social level, and at a political level.

So, the West is drawing back from East Europe, first by giving up the idea of its integration and by replacing this objective with the limited objective of surviving near it in the best of conditions. Or, better said, with the objective of letting the East survive as it can. Soon enough after the 1989 revolutions, the West has confined its ambitions to backing the transition oriented to the exterior. The other transition, the one meant for internal transformation, it leaves completely up to the East, so completely that it may not matter if it is not implemented at all. Whereas in the beginning, right after 1989, the West seemed worried by the possibility of such a failure, now it does no longer worry. By giving up the promotion of "recipes", by giving up the pressure for deadlines, measures and a radical character of the reforms, by accepting one by one not only the expertise and motivation of the natives but also their options with regard to internal changes, the West is issuing the clear message that the countries of East Europe will be what they are able to turn themselves into, all by themselves.

Starting 1993, with the ready acceptance of the victory of the Left in Poland, repeated in Hungary the next year, and of Yeltsin's dictatorship in Russia, the West is virtually giving up the drive for modelling domestic evolutions in the formerly communist East. What it still wants is its adjustment, even if differentiated, only to allow for international integration. Moreover, it is willing to adjust its own structures for the purpose, to extend the NATO, gradually and in a differentiated manner, to have the former communist bloc associated with the European Union, in the same stagewise way, and, generally, to find compromises allowing for the control of possible crises. Annoyed by the apparent resistance to settlement of the East's problems, concerned with its own problems – some of them generated precisely by the East-European revolutions – by the middle of the decade, the West seems rather preoccupied with defining for itself a new zone of prime interest in the Pacific, where the success is emerging from local characteristics and which seems to be developing into the new weight center of world economy and finance.

To the East generally, and to Romania which is our prime concern, the most important consequence is that the responsibility of the transition is now devolving not only to a great extent but completely to them. The idea that the West will not only finance, but in the end will push somehow, even pressing, the East-European countries on the way to development, is now obvioulsy false. Romania, which was anyway only peripheral, even in the West's most ambitious projects, must be the more aware of the fact that its future depends only on itself. It will get minimal financial, economic and political assistance, smaller or bigger, contingent upon the evolution of the strategic situation in the region. But the rest will depend only and solely on what will be happening on an internal plane, on how much it will understand its own transition and will be able to harness it.

2. The two transitions

Getting rid of communism was the East-European societies' response to the pressure of prevalently external factors. Even though for some of them mattered also significant domestic disfunctions – as was the case of the Catholic Church in Poland, most often even those were the mediated result of external pressures.

The most important external pressure was not political, but economic and financial. During the '70s and '80s, the developed West managed to build a world economic system the nucleus of which was the group of twenty or thirty advanced states, they too, stratified. Nucleus means that here the fundamental rules of world trade, hence of influences, of world production, are being established in the nucleus.

The communist bloc, which had managed that far to avoid a direct economic confrontation with the developed nucleus of capitalism, was gradually adsorbed into the world economic system. Or, its big industrial, commercial and distribution structures were completely inadequate to the rules and structures which the new world system was imposing with a strength which the communist bloc was unable to resist. The cause lay precisely inside it. As it developed, the communist industrial system grew increasingly dependent on its external ties, on its capacity to export finished goods in order to import the raw materials it needed so as to keep the installations and enterprises in operation.

Such a dependence was normal and was no reason of surprise. It had always existed and the communist bloc tried to cope with it in the "traditional" way in which any industrial bloc would try to settle the problem of supply with raw materials and of finding outlets: by building some sort of semi-colonial system. Just like the developed capitalist bloc, the communist bloc tried to single out a certain sector of the third world, defined by a lavishness of raw materials and scarcity of manufactured goods, that should make a safe, controlled market, acceptable as regarded the raw materials and also providing safe outlets for its industrial goods. That is how the "socialist" third world came into being, as a zone of political and economic influence of the communist bloc. This zone obviously interfered with the zone of the capitalist bloc and it was for its control that the main battles of the cold war were fought.

The capitalist world's faster development was a major handicap for the communist bloc in the competition with the capitalist one. Being unable to employ in that cheifly economic battle chiefly economic barriers, the communist bloc employed especially the political ones. The major economic relations were thus secured by primarily political relations, the most simple method being to conditions the military and political support, indispensable for the maintenance of a certain political regime, baptized "socialist" for the purpose, upon the priority granted in economic relations. Naturally, that was conducive to engulfing this zone, in its entirety, into the sphere of inefficiency, or of inferior efficiency, of the communist-type economy. The more marked this difference of efficiency between the two economic blocs was growing, the more expensive it was for the third world to remain inside the communist economic bloc and the bigger the pressure indirectly put on it.

But, although having lost the battle for the third world, the world of convenient economic resources and outlets, a battle that was of tremendous consequnece for the striking of an overall balance adverse to the communist bloc, it was first of all at home that it actually lost the war. For, the main weakness of the communist industrial system was not its inability to secure stable markets for raw materials and for its industrial goods, but the dependence on the developed nucleus of the capitalist economy if it was to secure even its simple industrial reproduction.

One of the less conspicuous things was that the whole communist industrial system was entirely imported from capitalism. Moreover, it was completely dependent upon the trade with developed capitalism in order to be able to reproduce itself, i.e. to be able to function. It was that dependence that forced implacably the communist economic bloc to participate in the world economic system and to willy-nilly accept the rules of the economic game set in the industrial centers of developed capitalism. From that moment on, communism was already defeated economically, since, like I said before, its economic, industrial, managerial structures did in no way match the structures of this world system. The result was obviously an exchange always made to the disadvantage of the communist economic system. Such a "mismatch" is bound to operate like a vacuum cleaner (suction pump) as, on the one hand, it pumps resources into the nucleus of the system, and, on the other hand, it pumps an even bigger "mismatch" back to the place wherefrom it was sucked, thus disbalancing the exchanges even more.

For a while, the communist system showed willing to pay, which naturally resulted in expensive imports and cheap exports, with the deficit balance of payments with the developed capitalist nucleus having to be compensated from other resources than the industrial ones. In absolutely all socialist countries, in various degrees though, one of the sources was curbing the people's consumption. Which, of course, meant a system of contra-propaganda to the official pro-communist propaganda, even more efficient than anything the pro-West radio stations could air.

Other sources differed from one country to another. Russia, for instance, tried, and did manage for some time, to compensate that permanent deficit by exports of unprocessed raw materials. In the '70s and

'80s Romania used for the purpose financial credits got from the international market, turning to advantage a congenial conjuncture and its political position as a Maverick in relation to the Soviet tutellage. But none of those sources could account for a system, a mechanism with continuous and stable operation apt to allow for the survival of the socialist industrial system.

The main cause was that it was increasingly less consistent with the world economic system from which it had still to derive its survival. When the mismatch became big enough, communism broke down, first and above anything else, as an industrial system. Two important things require attention at this moment.

First of all, the fact that the necessary changes for the formerly communist countries' economic integration with the world economic system are vast and complex and they require not only economic adjustment but also concomitant and sizeable political and cultural adjustments. New political mechanisms, new relations between the state administration and the population, as well as between the former and the economy, a new decision-making system in the economy and in industry and new relations and criteria of distribution of the resources and incomes, all these changes have to be achieved for the formerly socialist world to be able to integrate with the economic and political system built by the developed West for the whole world. If we are to consider the starting point, meaning the characteristics of the East-European communist societies, then the whole of these changes fully justifies the name of revolution for their global description. What is more difficult to accept is the idea that all these major internal changes mean only an adjustment to the exterior world.

To accept this idea, we must understand that the kind of integration entailed by this new world economic system differs in its essence from the one in existence until the last quarter of the 20th century. It can no longer be confined to a mere cooperation between two countries – what could be termed as exchanges between "national economies". The ties it requires are far more initmate, they entail more profound mutual involvement, hence also a similar legislative, institutional and bahavioral framework. It is from this that results the necessity of changes, not only economic, but also political, cultural and legislative, in the East-European countries. An economy like Romania's cannot be integrated in this European and world economic system unless it allows for a flow and, possibly, for a steady transfer in every domain (financial, material, technology, knowledge, people, etc.). And this mutual transfer, in order to be possible, requires not only similar statuses of property, of the freedom to move and decide in relation to the administration and governments or other factors, but also a certain political and legislative integration as defined, for instance, by the terms of association with the European Community.

The other conclusion, maybe even more important that the first one, is that all this revolution of adjustment to the exterior world, in spite of its vast and complex character, does not cover all aspects of the transition. Even if no domain of the political, social, economic, cultural life, is entirely ignored – from political democracy, the status of property and of foreign investments up to environmental protection policies and to social or medical assistance (health care) systems – still, none of these domains is changed in all its aspects. On the contrary, they are all adjusted only in one respect: the requirements of the external system. Every detail referring to the second group of essential necessities of all sub-systems in a society, the strictly domestic ones, remain indefinite.

So, here we are, facing at once not a single transition, but a double one. On the one hand, there is a transition oriented to the exterior, with the objective of turning the formerly socialist Romanian society into a society apt to adjust itself to the European and world systems that are just coming into being at this end of a century. It is a complex and difficult transition which, like we have seen, requires changes in all domains. Here, we have the benefit of a Western guide that, although not always very clear, is, in turn, coordinated by the very characteristic of the existing international system. Where the guidance is missing, we still have the model before our eyes. Here too, we enjoy substantive support. All assistance programs extended by the West, from the humanitarian and ecological ones to those meant for administrative and political restructuring or reform, are meant only and solely for this external integration. Which is only natural. This transition oriented to the exterior just has to be done. But, while doing it, we must not for a moment forget about the other one. Since we have to accomplish one more transition, this time oriented to the interior.

Romania wishes, frequently and unanimously states it: to integrate with the European system which is about to come into being around the European Union. For that, it has already committed itself to change its own structures and isntitutions in such a way as to have them "fit" the European ones. Let this aside, it still has to establish what kind of European society it wishes to grow into. And to develop the second transition, oriented to the interior, to turning the "European" Romanian society into one that should resemble the model it has chosen.

Here, with this other, interior-oriented transition, we have the benefit of neither models nor technical assistance. We only have the right or possiblity to make an option, but this is a questionable advantage as long as we do not seem to be very aware of the need to use them. There would be one more advantage, at least as questionable as the one mentioned before. The advantage of not accomplishing any second transition at all. There is no special external pressure to this end. There are some internal pressures, most of them put up by the population, but they are diffuse and wanting in precision, since the necessity of this second transition is not consciously felt at either the economic ot the political level. Actually, it is rather felt as an absence of the other one, of the former transition, and the simplest solution is to take it for its normal cost. This helps one not to bother and find out what is missing.

Like about any other country in the East, one can say about Romania that it is giving up the completion of the revolution which it has started (or rather, which it has made possible by overthrowing the communist political regime). It is only too little aware of the road opened at home and is wasting most of its efforts to adjust its internal structures to the necessary external requirements. Adding to this, as a second component, is the childish objective of winning an imaginary competition with the other East-European countries in the domain of the "reform".

The adjustment to the European system is the main purpose of the reform. This is what focusses also the West's support and pressure and, at least in this case, there is a clear direction of the change and some coherence, imposed rather by the coherence of the model than by the clear understanding of the objective. But even this coherence is limited. Since, most often, its objectives are superficially defined, as a mere resemblance to or reproduction of the West's familiar structures, from private property to local autonomy or individual rights, from political institutions to TV shows or luxury shops. Romania seems determined to adjust itself to post-communism, by imitating Western forms, patterns and regulations. Once borrowed in the Romanian society, they go through essential changes. A part, the most superficial one, which is most deeply involved in the adjustment to the West, the part of pure communication with similar or corresponding forms of the exterior world, remains mainly unaltered. But the other one, oriented to the interior, goes through essential changes of functionality. It is adjusting itself to internal realities and, instead of changing them, it starts to contribute to their reproduction.

All these forms, regulations, patterns are institutions of societies far more developed than Romania's. However, their introduction into Romania does not generate development. This profoundly wrong belief of the Romanian politicians and ideologists is surprisingly resistant. It reminds of a generally human behavior which is rather primitive precisely for this reason. Somewhere, in one of the isles of the South that hosted an American military basis, the native noticed that the Americans were taking all kind of goodies out of the friges. As the American left, they built wooden replicas of the refrigerators and were baffled and disappointed to see that no goodies would grow up inside them the way it happened with the American refrigerators. The illusion that the transfer of western forms to Romania is enough to accomplish the transition sounds like the aboriginals' frige story and the sooner we give it up the better.

This does not mean we should no longer import Western forms. They are necessary first of all in order to secure the integration with the international economic, political and strategic system. But we must not expect them to produce more than that. Then, we must focus on the internal transition, on development that is. This is the point. External transition, i.e. the integration with the international structures, mechanisms and flows, is far from complete. However, the main landmarks have been laid. More difficult and later, Romania has however been accepted to the international community and it has managed to operate the most important of the necessary changes for that. From now on, the way how the international integration proceeds is greatly dependent on the country's domestic features and on the evolution of the other transition, the interior-oriented one, rather than on the international political-diplomatic game. And this second transition requires more profound, more coherent and concentrated changes than so far. But they don't come of their own accord and, like we have seen, they will not be implemented or imposed by others for us either.

The society we are living in now is not a development-orientented one. Most of its fundamental structures and mechanisms are those of the former socialist society the development of which stopped around the beginning of the '80s. The changes after the revolution have altered many features of these structures and mechanisms. But the result has not been the beginning of development. Most of the changes have been only meant to allow sui generis forms of the old structure to multiply. And in some cases they forced them back into an even more remote time. In an era when the post-industrial society is regarded as a reality which is already growing obsolete, one of the steadiest characteristics of the spontaneous changes and adjustments taking place in Romania is to generate features specific to pre-industrial societies. Irrespective of their name, they are typical of underdevelopment. Their main source lays in the economy, but they develop correspondents also in politics, social structures, behaviors and even in domains that seemed to have definitely gone past that stage, such as the domain of education. And now, all these components are mutually supporting and stimulating, dragging us deeper and deeper into underdevelopment. If the spontaneous transition goes on, if fast and firm action is not taken in order to shape the interior-oriented transition with the direct objective of imposing development, Romania's fate might be decided for many years from now on. Since this tendency has already been entrenched and all it needs to become a fact that everybody should continue to do waht they have done so far, then it is the most probable.

But there is also a chance to avoid underdevelopment. It might come precisely from the fact that, although kept at the fringes for the time being, Romania is rejecting the periphery, out of national pride and out of the vanity prompted by its bèing still the biggest country of the South-East. Another chance can result from the freedom of movement which Romania seems to avail of for the first time throughout its history, still not engulfed as it is in any clear zone of influence. Finally, Romania's chances might be enhanced by a change of attitude. This might happen if, tired of repeating to all big powers of the developed world how important it is due to its strategic upperhand and to its potential, in a hope to be able to have them convinced that it is in their own interest to subsidise its failures, Romania makes up its mind to capitalize on these potential advantages. Almost like never before in history, the turning of a potential chance into a real chance depends only on two aparently simple things: the knowledge of one's own reality and the ability to turn this knowledge into the base of a coherent action for development.

The purpose of this book is to propose the building, for Romania and for its people, of a future that should not be like the one prefigured by the tendencies of the realities stabilized these last five years. The basic requisite is to change these realities, that are unpleasant and undesirable. This book is not addressed to those who feel pleased with themselves and with the world that has grown around them.

Sure, you cannot project a future unless you understand the present and a great deal of the past. Therefore, a first part of the book is an anlaysis of the present and of its short history of coming into being from the ruins of the former regime. This part is not the most important though. Far more important is the last part, which elaborates on what ought Romania to try and how. The road proposed here is not a discovery, it is an invention. It rests on a string of options that are, in turn, based on values which the author thinks should make the foundation of the new society that would be built. Different options, based on different values, will lead to another road and another society. A package of suc options are already in operation, because the present society does not resemble the one which is proposed by this book, nor will it ever come to resemble, unless major changes are wrought. But, options and assets are, like their very name shows, a matter of choice, of preference and, ultimately, of interests, either personal, group or national. And this choice has to be made by everyone individually, of course, after he has decided to do something.

I. THE FAILURE OF INFERNAL TRANSITION

1. Optimism of disaster

The writing of this book was prompted by the discontent with the way how the internal transition proceeded and, above all, with its results. The discontent is not singular. If we are to take opinion polls for granted, most Romanians are dissatisfied. They are dissatisfied with what has happened to the country's economy after the revolution. They are dissatisfied with the fact that most of the population has been impoverished and is living now even worse, in some cases, than before the revolution. More people are eating less now, although the shops are full, but they simply cannot afford the food they need. There are more children who do not go to schools and an increasing number of children and youth will from now on abandon school at an earlier age, meaning they will be less educated than the previous generations. The old persons who can no longer afford any kind of recreation and whose pensions are just enough for a bread-line living become more numerous. There are more and more sick people who can no longer pay for an absolutely necessary medical treatment. And there are more and more adults who don't have a job, who don't have the means to provide for themselves and for their families.

On the other hand, almost all bad phenomena and things have grown. Crime has grown, the city streets are increasingly insecure and new offences, unconceivable in the pre-revolution Romania, have emerged: drugs and criminals carrying fire arms. Corruption with the administration and economic managers has grown to the point of turning from an exception into the golden rule of business success. Health care services have deteriorated instead of improving, medicines are still in short supply in hospitals, patients are not properly looked after and their food is inadequate, for all the aid and philanthropic actions the community of developed countries has lavished on Romania. Diseases we used to think of as gone for ever have reappeared in the country, like malaria, caused by the degradation of the environment, while other ones are being caused by the recurring malnutrition and the permanent deterioration of the conditions of public hygiene. The cities keep being dirty, full of pits, inadequately supplied with electricity, water and heat, and public services, from posts and telephone to transport and public order are still below minimal European standards, although their prices have sky-rocketed these last five years. And, as a symbol of it all, the buildings under construction in 1989 have not been finished to this day.

Yet, official optimism is spreading all over. Rulers have been optimistic at all times and under all regimes and they have chosen to see primarily the full half of the bottle, full of achievements that is. The political speech delivered to the eldermen of Troy by young Paris more than three millennia ago stands proof that official optimism has always existed, even on the verge of disaster. Only few people are remembering now Ceausescu's speech delivered at the last congress of the Romanian Communist Party. Only a month before the revolution that would sweep away the extant political regime, its head and symbol was overlay optimistic, at least when he was addressing the others. Romania's post-revolution governments have been no exception in this respect. They have always enthusiastically listed the achievements. They have even sometimes termed as such things which, before the respective speech, we would have been rather inclined to see as failures. They have termed them as "surgical interventions" in the process of transformation of the society – painful indeed, but things that were just bound to be worse before getting better. To get in Paradise, it seems that the Romanians have first to go through Purgatory.

The optimism of balance-sheets is overlapped by the even greater optimism of the look into the future. At least once in every six months, the incumbent prime minister or, sometimes, the whole Cabinet, use to address the population, announcing that very soon, right from the next quarter of the year sometimes, the much waited for economic recovery will start. Every time, official statistics convince us that it is just around the corner, and experts can already perceive the gladdening signs of the revigoration although, in the everyday life, the positive effects will show a little later.

Obviously, with all these speeches, the rulers want to convince the population that they have ruled well, that achievements exist and these achievements will soon materialize in benefits for the ruled ones. Such attitude on the rulers' part must not come as a surprise. But, every time, a big part of the population has believed these speeches and these pink pictures of the situation. The basic idea of the man in the street, after having listened to such a speech made on TV or in front of the Parliament, is that things are not that bad after all, see, something has been done and it will be far more better soon. This lenient attitude of the taxpayer does not prove the rulers' credibility, much that they would like to believe it. It only shows how willing are the people to be able to hope, to confidently look to a better future, if not very soon, at least reasonably soon. To escape the troubles of the present, some take refuge in the past. Following their rulers, the Romanians choose to take refuge in the future.

It is not an easy thing since, of course, the official optimism has every time been denied by reality. This however has not discouraged the rulers' optimism and the people's confidence in them. Both the incumbent rulers and the rulers in the Opposition. They are rulers, all of them, but, of course, their sermons differ. Whereas the rulers that rule emphasize the achievements and make of them the base for future hopes, the rulers that oppose emphasize the failures and make of them the base for a future which, they too, see pink, meaning their switch from the opposition to rule. Either of them state the same good intentions and especially the same objectives, expressing the confidence that they are able to accomplish the objectives and the belief that "the others" are unable to do so, either out of incompetence or out of ill intention, if not even both. These objectives which, put together, make up the recipe of happiness of all and everyone in Romania, are not different from the objectives of the previous rulers. They entail the application of the same measures that had failed before and roughly the same explanations for the failure.

In October 1991, on taking over, Theodor Stolojan proclaimed the "zero growth" as his government's main objective. The zero growth, meaning the absence of any economic growth is hardly an achievement one can take pride in and only rarely have the governments set it as the ultimate target of their economic policy. But for an economy that had marked a decline in its gross product by more than one third in two years, stopping the production decline would have been an important achievement. On the other hand, the Stolojan Government was only an intermediate, "stand-by" government. Its only mission was to pave the way for the new government, resulted from the 1992 autumn elections, that would start the real economic growth. So, for political and propaganda reasons and since in its form of "zero economic decline" the objective was even less appealing, Stolojan articulated the concept of "zero economic growth" and it sold.

This conceptual novelty was the only real gain, because the economy went on declining. One year after that, the Vacaroiu Government, that would have started with the pink period of positive economic growth

according to the strategy devised under the Stolojan governance, endorsed the objective of "zero economic growth" as the main target of its
"new" economic strategy (which consisted mainly of the application of
the measures which the Stolojan government had started but was unable to complete before the elections). In the two years of rule after
September 1992, the attainment of that famous level of zero economic
growth was several times announced by official statistics. Moreover,
striking comparison now with the previous months and then with similar periods of the previous year, and other subterfuges which economic
statistics never gets tired of finding, the rulers did manage from time to
time to leave the impression that something really started to grow after
all. It was not always about the same indicator: sometimes it was industrial production, at other times it was export, or a decrease of the trade
deficit and so on. Anyway, that could produce the impression that signs
of an improvement appeared at last in some domains. However, at least
so far, the "Stolojan" objective has surely not been attained.

In the end, it is sure to be accomplished. It is impossible that an
economy should shrink infinitely. Like a stone thrown into a well is
bound to reach its bottom, no matter how long its fall, an economy too,
is bound to decline up to a level where the decrease in no longer possible and then any movement will take the reverse course. Even for an
economy going through a dramatic crisis like Romania's now, there
comes a time when a further drop of production is no longer possible,
be it even for the reason that it is producing so little. It is at that moment
that the much expected "zero growth" is reached, but it surely means no
achievement at all. Nor does this means that the economy has reached a
fine starting point, a spring board wherefrom the reverse process, of
endless development is just bound to be launched.

The Economic Crisis

We must abandon official optimism, give up the idle, groundless
hope that things will somehow get straight of their own accord, and
face instead the reality that now, five years after the December 1989
revolution, Romania has not settled any of the problems that caused the
collapse of the previous regime. It has even aggravated some of them
and has added new ones. The current economic crisis is just an extension of the pre-revolution economic crisis. Romania keeps being faced

with a chronical energy crisis. True, there is no more electricity shut-off for people's homes in winter time, or even in summer time when water supply in the storage lakes of the hydro-electric power plants decreases too much. But, the main reason is not that the electricity production has sensibly grown. The decline in industrial production resulted in a lower consumption of electricity in the economy. And no consequential step has been taken toward solving the energy issue. The thermo-electric power plants, especially those fuelled with coal, still operate improperly. The Cernavoda atomic electric power plant, a project inherited from the former regime, has not been commissioned yet, even partially. The problems of heat and hot water production and distribution in cities obtain. Homes are still cold in winter time, hot water still runs according to a time-table, and the cities' drinking water problems have grown after the revolution instead of finding a solution.

The energy problem still exists. True, it has somewhat changed features. To a great extent, for the reasons shown above, it no longer appears in the form of chronical electricity and heat shortage, but in the new form of very high costs of energy. The price of electricity has grown several times over since the revolution, and all these price rises make the prices of industrial goods balloon to the point of becoming impossible to sell.

Energy shortage was not the only crisis the former regime had on its hand. The technological crisis was at least just as important. Much of the Romanian industry had been technologically renewed in the '60s – '70s, thanks to impressive efforts of investment. Even though that renewal did not follow a well established program of priorities and did not mean the acquisition of the state of arms technology of those years, it meant a lot to the Romanian economy and allowed for an economic growth. By the end of the '80s and throughout the '90s there was no more technological renewal. The technologies bought two decades ago are outdated and some are also worn out. Moreover, their degradation started right in the '80s, because of the pressure put for replacing imports with autochthonous solutions even when it meant technical improvisation and sizeable deterioration of parameters. After the revolution, the technological renewal has been considered as an immediate priority. At least in words, the need for new technologies has been central to speeches, programs and debates. After five years of speeches, the rate of technological change is discouraging. Romania has kept spending most of the resources, including money borrowed from abroad, on maintaining in operation the extant technologies, setting aside extremely little for their updating or for buying new ones. And when that did happen, the buy was clumsy enough for the results to be at least doubtful. Two examples can be telling in this respect. One has become famous, as some tried to make a political scandal of it: the modernisation of the TAROM fleet through the acquisition of new planes of the Airbus and Boeing type. Well, the company is now on the verge of bankruptcy. The other case is the case of the Midia refinery which, after having updated and completed its technology, has come to top the list of enterprises waiting for the restructuring, as it is not only unable to pay for its investment but it cannot even operate any longer unless it takes new loans.

The economic crisis is caused to a certain extent also by a management crisis. Romanians did not even know such a crisis could exist until they found out that enterprises that ought to survive were on the brink of bankruptcy or were still in operation only because they refused to pay their earlier debts all while sinking deeper into the new indebtedness. As a rule, a management crisis with a company or enterprise should be settled by changing the managers, but a nation-wide management crisis cannot be settled because there are no new managers. Coping with such a crisis would take the re-education of the incumbent managers and the beginning of mass and systematic education of new, young managers. None of this is actually happening, so the managerial crisis will keep playing havoc with the economy and mainly with industry.

So many times has it been repeated that the Romanian economy is characterized by a productivity utterly inferior to any European or advanced standards that another mention of the fact would mean one too many. Yet, two aspects deserve being mentioned. The productivity crisis in the Romanian economy, especially in industry, emerged and grew under the former regime. Post-revolution Romania has inherited and aggravated it. Only one thing has declined in Romania more than industrial production and that is labor productivity. Some of the causes of productivity decline may be claimed as being political in nature. They might, but I do not think it matters. I do not believe we should deem the explanation above the result. The result is that this labor productivity crisis continues and has even grown worse and five years of post-revolution reforms have not made things any better. The same can be said of the quality crisis that goes with the other crises in the economy. The old regime had conducted a deliberate policy of lessening the quality of certain consumer goods in order to curb the rise in their prices or not to need to import raw and auxiliary materials and parts. After the revolution that policy stopped, the import of higher-quality components has grown but the products' quality has not followed suit. It has even declined in some cases. True, these quality failures are no longer caused or can no longer be blamed on the absence of imports. Only now has it become obvious that they are the result of all the other crises mentioned so far: obsolete and poorly performing technologies, management deficiencies, low productivity and undisciplined manpower, etc.

Industry surely suffers from more diseases than I have shown here in order to demonstrate that, five years after the revolution, we are still faced with the same problems that Ceausescu too, had unsuccessfully tried to solve. It is the same with agriculture, transport and trade, including foreign trade, with the financial system. The fact that the former political regime was overthrown and Ceausescu (which is just a name for a larger group of political leaders) is no longer running the policy and the economy alike, has brought nothing new either in the approach to or in the settlement of these problems. We are none the closer now to their settlement than we were in December 1989. If we expected the political victory of December 1989 to be followed by tremendous changes in the economy, our expectations have only partly come true. Important changes did occur in the economy, some of them wrought precisely by the new rulers, by the name of "economic reform". Other ones, even more numerous, have developed spontaneously, as the unexpected result of the chance action of millions of people. Some of the introduced changes were abortive attempts to modernize the economy. Most of them were however oriented toward a redistribution of the control of resources. This puts in scientific words a reality that, in straight and plain language means that for five years on end we have been working on how to share among ourselves the tremendous wealth of formerly socialist Romania, and less or not at all how to solve the problems that have made of this tremendous wealth rather a burden than an advantage.

The December 1989 revolution was exclusively political. It could not change the economy overnight as it did with political system. But the crisis of the socialist economy was undoubtedly one of the main reasons that ignited the revolution. The political regime was overthrown when it became clear for everyone that it was stubbornly opposing changes that were so obviously necessary in the economy. And, although there was no clear vision of the changes, nobody fancied them as a long economic crisis, as an endless collapse of the economy that should not be matched at least by its changing. Started politically, the revolution had unquestionably an economic and social finality to attain, which is not even incipient, though, let aside accomplished.

The Minority That Gets Rich and the Majority That Gets Impoverished

The economic crisis is the only one which cannot be denied as a crisis. It is only too obvious and the results just cannot be interpreted in much differing ways precisely because of this conspicuousness. Therefore, the main way of countering this unpleasant reality, employed by rulers and population alike, is being optimistic about the future, this endless repetition of therapeutic slogans like "it is just a transition, it will pass, sufferings and losses are necessary, it is going to be better soon", etc. But there are other domains in which the crisis is at least as severe, yet its elements are so new that nobody understands precisely what to make of them.

The most serious of them all is the social crisis. It is generated by the brutal, almost violent switch from egalitarianism to elitism. The Romanian society before 1989 was an egalitarian one. Even if not everybody lived the same, and in some respects the differences were extremely big, that intention of egalitarianism was asserted as legitimate. It was a rather improperly understood egalitarianism, because its objective was to provide for minimal instead of maximal levels. It was to a great extent built on the principle of killing also the neighbor's goat since your own has died. The general idea was that everyone had to make do with a minimum considered as both necessary and possible. Socialism was figured out in such a way as to represent a system of egalitarian distribution of poverty. Except for several categories that were privileged by the closeness to the power centers, nobody was allowed to go past that minimal level imposed as a generalized average level.

The revolution smashed that egalitarian principle and replaced it by an elitist principle. It is never clearly stated, because it is politically counterproductive, especially from an electoral point of view, but all steps and actions taken are translating it into life with a steadiness that has not been applied to other transformations as well. The elitist principle states that inside a society there emerge elites and they are entitled to more, even far more than the common people of that society. The way how such elites can come into being has never been clearly explained, but they have actually burst out right after the revolution, sorting themselves out in at least two categories: a power elite and a money elite. In the beginning, they were apart, as the way to power and the way to wealth seemed to represent two completely different mutually excluding trajectories. Very soon though, one or two years only after the revolution, the two elites started to draw closer to each other, since they obviously needed to be mutually supportive. The political and administrative power needed money to hold on, while the wealth elite needed political and administrative support to keep its money safe and above all to make even more money.

So, a first characteristic of the social crisis which is developing in Romania now, as a direct consequence of the revolution and of the transition that followed, is a social polarization. The two elites, on the one hand, and the mass of the population on the other hand, evince a tendency of growing more and more apart in terms of incomes, living conditions (from food, housing and clothing to the access of education, spare time and social services) and even of such elements of the quality of life as human rights or individual freedoms. Theoretically, they ought not depend on the social station, but in actual fact they do. For, the administrative system, the judiciary, police and even public opinion are tending to give a preferential treatment to elites and to disadvantage the "common" people. We can talk a lot as to wehther polarization is or is not necessary, useful, maybe even desirable. One may argue, and some do, that elites are necessary and that every country has prospered also thanks to the existence and activity of its elites. Such a discussion was in fashion in Europe all along the past century and much of this century, until about the end of World War One. The matter is mooted again in the developed countries now, but, obviously, from a different starting point.

But, what renders all this debate and arguing pointless in Romania is that the polarization occurs not only through the separation of the elites from the mass of the population, but also through the generalized regress of the living standard and quality of life of the majority categories. Polarization in Romania occurs through a double move. Whereas the elites are acquiring more and more power and bigger wealth, thus rising above the average level in every respect of everyday life, the big majority of the population fares the other way round. The population is increasingly losing power and, above all, it gets poorer at the same speed at which the elites get richer. So, not only do the elites tangibly raise their living standard above the pre-revolution one, which is not bad at all, but also and concomitantly the polarization occurs because the mass of the population sees its living standard decline far below what it had before the revolution. And in Romania this is unbearable. Romania had an extremely low living standard even before December 1989. Its further decline is unacceptable. Still, it started to drop already in 1991 and has done even more so in the last two years.

That is why the talk about elites is pointless enough. It is not the elites that should make the main concern, but the mass of the population and the negative social movement at grass roots. It might not be dramatic, it might even be wholesome that a small number citizens, say one per cent of the population, get rich piling up millions of dollars in private wealth. But it surely is extremely grave that over ninety per cent of the population has been impoverished materially and is going through spiritual, human and even biological degradation. And this is unacceptable. For both humanitarian and pragmatic reasons. No matter how cynical, we must still realize that a society's main potential is its people's quality, and poverty is the main factor of debasement of this quality.

Just as worrying is the fact that a void is growing between these two poles, between elites and common people or, if we are to employ the Western names, between the haves and haves not. The idea borrowed from the West about the ideal structure of a modern society says that it ought to have a rarefied, powerful and rich elite at one pole, and another, equally small, group of persons disadvantaged by economic, cultural and even physical handicaps, at the opposite pole, with the bulk of the population, making up the so-called middle class, between the two extremes. The idea that Romania too, is bound to see the emergence of this middle class, which makes a society's most active and dynamic force, its backbone or whatever you like to call it, has been enthusiastically espoused by all parts and all politicians. It is a generous idea entailing at least two major advantages. First, it shifts the attention and talk from the two poles, embarrassing as they remind of a social crisis. Second, it allows for a comeback to the generally favored way of painting the future in a pink shade justified only by the extreme unpalatable colour of the present. And so, the happy ideal of the middle class can be depicted for the inferior pole, the disadvantaged, impoverished and degrading pole. In actual fact, there is no sign, no tendency and no process to justify the hopes associated with the emergence of this middle class. Romania is not about to develop a social structure specific to the modern and developed societies, it is just about to remake the social pattern of the inter-war period. The difference is that, instead of a big mass of poor peasants, we will have an as big mass of poor industrial laborers. A glance cast at the poor, half-urbanized countries in Latin America or Africa is telling of the prospects.

A third reason for worry, associated with the emergence of the new post-revolution elites is their own behavior, since the formation of the elites being matched by the marginalization of the bulk of the population is more than just an unfortunate coincidence. Just the opposite, the two social moves, one of rising above the average level, characteristic of the elite, the other of sinking beneath it, characteristic of the population generally, are interconnected. Better said, the former is generating the latter. The coming into being of underprivileged majority pole is the result of the emergence of elites. The latter simply accumulate more and more power and money, eating up the share of power and incomes that would otherwise go to the population. There is an important difference in this respect between the elites that have asserted themselves for five years in Romania and the elites of the modern societies. The latter are more functional in society, performing a well defined economic and social role. They stimulate the generation of more wealth and power in society and, true they claim a bigger part to these surpluses. But, they claim and take less than they manage to produce in excess. So, they and their privileges are acceptable simply because as they get richer and more powerful, the whole society, all citizens that is, get richer and more powerful. And although every individual citizen gets so less than the members of the eiltes do, when it comes to measuring the power and wealth accumulated by all citizens taken together, the end-result is far bigger than the additional power and wealth accumulated by elites. So, the elites keep being eiltes, but the difference between them and the common people is rather being attenuated than increased.

It is obviously not what is happening in Romania now, and that is precisely why we have a social crisis on our hands instead of a more process of social restructuring. The social crisis mainly consists of a package of social phenomena, some of them hard to distinguish in the everyday life, other ones far more conspicuous, as is the case of poverty. All these phenomena are overlapped also by an ideological construction, meaning systems of values, ways of thinking and typical behaviors, which are at least worrying as the social processes themselves. Of course, the tune is set by the elites. The speed at which they have come into being is amazing. As for money elite, this small group of people's velocity in stockpiling tremendous wealth – at Romania's scale – has baffled even the Western millionnaires. Rates of profit like the ones got by the Romanian class of nouveaux riches are not only unusual but even unacceptable in a normal society.

This fast process has been matched by the emergence with the elites of ways of thinking, of appraising the reality and of behaving in it quite inoperative for the society and even for the elites themselves. The developing elites have developed an ideology according to which they are entitled to everything and allowed to do everything. Even if formally some things are forbidden, the interdictions must not apply to elites. Any means is good if it helps reaching a goal. Graft, theft, power abuse, negligence and lack of responsability, all these social doseases of the transition are only specific forms in which the elites are asserting their supremacy and their wish to speed up their formation. It does not matter how you make money, as long as this makes you richer and richer. It does not matter how you come to concentrate power if this ends up by giving you more power. And, what is more dramatic is that these unwritten rules, criticized more loudly precisely by the elites, have come to be accepted by the whole population as normal transition things. And so it happens that, out of passivity, despondency and individuality, it is precisely those who are dispossessed of both wealth and power that come to support this process. The end result is a famous Romanian comedy character's inferance:"a society wanting in principles means that it doesn't have them!" But with the character's author, Caragiale, the comical is a blanket for bitterness. The situation is far more dramatic when it is about specific social reality.

The unbiased conclusion is that in the social domain the revolution has had quite different effects than the expected ones. Just like in other domains, the political or economic one, it made a good start. It successfully implemented the first stage, of tearing apart social patterns that no longer satisfied anyone. But the initial destructive stage has not been followed by a constructive one. The revolution brought nothing in the place of what is dismantled and the reality, that does not settle for voids, has triggered a long train of spontaneous processes of change. Even before we got aware of them, their effects have started getting entrenched, generating tendencies that are not only rendering the present uncomfortable but are also making us worry about the future.. As regards social realities, the revolution made a good start, but it stopped before finishing its job. As with the economy, in the political field too, it has remained unaccomplished.

The Confusion of "Entering Europe"

It is not extravagant to say that one of the reasons why the Romanian revolution started and was successful was the international isolation Ceausescu had brought the country to. Romania had always strong ties with the exterior world, not only as an economic partner but also as a reference point in the everyday life. In spite of the restrictive regime of contacts with the foreign countries, especially with the West, it was toward them that were oriented both the industrial managers and the population in Romania. That traditional orientation of the Romanians was reinforced even more by the foreign policy conducted by Romania after 1968, characterized by a primarily West-bound orientation. The reasons were surely of a mainly economic nature. Romania needed the West as its main financial source – to finance its development, and technological source alike. Especially after the '60s, when, either as the result of a strategy, or because of conjunctures, the Romanian industry was more and more oriented to petro-chemistry, and the bulk of the oil resources were being controlled by the West and selling through its market.

In the second half of the '70s, Romania's policy, mainly West-oriented, started to change. Trying to capitalize on its development superiority over the third world countries, the Romanian economy turned to massive exports there, in exchange for raw materials indispensable for its functioning. That switch accounted not only for the first major foreign policy change after the 1968 opening to the West, but also for the first stage in the country's process of political and economic isolation internationally.

Apparently, of course, things were not like that, but the significance of such a mutation was deeper than the mere theory of the traditional exchange of manufactured goods for raw materials. In actual fact, the socialist economy in Romania, that had already its encounter with the international market with the opening of the relations to the developed West, was returning to the apron of political relations with the shifting of the weight center to the third world. Ceausescu's African and South-American tours and the development of preferential relations with some of the Near East states had the mission to develop commercial and economic privileges upon political criteria. Latin America has never been a success for Romania's foreign policy and foreign trade after all. The visits, both prior and after the revolution, have remained simple protocol actions, when they did not have chiefly touristic purposes. But Africa, lying at a crossroads of Western, Soviet and Chinese spheres of influence and having its trade partners defined by the big powers that were guardians of the local political regimes, was ideal for such a strategy. And, as communism was growing more isolated on an international plane, in order to avoid an economic confrontation which it would only lose, the political relations tended to be the essential criterion of economic ties.

And so, little by little, Romania's economic orientation started to be guided by political criteria instead of commercial ones. The boomerang effect consisted of maintaining the appearance of viability for an economy – industry above all – that would not take the needed stride to modernization required by the attempt to remain in the Western market. And as the Bucharest regime grew less popular and more isolated from the developed world, it was ever more inclined to confine also its commercial relations to the countries that shared its situation, that were just as isolated or little approved of because of the political regime as Romania. That was the case of Sadam Hussein's Iraq, Gadaffi's Libya, fundamentalist Iran and many of the black Africa's countries.

In the second half of the ninth decade, when the West switched from coolness to reprisals in relation to Ceausescu's regime and he answered in coin for coin, at a disproportionate scale of course, Romania's international isolation became almost complete and the country slipped into some kind of economic autarchy as if it were fighting a war with no allies. The Romanians profoundly disagreed with such a policy. As the communist regime was limiting the contacts and communication with the West the people and economic leaders were evincing more interest and greater inclination for it. From Western radio stations to Western cultural products, Romania would hungrily take in everything that came from the West. In that respect, the revolution meant breaking free of an artificial restriction and a big step taken by the country toward reintegration with the international community.

In December 1989 it seemed that the revolution meant a complete success in that respect, and Romania would be readmitted to the "civilized", meaning developed world, like the prodigal son in the Bible. On live cast in Romania and shown on all major TV stations in the world, the Romanian revolution generated extraordinary empathy with international public opinion for Romania and Romanians. Romania became instantly the main concern not only of mass media but also of the humanitarian institutions and organizations and it seemed that politicians too, would be carried away by that wave of general enthusiasm. Such an opportunity may have really existed and the politicians of the revolution, inexperienced with international relations, may have missed it. It is just as possible that the experts of the Western cabinets should have had from the onset an appraisal and an attitude toward Romania different from those of the public opinion. The fact is that very soon the country was just as isolated inetrnationally as it had benn before the revolution.

Five years of political efforts followed, for Romania to come to be accepted by the international community at a political level. Ever so slowly Romania has become an associate of the European Union, has been admitted to the Council of Europe after an extremely humiliating bargaining, has been reinstated in the Most Favored Nation Status by the United States, after a refusal in 1992, has become one of the members of the Partnership for Peace built around the NATO and has got, after much bargaining and hesitation, loans and credits from international financial institutions. In 1993 and 1994 all these shy steps into the international area were naturally recorded as political achievements, but in actual fact they have only attenuated instead of annulling the marginal condition to which Romania is still confined. All in all, they only mean that Romania has ceased being regarded as an outcast, some sort of Iraq or Libya in the middle of Europe. Nor is there any real reason for shunning it like this and in the end even the Western politicians have understood it. Yet, this has not prevented Romania's being considered a third – or fourth-hand country, some sort of necessary evil which one can neither completely forget about nor want to be in closer touch with. The rulers think it has been a political success that Romania was promoted by Western economic and financial ratings from the group of greatest risk countries to the next one. In a way, it is a success, since it means a mending of the wrong image of the post-revolution Romanian politics. This last but one group of risk rating is not necessarily an incorrect appraisal. Unfortunately, it expresses the place which Romania can hold in the world for the time being, considering its internal characteristics.

Romania's international relations have been maybe the most debated problem in Romania's internal political life. For five years on end, the Opposition has made of the international pressure and the failure of the official policy the main theme of election campaign. In turn, the rulers have hurried to blame their own failures on the Opposition, accusing it of having sabotaged the country's national interests on an international plane. And, when none of such like explanations seemed to be enough, there were always the Hungarians there to blame. It is because of the Hungarians that Romania and its governance have such a bad image in the West and that the country keeps being regarded as an outsider although, of course, the Romanians think quite different of their own importance and due place on a world plane.

The international relations make a maze of contradictory and rather disconcerting interests for everything. Especially after 1989, the Western countries have proved not to be acting either consistently or in consonance on an international plane. They have behaved in the same way also with Romania. It is also probable that all explanations be partly true. Romania's political leadership after the revolution has never been and is not now either in much favor with the Western administrations and it is obviously not to the liking of mass media. The political leaders of the Oppsition have tried to stimulate the Western pressures in order to pave their own way to power at home. And Hungarian lobbies exist in all developed countries and they have never been congenial to Romania. But, absolutely none of these conjunctures, or even all of them taken together can justify Romania's current situation. The fact is that, finding itself all of a sudden in the situation unusual for it, namely of no longer depending decisively on any big power, either in order to obey or in order to oppose it (as Ceausescu had done with the Soviet Union in the '70s and '80s), Romania has no longer known what foreign policy to promote. Therefore it has conducted no foreign policy at all.

It does not pursue any foreign policy now either, meaning that the current ambiguous and marginal condition will continue also in the future. The Romanian politicians, both rulers and opponents, have remained prisoners of paradigms and of a conceptual language characteristic of the period prior to 1989. The big Romanian foreign policy debates are still conducted in terms of pro- or against Russia (pro- or against the Soviet Union until the second half of 1991), pro- or against the European Union, United States, NATO, a.s.o. Not even the promoters of these policies see it clear what would justify one or the other of the options or what would get Romania by promoting either of the alliances.

To put words in a nutshell, Romania does not have a foreign policy. It does not know what to expect from the international community and, more generally, if it does expect something from it. The political rethoric about "the place in Europe" still sounds like a talk about a natural right and a dinner party etiquette at the same time. To Romanian politicians the "place in Europe" is rather a matter of pride. Nobody thinks of commercial, economic, political or cultural objectives. Even less are the Romanian politicians thinking that the mission of international policy is to get changes, advantages, favorable conditions on an internal plane. Isolated from international economic and social realities by misjudged superiority, by indifference, the Romanian foreign policy is drifting with the current, carried away by vanities and everyday problems.

The current is the European integration that has become some sort of a rather shallow slogan of Romanian politicians and diplomats. European integration is an extremely complex process the hard nucleus of which is made of the economic, financial and cultural integration of the West-European countries. The integration policy is the main instrument by which those countries are spending up and negotiating the conditions of economic, financial and cultural integration. But, as the Romanian foreign policy is indifferent to the domestic policy, the European integration bears to us especially the significance of Romanian politicians' participation in every kind of meetings, talks, conferences, at the highest levels. It is rather a matter of international prestige employed as an asset in the domestic political relations. Things are not like this and we will feel it soon enough. Romania's association with the European Union was negotiated by Westerners, especially economically, and by Romanians especially politically. But the joining in the European Union will be above all a process of economic and cultural adjustment and integration.

The role of vanity in the Romanian foreign policy is not negligible. What makes it possible is the same incongruence of the foreign policy objectives with what is happening inside. Therefore, much of the Romanian diplomatic activity is mere international tourism. I will mention here a real story, telling the whole post-revolution Romanian foreign policy. A senion Romanian official asked his experts about one of the world's biggest economic and financial powers: why no minister of that country was willing to pay a visit to Romania? The answer was clear: because they had no problem to settle in the relations with Romania. But the Romanian dignitary's inability to find an answer by himself is indicative of the difference of outlook on foreign policy. Whereas to the Romanian dignitary the meeting was important because of the prestige he might derive, of its political significance, for the Japanese one (for it was about Japan), what mattered was the content of the talks and not only the importance of its having had place. And for that content to get beyond were delcarations of good will (or "mutual information", as was the official phrasing of the announcement that there was nothing to discuss), it takes an infrastructure of economic, cultural relations and interests.

Of course, Romania is not the only formerly communist country whose foreign policy is fumbling in absence of clear objectives and out the inability to single out foreign policy targets that can support internal changes or get attuned to their necessities. All tension and political arguments between Romania and Hungaria, for instance, start precisely from the fact that this time Hungary more than Romania is employing the old criteria and conceptions regarding the foreign policy. The economic, tourist, neighbourliness relations between the two countries are developing in utter contradiction with the political ones, which have remained stuck in the sentimental-demagogic problems of nationalism and, in Hugary's case, in the yearning for the "golden age" of the Austro-Hungarian Empire. But it is no consolation at all to know that such a policy is not singular.

Like in every domain, in the international relations as well, the revolution has broken barriers and opened opportunities. Consequent to the revolution, Romania has given up the odd policy of self-isolation, and the international community has shown ready, even though unenthusiastically, to recuperate the blank that Romania used to be. But, like in all the other respects, things have stopped at that beginning. They have never been completed and have remained at the ambiguous stage characteristic of the transition. They have remained pending and waiting to be given some direction.

The Absence of Governance

Whenever one strikes a balance of the revolution- what has been achieved by Romania since December 1989 to this day – the main place is held by the political changes. True, the whole political system has been changed. None of the political institutions of the former regime has survived the revolution, even though some political characters have migrated from the former institutions to the new ones. Although this continuity of certain politicians is the favorite target of the opposition's criticism, in actual fact it matters litlle or not at all, when it is compared with the institutional change. But the change of the political system/polity, of the institutions and rules of designation of their leadership is still only half a change. As shown before, in all domains the revolution operated this first half of the change, this beginning of a transformation. The most radical start has been made in politics, as it is but normal, since revolutions are a major political act. The revolution dismantled the political system of the former regime and a new one emerged on its ruins.

But, for all these political transformations, once they were tested and have come to stabilize, the satisfaction of the sum-up has started being shaded by some questions first and, lately, by discontent. All opinion polls show that the population is dissatisfied with politics. Not with the new rules of the system. Not with democracy, not with political pluralism and free elections. The mass attendance, both at the elections since 1990 until 1992 and at the referendum on the Constitution prove that people are interested and still pinning their hopes to politics. But they are disappointed by the way how politics is being done now.

It is not clear what this means. The same people who strongly declare they do not like what is happening with Romanian politics are stammering when they have to explain precisely what is not up to their expectations. But the main institutions of the political system – the Parliament, political parties, political government – have much eroded their credibility. Even the most stable institution in point of popularity, the country's President, has started being associated with the general confusion that prevails in Romanian politics.

The politicians, at least some of them, are just as dissatisfied with their own parties, with the Parliament where they carry on most of their activity, with the fight they wage and the subjects on which they fight. A phenomenon that is growing statistically significant is the politicians' "desertion" into the business world or, even safer and more alluring, into the state administration, from diplomacy to ministries and prefect's offices. Something is happening with Romanian politics, something that nobody likes, although it has not become obvious yet to public opinion what name ought this phenomenon to be given.

In actual fact, politics, the way it is being done now, has gradually and radically departed from the reality which it has ceased governing. Hence the disappointment of all and one. As a political act, the revolution was not so much aimed against a political system, against a party and a person, as rather against a certain governance. People got out in the street and demanded Ceausescu's resignation when it was obvious that his rule was pushing the country more and more toward a disaster. And they demanded a different governance, a different direction, a way of leading the country out of disaster and not toward a greater one. Everybody agreed that what was needed was a change of political institutions and of rules of political life (it is often called "political game", but it is no game; it is an extremely serious thing on which the life of all of us depends). But nobody thought that the institutions had to be changed just for the sake of having new institutions. New institutions and different rules would have had to be only the means to achieve the new governance. The disappointment comes from the observation that, although having new political institutions and new rules to run them, instead of the bad governance of the time before the revolution, now we do not have any governance at all.

In the first years after the revolution, everybody was delighted with the new political institutions and with their way of operation. The boring debates in the Provisional National Unity Council used to be on live cast on TV and the people used to watch for hours on end the idle discussions not because important problems were being solved there, for they were not, but because it was fascinating to see the new politicians getting used to the institutions and the institutions themselves getting used to working. It happened the same with the Parliament debates after the June elections. Now, over 80 per cent of the population is bored and disappointed with the Parliament and its members, although it voted them in the elections. And this happens because the new institutions, even polished, went on revolving in vain, without producing what everybody expected them to give – a governance of Romania that should change the downward course imposed by the previous rule.

Well, there is no sign that this absence of governance will be mended in a near future. Moreover, the rulers have gradually started to "free themselves" of any responsability concerning the appearance of reality, and especially concerning the way of living in Romania. The official doctrine of the previous regime established a direct and simple connection between reality and politics. Reality was the product of political activity of the communist party, more precisely of its leadership. Since it controlled everything in Romania, the country's political leadership was seen as the source of all things, good or bad. Therefore, when reality became unbearable, the leadership of the communist party was considered as the main cause of the evil, and the revolution marked the people's determination to change it by force, given it had been unable to change itself (at the 14th congress of the communist party, in November 1989, only one month before the revolution). That cause-to-effect relation between reality and leadership was espoused also by the leadership emerged right after the revolution. Therefore, the measures which the revolution leaders took soon after its victory were meant to mend the reality, to warm up the cold homes, eliminate the shortage of food and imported products, to do away with the electricity stoppage, etc.

After the May 1990 elections, the Opposition started to criticize the country's pre-election government for having caused an abrupt and artificial improvement of the living standard in the January – June 1990 period. The short way to buying the votes of a naive political electorate, says the Opposition now. But it did not object at that time, nor could it. It could not cross anybody's mind on those days to shut off again the electricity from homes or to leave the food stores empty. When, worried by the fast draining of the reserves carefully set aside by Ceausescu's thrift, the rulers wanted to turn off the tap delaying, for instance the passage to the five-day workweek, the population violently reacted. And the rulers yielded, as would all those who followed in office ever since the revolution. Partly because then the power was too weak, too little legitimate in order to efficiently withstand the pressure of any significant group that would rose against it. But, partly also because they were optimistic themselves about their ability to change the reality, through a fast economic revigoration.

Later, after elections and after the launching of what was called "economic reforms", the ideology of the former regime about cause-to-effect relation between the society's leadership and its reality was replaced by a new ideology unjustly related to "the market economy". According to it, the responsability of the rule is dramatically shrinked and the reality starts being rather the result of the action of independent mechanisms considered to belong to the market. The impoverishing of a part of the population, inflation, mounting prices and unemployment are caused by "objective" laws on which the governance has neither the ability nor the intention to work. The absence of a governance started in Romania with the diminution of the government's responsability for what is happening in the country.

For a change, the government's explicative capacity has grown. Concerned with answering the accusations of the opposition that blamed the rulers for all the negative changes that prevailed these last five years, especially as regarded the economic evolutions, the rulers started to give explanations. That was something quite new in Romania: a prime minister or head of state showing up on TV to explain to Romanians that all evils that have befallen them after the revolution were caused by "objective factors", from the world economic crisis to the enterprise managers' incompetence. Irrespective of the blamed factors, all speeches have been meant to explain that it is not the government's fault. Moreover, the government cannot and must not interfere. But it can competently explain why are things turning from bad to worse.

There was only one step from explaining why the intervention was impossible to giving up any intervention. The step was soon taken. It is a somewhat paradoxical demarche since, while ridding itself of responsibility, the government was starting the implementation of reforms meant to change radically the institutions and structures of the economy. But, on a more attentive analysis of this apparent paradox, the attitude proves to be similar with the one that dominated the political change. The rulers assumed the task of changing the system of institutions and rules in the economy, the way it had changed the political one. But, they did not assume any responsability for the way how the new institutions and rules would function and even less so for their effects. This is precisely what the absence of governance means.

It is difficult to talk about the absence of governance because almost nobody understands very clearly what governance means. The country's last real rule was the comunist one. The comunist rule was a rule that generated a grave economic and social crisis, but it was a genuine rule. The leading stratum used to set targets regarding the operation parametres of institutions and economic, social mechanisms and even regarding behaviors and then it would articulate complex combinations of measures for their application. It would draft new laws, set up institutions, then it would send its army of party activists to press and control everybody that might influence the decisions, would threaten rebellious managers with the firing or even with the jail. When targets were unrealistic they were obviously not attained, but the governance mechanisms were however set in motion for their attainment. It is equally true that, of all possible governance mechanisms, the communist rulers mainly used the most primitive ones, relying on administrative pressure, but they did use them. Just like they used (or tried to), less efficiently and at a smaller scale, also more modern mechanism of preferential allocation of resources and of stimulating positive behaviors (the social shares are an illustration of the failure of such an attempt).

The successive rulers after the revolution found themselves in the embarassing situation of either conducting a communist-type governance or giving up any attempt to govern. In the first months after the revolution, they had the benefit of the people's extraordinary willingness to participate in governing through the mere implementation of objectives set by the executive. But at that time the excutive was busying itself with other things than setting objectives for the change or simply for governing. The inability to set objectives has then become chronical and the governance, just like politics, has gradually departed from reality to the point of coming to live in an artificial world, confined to administrative palaces in Bucharest and completely cut off from the outside world.

2.The Need for Action

Quite sure this long string of discontents and failed expectations of the revolution might be even longer. Other ones too, could be added, apart from the economy, social structures and politics. Education, social assistance and medical care, social security, culture, urbanism, environmental protectiom, all of them are going through their own crises and, instead of changing for the better, as all of us hoped at the beginning of the revolution, they are faring increasingly bad, like all the other ones. But what matters are the conclusions that can be drawn from this picture of reality.

Firts, it is obvious that it is not about a chance aspect or detail that can possibly mend all by itself. It is obvious that all important domains of reality are changing, but they are changing in a way that differs from our expectations. Especially in the major domains, the change obviously does not match the expectations born out of the revolution. The revolution was not done to speed up the economic crisis generally and the industrial one particularly. Such a result is precisely the opposite of the objective proclaimed during the revolution in the famous Declaration-Program, that must by no means be forgotten. Also, the revolution never had the purpose of developing a powerful and rich elite on account of impoverishing the population and of reducing the power it is naturally entitled to. If an elite is necessary, very well, then it is accepted (let us remember the general requirement for competence that went with the revolution), on condition that the domination of the former political bureaucracy, of the "professional revolutionists", should not be replaced by the domination of a new bureaucracy – the money and administrative elite. Last but absolutely not least, the revolution was not done for Romania not to be governed at all and for the transition to proceed at random. On the contrary, the purpose of the revolution was to change the governance not to annul it.

Another preliminary conclusion is that all these changes, not at all wanted and expected, were triggered by the revolution. Had it not been for the December 1989 revolution, they would not have taken place at all or would have proceeded in quite different forms. The economic crisis would have deepened further. Certainly, the international isolation would have ended up in a confrontation with the international community, but North Korea's case proved that one could nagotiate with the West even in absolutely dispropotionate conditions of power and influence. Sure, Romania is no North Korea, but let us not forget that a little before the revoltuion, Ceausescu was doing precisely what the Korean leaders would do five years later: he was threatening the international community with the ghost of an uncontrollable nuclear military potential. Then, the giving up of the old governance would not have occured in the absence of the revolution. The 14th congress of the Romanian communist party is a premptory proof in this respect. The congress was Ceausescu's big opportunity to understand the tendencies of change in the contemporary world and especially in East Europe and to follow the prevailing trend. Ceausescu did not miss that opportunity at the congress, he rejected it. According to his plans, Romania was to stick to a road which would have surely led to an economic and social disaster but would have preserved the ruling class. It was the revolution that rejected that opinion and abolished it. It simply removed the leaders that promoted it, it abolished the institutions on which they counted or which they were dominating, from the Securitate (Security) to the Grand National Assembly and created the possibility of replacing an already surrealistic governance by a new one. Just like the other possibilities, this one too, has not been taken advantage of. But it is the most important of all, since it is a prerequisite for the other ones. Neither the economy, nor the social structures and the people's everyday life can change for the better in the absence of any governance. Because it is precisely the governance that ought to initiate and assure the carrying through of all the other changes.

The revolution started the changes, but once started, the changes have not continued of their own accord. Nor is it possible to have such a transition, which nobody gives direction and shape, but which automatically leads to the society dreamt of by everybody. Since it began, since it was successful in its first part, meaning the destruction of the base or infrastructure of political, economic and social realities that were based on a regime that had become undesirable, the Romanian revolution of December 1989 was triumphant. But, since it has not continued and has failed to attain its implicit objectives, it has remained unfinished.

The third conclusion is that although the revolution failed to change the reality into what everybody expected or wanted, it does not mean that reality has remained unchanged. The transition has taken place and it still continues. The old economy is being gradually replaced by a new economy. The social structures of communism are falling apart and new structures are coming into being. The political system has changed its rules and institutions and it does fonction, even though the public opinion is dissatisfied with its functioning. As a whole, Romania has changed but it has done so in a way that nobody says it is what they would have wanted. The transition is going on but it is spontaneous. The absence of any control of transition in itself would not be grave if it led to a Romania in the least similar to what we expected it to be back in December 1989. But it is clear that it is leading to a reality that may be a blind alley just as bad as earlier communism. The words "it was better before" are ever more frequently heard. And they are not spoken by the former elites of communism, by those for whom communism meant first of all privileges and advantageous positions. They are spoken by the same categories which were disadvantaged also in communist times, from pensioners and industrial laborers to research-design intelligentsia. Communism was no good to them but give up communism just in order to sink into the third world is absolutely not the wanted solution.

There was a revolution in Romania. The revolution changed the bases of all components of a society that in the last years had proved it either could not or did not want (which is just the same, since not to want meant not to be able to want) to better its structures. This change of the foundations of the former society triggered the transition. But the results of the transition are about to cause as much dissatisfaction as did the pre-revolution society. Only this time there is not even the chance of repeating the revolution left unfinished. But there is the chance of taking over control of the transition.

Our first step toward using this really ultimate possibility is to get aware that we are not content with how the present looks. This does not mean only to shout that we don't like it. It also means to understand what went wrong, what realities, for the changing of which the revolution created the necessary opportunity, have not changed, and what other realities, from among the new ones, do not fill the expectations generated by the revolution. It means that we should make a critical analysis of the transition.

Such a critical analysis of the transition is necessary but not sufficient. If we merely find out what does not suit us, we have taken one step ahead but have not settled at least formally any of the difficulties we would like to see eliminated. The next step is to find out what ought to replace the wildcat transition that has been going on these last five years. For what we need an outlook on transition and on its management. Such an outlook on the future would allow us to project a normal follow-up of the revolution. But unless it is matched by an analysis of the conditions in which it could take place and by the singling out of the means to attain it, that outlook remains mere utopia.

With this last chapter, the transition would get its due place, at least in words. Instead of a wildcat transition which nobody controls and nobody even tries to oppose, we would have a feasible project of transition, devised as a natural follow-up of the revolution ignited in 1989. From that point on, we would only have to implement the project. But this no longer depends either on theory or on projecting the reality; it depends on concrete political action. Of this latter aspect whatever we say is not enough. The mere description is not enough. What is needed is action.

II. THE REVOLUTION

1. Reconsideration of the Revolution

A Challenged Revolution

There has been less and less talk of the revolution lately and people have started to have mixed feelings about it. The passions and interests of the home and international politics unleashed after 1989 had the revolution as their special target. It was referred to in every way likely to influence or justify attitudes and objectives that otherwise had but little connection with a revolution. The politicians that were dissatisfied with the sharing of benefits resulted after the revolution are inclined to disconsider and minimize it. In order to justify their own failure and especially to de-legitimate the incumbant rulers, they have given a helping hand in all speculations about "plots" or "coups d' etat" that allegedly replaced the revolution. The mass media, always looking for the sensational, have never got tired in five years of looking for obscure forces, hidden by intelligence services across the world, behind the great popular uprising of December 1989. And they have decided not to mind the humorous side of it. To these efforts for dwarfing the significance and importance of the December revolution, "the others" only oppose a rather unimaginative festivism. One can easily distinguish the clichees of the other festivism that had bored the Romanians so much before 1989 with the exaltation of the "golden age/era". And maybe this clumsiness would not be so conspicuous if the festivism did not betray the wish to use the revolution in order to legitimate positions, advantages, and in the case of the "heroes of the revolution" – the privileges.

In fact, the December 1989 revolution was the most important event in Romania in the last half century. It radically changed the lives of millions of Romanians, the country's situation in the world and triggered a process of change the evolution of which is hard to foresee now. By its implications, it might well be the most important event throughout the country's modern and contemporary history, since 1848 Revolution, which, although suppressed, ushered in the period of Romania's modernization and "Europenization". This new revolution, although victorious, is still at a crossroads, because neither its consequences nor its subsequent evolution are decided yet.

Of all possible ways of treating the december 1989 revolution, to underrate it is the wrongest. And we can do it if we ridicule it or if we take it for an espionage novel. It is nothing wrong with investigating the december events and the way how institutions and personalities acted and reacted at that time. Also, it is nothing offending in telling jokes about the revolution. But all this must not prevent us from appreciating the revolution and the horizons it has opended, with their due value and significance. Above all, it must not prevent us from turning to advantage the possibilities it has offered. The possibilities are still here for us to pick. From this perspective, the revolution is not completed yet, because it has not exhausted its consequences. But they must be understood and modelled as one can. However, we must first understand the true significance of the revolution.

Changing the Future

Revolutions are phenomena so rare in history that only little is known about them. One does not know what to expect; it is hard to tell precisely when they have ended; and very often, their objectives are changing on the run, so that the changes they trigger are sometimes only little associated with the reasons that generated them. In 1989, Romania lived through a revolution without realizing it very well. We can recognize it as a revolution by that it was an attack from the inside and essentially directed against the extant political regime. Both features are important. The fact that it was from the inside means that the society itself no longer accepted the then political regime. The Romanian revolution in 1989 was a revolution viewed from that angle, whereas the change of political regime in Japan in 1945, for instance, implemented upon the orders of the US occupation army command, was not a revolution. Following the same criterion, it is debatable whether the change of political regime in 1946-1948 in Romania, that was just as essential, was a revolution.

It does not matter how did the revolution start and which was the event or string of specific events that made people get out in the street in December 1989 to ask for Ceausescu's resignation. What matters is the effect of that mass action. For that reason, all debates on the possible "plotters" and a possible involvement of foreign intelligence services in igniting the events in Timisoara, Bucharest and the other cities are irrelevant for this question: was it or was it not a revolution.

The essential character of the change is just as important. And it does not cover the political regime only. The revolutions give rise to essential political changes in order to allow for in-depth economic and social changes. In Romania, the revolution caused the collapse of an East-European type communist polity and replaced it by another polity which, as shown above, relies on different institutions and rules of acceding to and maintaining the power. Also, this change of political regime was not meant only to overthrow some leaders that had become unbearable for everybody. Its mission was to allow for radical changes in the economic and social structures and institutions and in Romania's relations with the world at large. These changes having taken a course which does not satisfy us must not prevent us from appreciating the revolution as such. Although not being what we expected or wanted them to be, these changes exist. This does not alter the revolutionary character of the December events.

It was a real revolution. Pleasant or unpleasant, the consequences are here for everyone of us to see them. Starting December 1989, Romania's history has changed its course. In the years that preceded it, a long train of phenomena and processes had got stabilized and their tendencies were clear. The December revolution utterly disrupted them. The future, which was predictable in November 1989 or earlier, was simply smashed. None of the expectations and forecasts made before 1989 with socialist Romania's economic, social and political realities as a basis, will ever come true, even approximately. The revolution meant that passage from a probable future to another one, which was impossible before its victory.

The Revolution without Enemies

The reconsideration of the revolution is not complete unless we reconsider also the particpation in the revolution. For, one of the peculiarities that distinguished the Romanian revolution of 1989 from the revolutions we know from history books is that virtually all social categories and classes participated in it and supported it. By the end of last century, on analyzing the class struggle in developed Western Europe, Engels had already proclaimed that victorious revolutions had become an impossibility. The reason was of a military nature – the modern weapons had become so sophisticated and efficient for mass destruction as no popular insurrection could be successful against an armed force resolved to offer resistance. It was a misjudgement, since he did not anticipate the possibility of a civil war, when the political force opposing the incumbent regime is capable of organizing for itself an army like the state's one. The revolution in Russia, in October 1917 and the revolution in Latin America, East Asia and Africa proved that such a victory is possible. But it takes a long period of bloody war. The other possibility was illustrated by the Romanian revolution.

The Romanian revolution, as well as the other revolutions in East Europe, did not mean the raising of one or several social classes against a ruling class. The revolution did not proceed as a fight between social classes, but as the people's rising against a political elite. Moreover, even that uprising against the elite was secondary. It appeared and had an important role in the revolution because the system had to be identified and personalized somehow. But the revolution was against the political system, against its institutions and, above all, against the policy they promoted. It was everybody's fight against a mechanism and an establishment and not a fight of ones against the others. Although some persons were identified with the establishment and its policies, that was rather a mechanism of the mass psychology. And that small group of people who were identified with the establishment, or who identified themselves with it, refusing to change it when they had an opportunity, found themselves isolated and having to face the whole population, even those who, formally, would have been supposed to back them, like the militia, security, army and judiciary. This is precisely why the success of the revolution was so positive, fast and, apparently, so easy.

In other respects, the Romanian revolution was unique in a Europe of anti-communist revolutions. There were revolutions also in Poland, Hungary and Czechoslovakia, since, ultimately, the establishment/polity was radically changed, and that change triggered the change of the type of economy and of the social patterns. But, the changes in those countries were achieved with the support of the incumbent establishment and through its agency. After the model launched by Gorbachev in Russia in 1985 (which seems to have imitated the Czechoslovak experiment of 1968), the changes were achieved through a string of successive reforms introduced precisely by the establishment which was falling apart. The big battles were fought between competing elites of the same political regime.

The political elite existing in Romania – the leaders of the communist party – did not split into supporters of the establishment and its reformers. Many people, including Western observers and analysts, hoped for that to happen at the 14th congress of the communist party. Popular discontent was building up, as shown by the workers' demonstration in Brasov in 1987, as well as by a host of small political incidents emerged in preparing the congress, and they fuelled hopes that Romania might follow the "recipe" already tested in the other communist countries in Europe. But that did not happen and then, instead of reforms, Romania lived through a revolution.

The absence of any organized support in favor of the revolution was fully compensated by the absence of any organized support in suppressing the revolution. Paradoxically at first sight, the revolution in Romania had no enemy. On the moment when the institutions of the power were seriously challanged – on the morning of 22 December, when the Bucharest population got out in the street –, they collapsed, offering no resistance. They were perfectly able to do it. They had the means. They had even plans prepared for such an event. Engel's reasoning was correct in that respect. What did not exist was the engine of such a reaction, meaning the will to resist. From that angle, the December revolution did not have enemies. The weak opposition it encountered was individual, not institutional or social. And it is extremely significant that, to counter the revolution, Ceausescu resorted to the means he availed of as a head of state, but not to the communist party. His failed attempt to mobilize the population to his support on 21 December, was not followed by the most normal of all measures – the attempt to mobilize the communist party to back him.

The revolution overthrew a power system and, after some wavers, it established another one. The major achievement naturally was the overthrow of the communist power system. That it was possible is still amazing the world and the Western analysts of communism. The fall of communism was the only thing which they would have never forecasted and which they did not believe even when it happened. Among other things, Romania suffered a lot and still suffers on an international plane because of the lack of understanding of Western specialists and of the mass media. What neither Western specialists and journalists nor some

Romanian politicians understood is that the revolution availed of a long period of preparation, which coincided with a period of continuous weakening of the former establishment's power structure. The revolution destroyed that power structure. There are plenty of misperceptions, the most disseminated of all being that communism was maintained by the mere police repression. It is not possible to understand how could it be, if one remains in the land of legends and does not understand first of all the content and appearance of the power structure of communism.

2. The Power System of the Communist Society

No matter how it came to power, imposed by the Russian armies or sustained by the population, or by a combination of both, communism soon developed its own power system which, but for small national variations, was the same in all East-European countries. In Romania, one of its salient features was the "Ceausism", a variant of personal dictatorship quite different from the famous personal dictatorships that fill the sort history of communism: Stalin's in the Soviet Union, Mao's in China and Kim Il Sung's in North Korea. Those personal dictatorships however represented only the spectacular and visible part of a far more intricate power structure. Such a structure was beheaded by the December revolution, but the success of the revolution cannot be understood either in Romania or in the other East-European countries or in the Soviet Union, unless we understand that a part of the socialist power system particpated in the revolution, using it as an opportunity to settle to its advantage a power conflict that was proceeding since long beneath the surface.

The Administrative Bureaucracy and the Political Bureaucracy

On its advent to power, the communist party did not find a vacant place. Actually, it found it more filled that it had imagined. The real political suprastructure of the country, which the communist party would have had to replace by taking over the power, had been dismantled as early as 1940. Although the political parties knew a revigoration right after 1944, they did not come to make up another power structure, nor could they, considering that the country was under military occupation. The power had already been concentrated in the hands of the government bureaucracy that, thanks to the war, was possessed even by the necessary experience of cooperating with or dominating the other bureaucracy, typical of any modern society, namely the industrial bureaucracy. The industrial bureaucracy, represented by the bureaucratic structures of industrial enterprises, of the banks and insurance companies and of big corporations, usually holds the main control over the economy. In the mid-century, backward Romania, that only had about 300,000 industrial workers (including the ones of businesses with less than 25 employees), the industrial bureaucracy was even less numerous and it was weak. What mattered first was the other, administrative bureaucracy, the host of townhall and ministry white collars who kept under control Romania's peasant population.

The abolition of the political parties of the monarchy were gestures with a rather symbolical value, precisely because the power structure in post-bellum Romania was relying on administrative bureaucracy. The true act of taking over the power was the formation of the government. With it, the communist party placed its politicians in the position of legitimate and absolute rulers of the administration. At the same time, it established another group of politicians, the true political leaders of the party, with the task of controlling the former.

Sure, the communists proceeded to numerous purgings and appointed their own, reliable people to the key posts of that administration, to prefect's offices and townhalls, police, judiciary, etc. But they did not change the establishment essentially. Or, what matters for a bureaucracy are the structures and the way how to, operate and not the people who hold more or less crucial posts in the structures at a certain moment. The main feature of any bureaucracy, administrative included, is that once a person is included in its structures, his personality, opinions and generally everything that distinguishes him from the other people, or from those who held the same position in the bureaucratic structure before him, become inconsequential. They influence but little or not at all the functioning of the institution as a whole or its output. That is precisely why it is a bureaucracy instead of anything else.

What the communist party tried to do was not to dismantle the administrative bureaucracy and its dominance, but to subordinate and use them. For that purpose, it developed a bureaucracy of its own – the political bureaucracy of the party activists -, that paralleled the technical-administrative one, both in the leading bodies and in the territorial ones and, even before the nationalization, but obviously far more widely after it, also the industrial one. Very soon, virtually right after taking over the power, a system of distribution of the power was articulated, which relied ont two bureaucracies – the administration and the communist party.

No real conflict ever existed between the administrative and political bureaucracies. Generally, the administrative bureaucracy in autoritarian systems does not interfere with the struggle for power, because nobody challenges its own power. The fight is waged for the seizing of the specific position that allows for the political leadership of the bureaucracy. The administrative bureaucracy never holds that position itself. But somebody has to hold it. That need results from the inner characteristics of the decision systems of a bureaucratic type. A bureaucratic decision, at least at the higher echelons, meaning where it still has a high degree of generality, is always made on basis of two sets of criteria. The first set is defined by the bureaucracy itself. Its criteria are always presented as technical criteria and they do have a very sophisticated technical form. Partly, they really are technical, because they comprise or take account of all technical characteristics of the context and object covered by the decision. Partly, they contain in a technical form the decisions that are indispensable for the reproduction of the administration and for the distribution of the power to its advantage. But these decisions criteria are not enough to eliminate all alternatives, hence to define a decision. Even the technical conditions are filled and the reproduction of the bureaucracy secured, it still may happen that there should be several solutions for the same problem. It takes the introduction of other criteria in order to reduce their number to one and allow thus for the making of a decision. These are the political criteria. In order to be able to operate, the administrative bureaucracy needs these criteria, hence also a political body to articulate them and also to assume the responsability for them. For, as far as the bureaucracy is concerned, it is exonerated of responsability as long as the criteria which it introduces are presented as unavoidable technical criteria.

This detailed analysis is an attempt to put in scientific language the simple affirmation that an administration is indifferent to the political leadership because the latter never challenges its power. And an administration can serve any political power just as well. Better said, it has served them all along the history, at least those that never threatened to diminish its power. Once this higher political authority established as the leadership of the administration, the administrative bureaucracy seriously restricts its options and alternatives. Obviously, it does it through its own characteristics of operation and the "technical" aspects of the decision. The result is that a compromise always develops, some sort of symbiosis between the political power and the power of the administration, in which they are mutually supportive and restrictive.

For the communist party which was just taking over the power, the main problem was to secure an efficient control over that bureaucracy. Taking over the central government and the rule of the local administration was a first step. One more step was to bring in people truthful to their own policies. But that was far from enough. Like I said before, personal truthfulness to one policy or another mattered but little in a bureaucracy like the administrative one. Once included in the system, a person would discharge first of all a bureaucratic function and would get caught in its rules. Therefore, the communist party built another bureaucracy, political this time, the bureaucracy of the party activists, that in a first stage had the role to control the administrative bureaucracy and subsequently acquired the far more important role to control the industrial bureaucracy.

Anyway, by building this other, political bureaucracy, the communist party defined the main stage of the fight for political power. In a multi-party system it would waged among parties, better said inside the rarefied circle of their leaders. With the communist party, the fight was waged inside the political bureaucracy and was clearly its leaders' main preoccupation.

Challenging the Power:
Coming into Being of Industrial Technocracy

This combination of bureaucracies efficiently operated through the '50s and '60s, having as main political goal to concentrate all resources toward industrialization. But industrialization brought to the stage a new actor in the competition for power: the industrial bureaucracy. In an industrial society, most of the resources are concentrated in industry. It is there that are to be found money, means of production, manpower, raw materials and, above all, it is there that are produced all or almost all goods needed by the society. In an industrial society, the true power consists of the control of industry (including transport, banking system, trade, which are parts of the industrial system). And this power is now concentrated in the hands of the industrial bureaucracy, the bureaucratic network that starts with the company or enterprise managers and ends with the petty clerks or production flow engineers, which we will here-after call industrial technocracy. In Romania, as industrialization was gaining ground and the bulk of the resources was shifting from rural areas and agriculture that were easy to control by the administrative bureaucracy, to rural areas and industry, the industrial bureaucracy be-came an increasingly important factor in the distribution of power.

Whereas the administrative bureaucracy was never a real competi-tor for the political bureaucracy of the communist party in the fight for power, things were different with the industrial technocracy. Industrial technocracy has but few reasons to unconditionally obey by a political bureaucracy. It surely needs to permanently cooperate with the latter, but it would rather control the political decisions itself instead of ac-cepting the modification of its own decisions according to the impro-vised criteria of conjunctural political reasons. And it is even less in-clined to obey when such criteria are derived from a relatively primitive political idology and, since it was built in the period prior to industriali-zation and for the precise purpose of launching the industrialization, it was obviously growing outmoded once it reached a certain level of development. Too much power was at stake, too many resources, finan-cial, material and human, and too many implications of their use, from social ones to international relations, for the industrial technology to let itself dominated ungrudgingly by a small and important bunch of po-litical activists.

In an industrial, say capitalist, society, the political bureaucracy usu-ally finds a way with the industrial technocracy, resorting to compro-mises and opposing to its fragmentation the unity of the tremendous machine of administrative bureaucracy. By treating its own bureauc-racy as if it were an industrial society whose incomes are derived from taxes and rates, its political summit becomes a technocracy itself, which enters into normal relations with the other technocracies. Politicians also manage to outpower the technocrats in industry not only by relying on some of them in order to oppose the others, but also by the possibil-ity they have to build through legislation and administrative regulations an environment to which the technocrats have to adjust themselves. However, the power relations between technocracy and politicians are permanently oscilating, and the balance may lean to either side. Japan is probably the most explicit case of politics controlled by technocracy, and Italy seems to be following suit, after the decay of the post-bellum political elite. On the other hand, the West-European socialist governments were typical cases of supremacy of politics over the industrial technocracy.

But, by nationalizing virtually the whole economy and then by shaping the industrialization according to the principle of its unitary administration, socialism annihilated the last weakness of the industrial technocracy – its fragmentation and internal competition. The whole economy, and industry above all, have turned into a network the components of which – the big industrial enterprises – were mutually conditioning as much as they were mutually supportive. Moreover, the network extended also to the social services of industry – which otherwise had a certain autonomy – such as scientific research and design, trade and education. The result was the coming into being of only one industrial technocracy, apt to control everything, except for politics and administration, on the one hand, and for the institutions which political leaders developed on purpose, in order to secure their control over the society, such as the political police of the judiciary.

The first episode coincided with Ceusescu's coming to the limelights of the political stage. More precisely, his advent was one of the side effects of the battle. By mid-'60s, with the completion of the first stage of industrialization, that industrial technocracy had become powerful enough for a first attempt to get involved in the political decision, if not even to take over the control of the communist party. Romania had reached a critical level at which the political leadership, relying only on communist slogans and on the fidelity to the party of people that were maybe meaning well but simple and not possessed of the instruction required by the economic complexity generated by industry, was not enough any longer. In turn, industrial technocracy had managed to have its own representatives inside the political bureaucracy, and they were now pressing for the renewal of the political bureaucracy through its integration with the summits of technocracy, and for important political changes, tantamount to a reform of communism. Like in all cases of political crises, the battle was fought behind closed doors, meaning inside the political bureaucracy. Its result was a compromise. The political bureaucracy retained its power, but accepted to change its composition in such a way as to come to a normal communication with the technocracy. A string of reforms was launched, but they were soon stopped, as it was noticed that one of their effects might be the loss of administrative control over some of the most important financial and material resources.

The decisive period for that battle was "the Prague spring". At that time, Ceausescu scored a double performance. By taking advantage of the popular support to the anti-Soviet and pro-Czechoslovak policy, hence to the pro-West policy which he moted, he managed to consolidate his position in the power structures, accumulating, besides the leading position in the party, also the leading positions in the state rule. The fight for taking over the rule of the state administration – the administrative bureaucracy was the main object of the political dispute between party activists and technocracy – was won by activists, the political bureaucracy that is, although it took a while until the control became effective and unquestionable. Second, by taking advantage by the threat posed at that time by the Soviet Union to Romania, he managed to shift the whole dispute from the field of internal economic and political reforms, to that of nationalism and patriotism, in form af anti-Sovietism. True, the promotion of reforms automatically meant also opposition to the Soviet Union, but Ceausescu managed to empty that opposition of its reform-oriented content, keeping only the national content. That field of nationalism and patriotism would be his favorite throughout the time when he stayed in power, by December 1989. It was justified in many instances, but the problems to which national issues too were adjacent, could not be settled exclusively or primarily in that field in neither of them.

The End of the "Golden Era"

The fact is that technocracy lost the first round of the competition although for a while it harbored the illusion that it had won. The years that followed, the '70s, marked Romania's fast industrial development and the extensive growth of technocracy. Therefore, when in successive stages Ceausescu eliminated the political summits of that technocracy, ensuring the political bureaucracy's exclusive control of the political power, the industrial technocracy did not feel it as a blow. Partly, because it was too busy with branching out in the adjacent sectors, of which the administration was the most important. The setting up of the central industrial departments and the mushrooming of the economic ministries accounted for the main process of the industrial technocracy's penetrating the administration. And, by the early '80s, the administration was the main ground of confrontation between the two bureaucracies – political and industrial. It was only the main site for development of compromises and of a modus vivendi that should make both competitors comfortable. That period of relative "peaceful coexistence" between the two structures was the "golden era" of socialism in Romania. The competition for power between them never stopped, but its stake was still not the very survival of one of them. Consequently, the competition continued but it was not fierce.

Starting with 1980 though, Romania knew a deep economic crisis, and that opened a conflict for the settlement of which compromises were not enough. In the second half of the '80s, the conflict acquired political dimensions. The second stage thus started of the story of the competition for power between the political bureaucracy and the industrial technocracy. That time, the industrial technocracy had to fight for its own survival. It was the same with the political bureaucracy for, the stake of the game that time was keeping or changing not only some political characters, but the whole system of distribution of power in society.

It was all because around Romania the world was rapidly changing, leaving an industrial era behind and entering a new one. The technological revolution would eliminate the role of skilled industrial workers as the mainstay of production. First, it would shrink their numbers, as the share of workers was declining both within the total active population and within the total manpower in industry. Even more dramatic though, was the decline in the importance of their industrial functions that would be taken over to an ever greater extent by machines or by a growing new industrial bureaucracy that had to do with computers, marketing, financial speculation and technological development. The skilled workers, that used to make the backbone of industry before, would see themselves forced to take refuge more and more to industrial services: maintenance, special operations, the manufacturing of luxury or single products, etc.

The revolution started in the developed West in the '60s, but it came to change the mechanisms of the international market only by the beginning of the '80s, with the advent of what was called "Reaganism" in the United States and "Thacherism" in Europe, or a new liberal "revolution" in books of political economics. But to Romania, caught as it was in the scissors of prices in the international market operated by the representatives of the new type of industrial economy, the only reasonable solution was to get integrated with that process and change as soon as it could its own industrial and especially social structures. The industrial technocracy, through the agency of its elites in scientific research, design and foreign trade, was pressing hard along that line. But, to the political bureaucracy, the dwarfing of both the numbers and especially economic importance of the skilled industrial workers was tantamount to accepting the destruction of its social base. Not because the industrial workers were overly dedicated to the party secretaries and would fight to keep them in power. They did just the opposite in December 1989! But because, in the political equation, the communist party's bureaucracy could derive legitimacy only and solely from its representing the workers and leaning the balance of power to their advantage, in order to counter politically the technical and technological power that made the monopoly of the industrial technocracy. Having to make an option between accepting a profound economic crisis and industrial change, the political bureaucracy at head with Ceausescu chose to accept the economic crisis, because an industrial change would have meant also a change in the balance of forces in the power mechanisms. And so, it made of the technocracy the main target of a process if not of destruction, at least of limitation and marginalization.

In a way, it seemed to be a revival of the gone times of the '50s, when political truthfulness to the communist party was more important than professional competence and the unconditional obedience by the party leadership's commands was reinstated as the leading criterion of decision and activity. One must admit that Ceausescu and his political bureaucracy accepted without hesitation and in full awareness the economic and social consequences of the policy they had chosen. They also developed an ample complex of measures of all kind, from reinforced political surveillance and altered foreign policy orientations to the effort for developing an internal outlet for the "traditional" industry, through tremendous investment in public works, some of them useful, like the Danube-Black Sea Canal, other ones useless, like the People's House, all of them just as expensive.

After 1985, the year when the Soviet Union launched, shy at first, the reform then the giving up of communism in East Europe, the industrial technocracy switched to direct, mute underground fight, material-ized both in sabotaging the official policies and, especially, in de-legiti-mating the political bureaucracy and exonerating both the communist party with its three million members and the administration, whose sup-port was absolutely indispensable for the success of any change.

Three oh the elites of technocracy played an essential role in all that process. One was the elite of research-design, higher education, data procession and the like, that was the most involved in technological development and had become some sort of technical aristocracy of the economy. It is that elite that articulated the unwritten ideology and pre-pared and dominated the December revolution and much of the period that followed, the ideology of technical competence which we have already seen in action. Paradoxically, that elite would be pushed aside by the transition, precisely because the transition has not been able to settle the economic crisis and to orient Romania precisely toward what that elite had proclaimed as a base for social and economic change, meaning the technological change. The second is the elite of representantives of technocracy in the administration's structures, in ministries, central industrial departments and other central institutions of the State Planning Committee type. It has secured an oppositional unity and the connection with the managers of the big industrial units and the technocracy at their level, the only one that was in direct touch with the industrial workers and could attract them to the process of contestation and change. Likewise, it ensured the administration's co-operation during the revolution and right after it. The third technocratic elite, which has almost never been mentioned as such in Romania, but without whose cooperation neither the revolution nor what followed have been possible, was the military technocracy.

The army was the main paradox, hence, the main weakness of the communist power system. The initial communist army, the Red Army of the October revolution, was simply the armed people directly led by politicians. That was the role of the political commissary in the army. The second world war eliminated such armies and replaced them by professional armies, resting on technology and dominated by engineers and technicians of war. Romania's socialist army too, was "stuffed" with its own political bureaucracy, but, just like in industry, and even faster and more thouroughly, in the army it was marginalized and pushed outside the real sphere of power. The authoritativeness of the political aide rested only and solely on the commander's geniality. On the other

hand, the army was even more responsive than industry to the technological degradation that went with the communist party's policy after
1980, and the military more allergic to the attempts of the political bureaucracy to strengthen its own control. Therefore, in all East-European
countries, the armies backed the revolutions. Romania made no exception in that respect. Moreover, in the Romanian revolution, the role of
the army was essential. Nor could have any revolution been made in
Romania without the army's first tacit, then outspoken consent. As a
matter of fact, the turning point, the moment of triumph of the revolution in Bucharest, just like in Timisoara for that matter, was the moment
when the army sided with the revolution.

The third stage was that of the revolution, that decided in favor of
technocracy. The December 1989 revolution overthrew the political bureaucracy of the communist party. The power resulted from the revolution – the National Council of the National Salvation Front and the
Provisional National Unity Council and the governments that followed
– handed over the political power to the industrial technocracy, or, more
exactly, to a combination of industrial technocracy and administrative
bureaucracy, the foundations of which had been laid as early as the
'70s.

3. The Preparation of the Revolution

The multitude scenarios and suspicions about the "plots" pursuing
the manipulation of the revolution by small groups of anti-Ceausescu
conspirators for their own interest, was fuelled first of all by the apparently incredibly easy success of the revolution. Especially the West but
also much of the country's population and, paradoxically, even the dissidents, overrated the repressive force of Ceausescu's regime and its
political stability. That image deterred many of the potential acts of
opposition against his rule and reinforced the belief that Ceausescu's
regime could be overthrown only in extraordinary circumstances, wtih
great difficulty and, probably, at the cost of heavy casualties. Against
all those expectations, Ceausescu's regime fell after one and a half days
of peaceful demonstrations in Bucharest and a week of bloody clashes
between demonstrators and order-keeping forces, including the army,
in Timisoara. When, after the outburst of demonstrations in Timisoara,
violence was unleashed and the crowd was fired at, a great many peo-

ple were sure that the story of the Tian-an-men square would be re-peated in Romania. The army had firmly suppressed in China the stu-dents' attempt to overthrow the rule, but it was more or less tacitly backed by a part of the higher leadership of the Chinese communist party. In Romania even that backing did not exist. However, the revolution was successful after the Bucharest population joined Timisoara's. One by one, all the institutions that were supposed to support the regime drew back: the militia, the security and the army and, ultimately, even Ceaus-escu's personal guard. Ceausescu's rule fell not so much because of the heaviness of the blows against it, as rather because there was no one to back it any longer.

Another source of confusion created about the revolution was its specific. The December revolution had but little resemblance with other revolutions, better said with our own representation of the revolutions. There was no political force, more or less underground, constituted be-fore the outburst of the revolution, to organize and lead it politically. No matter how many dissidents, no matter how great their popularity and how numerous the small groups of "conspirators" that would have tried to project the unfolding of the revolution, they did not led it in any way. This does not mean that the revolution was not prepared and that some of its events were not triggered purposefully.

The Ideology of the Revolution

The most important part of the preparations for the revolution started long before 1989 and it consisted of the emergence of an ideology that challenged the extant political and social regime and proclaimed the necessity to change it. Such an ideology never appeared in Romania in an explicit, meaning written form, but it knew underground develop-ment, against the background of general discontent with the steady de-cline of the quality of life and, quite paradoxically, by using elements of the official ideology. The process started with a dramatic deterioration of the communist ideology, in a way rather similar to the emergence of heresies within a prevailing religion.

Unlike other ideologies, the communist one claims to derive its affirmations from scientific knowledge. All social classes and groups in a society are interested in misrepresenting the reality, except for one: the proletariat, the industrial workers that is. For that reason, the only correct perspective of knowledge is the one that deliberately starts from the industrial workers interests. But the idustrial workers have neither the time nor the knowledge required to study the society and draw from that study the conclusions fit to underlie their political activity. The task is assumed by the communist party, which take upon itself the role to politically educate afterwards the workers and to lead them toward changing the society for their benefit. Communists, in their capacity as politicians of the proletariat, are what they are precisely because they are possessed of a superior cognisance and, based on it, of a higher competence. Competence is the asset claimed by communist leaders and employed by them in order to legitimate their right to power. And with the same competence they legitimate their authoritarianism as well. Cognisance is not democratically sanctioned by vote. The truth is still the truth, whether the people agree to it or not. And it is pointless to organize voting, even if democratic, to tell the truth from the fake. That is why, when the power in a communist party was concentrated in the hands of one leader alone, his main attribute was heigher competence. Communist dictators are geniuses. Other dictators are inspired by the divinity, are bearers of traditions or of some purity, or they are simply powerful. Communist dictators, from Lenin to Ceausescu, through Stalin, Mao or Kim Il Sung, are simply so competent as they are considered to be geniuses.

It was precisely this superior competence of communists as leaders of the workers and of the communist leaders as the party's leaders that was attacked and smashed by the alternate ideology that was emerging on the ruins of the official one. The fundamental theorem of that new ideology says not only that the party activists, the political elite of the working class, are not its most competent representatives, but that they are the least competent ones, and their leaders, far from being geniuses, are either stupid or insane. That ideology was not given written form, but it is very important to understand that it was precisely its orality that made it extremely popular and helped a lot in its communication, all while rendering actually impossible its countering by official means. It was circulated in form of anecdotes and jokes about Ceuasescu and his wife, of "sure" news relayed from close sources or of "own" experiences of those who got in touch them and of an extraordinarily long casuistry of party activists' absurd or harmful actions. To put things in a nutshell, it took on the form of orally transmited folk literature, the more convincing as no interested source could be traced. An everyday ideology thus developed in years, that could be summed up in a few fundamental sentences. First, it said that things in Romania were bad, which was in fact easily to see and countered the official thesis that Romania fared better than ever. Second, the living was bad in Romania because the country was badly rules. And the country was badly ruled because it was ruled by incompetent people, the party activists, ruled in their turn by a madam – Ceausescu. The thesis of Ceausescu's insanity or at least of the insane character of his decisions was not difficult to sustain, especially in the last years of his regime, when the decisions made seemed to be more and more arbitrary and less and less in touch with reality. The yawning gap between Ceausescu and reality was well known, starting even from those who had to forge statistics, reporting record productions in agriculture and industry, and ending with those who were seeing the whole districts in Bucharest torn apart after the presidential car had traversed the zone.

But, the popular ideology did more than just blaming the country's economic and social disaster on the rulers. It offered also a credible alternative. The fundamental idea was that both on an internal plane and on an external one, Romania's crisis was artificial. On an external plane, it was clear that nobody had anything against Romania but against Ceausescu personally. Romania's isolation was obviously blamed on Ceausescu's rather personal initiative. On an internal plane, the idea was that Romania was a rich country with a big potential. Both the country's wealth and its potential were being however irrationally wasted by the rulers' whims. But there were also people who knew how to turn to advantage the wealth and potential. Those people were the country's technical intelligentsia. Sufficed it to give liberty, meaning authority, meaning power to the normal rulers of the economy, of enterprises, of cities, for them, the people specially trained to solve the problems, to do it. It was about the industrial technocracy. It was supposed to know how to rule Romania in such a way as to have things go well, but it could not do it because of the political bureaucracy.

Such an ideology is typical of the everyday thinking and this is precisely what explains its great success and its ability to be disseminated in simple forms, needing no written texts and sophisticated elaboration. It offers a simple and credible explanation for the reality. Central to the explanation is to identify the culprits, answerable for the extant evils. The ideology also comes up with the solution: replace the impotent (or ill willing) rulers with those who are naturally competent, the industrial technocracy that is. To legitimate this claim of the industrial technocracy a very interesting and consequential change appeared in the society's general explanation. The fundamental problems in the model of society the communist ideology built were political in nature. The political nature of the problems justified the politicial nature of the leadership and the central role attributed to the (communist) political party. In the new ideology, the society's general problems were considered to be only the effects of purely technical problems. Likewise, the solutions were of a technical nature and consequently, they had to be entrusted with technicians and not with politicians who were not possessed of any thorough technical training.

The new ideology had a fast and spectacular success. Although its orality was maintained all the time, it was however well supported by publications that had the indirect function of substantiating with arguments the technical character of the society's problems on the one hand, and of gloryfying the tehnician on the other. By the end of the '80s, that new ideology had already eliminated the official ideology which was poorly preached and more and more replaced by the mere glorification, verging the absurd, of Ceausescu. Obviously, the effects of such a propaganda were quite different from the expected ones, but all the vast campaign conducted in mass media for turning Ceausescu into a personality like Kim Il Sung was less directed toward convincing the public opinion (absolutely all those who participated in that propaganda spreading knew it to be inefficient with the population), and more meant to flatter Ceausescu himself. The whole official propaganda activity, so impressive for the West, had Ceausescu himself and the handful of his aides as the only favorable spectators and listeners.

Decomposition of Communist Party

Parallel to development of an ideology that was de-legitimating more and more the extant regime and concentrated the blame for its failure on Ceausescu, his family and an ever smaller number of figures around him, there was a shrinking of the social categories, groups and institutions willing to give him support. The most important of them all was the dissolution of the communist party. In the last years, it was matched by an ever more marked lessening of the support the state administration and institutions wre willing to give to the group of political and administrative leaders placed on top of the power pyramid. That support vanished completly on the revolution days.

The dissolution of the communist party started long before the revolution. It did not consist of its numeric shrinking, but of the increasing loss of significance of belonging to it. Unlike the traditional parties, the communist parties, that start from the idea that any activity has a political content, hence it needs political coordination, are not organized according to a territorial principle but according to work places. Consequently, the communist party is not a party of citizens, but a party of laborers, irrespective of their domain of activity and of the work they do. Therefore, the structure of the communist party simply overlaps the structure of the industrial bureaucratic organization. The communist party's territorial organizations are simple territorial groupings of these industrial organizations.

Such an organization was probably efficient at the time the political objectives different from those of the industrial organizations and when their technical managers could be considered, if not necessarily as enemies, at least as indifferent to them. That period ended with the consolidation of the power of the communist regime and the activity of the party organizations in enterprises gradually lost its content and authoritativeness alike. It lost the content as polotics proper yielded to economic, industrial and social politics and the content of the problems were turning from political to technical. It lost authoritativeness as the political decision itself was getting integrated with the normal flows of bureaucratic decision. Once such an integration achieved, the other decision-making flow, along political bureaucracy, was becoming pointless. Under the circumstances, the political organizations in enterprises became pointless in their turn, and their activity remained just formal. The decisions would be made at the level of industrial bureaucracy, based on other decisions which, in turn, would be relayed through the administrative bureaucracy. For a while, at the beginning of industrialization, the party organizations in enterprises did play a role in disciplining the fresh industrial manpower, recently brought to industry and to town, thus becoming some sort of non-administrative pressure at the service of the industrial bureaucracy. But, by the end of the '70s that function too, became minor. Everything the communist party still did at the level of common members in the last decade of activity was propaganda in favor of its higher leadership and, in the very last years, only in Ceausescu's favor.

As the alternate ideology was growing more and more disseminated and appreciated, even that activity lost any real content. In the last period of its existence, the communist party had become a gigantic cocoon inside which the butterfly had died. To be a party member had become a mere, formal condition to accede to certain social services or, for intellectuals, to a normal career. Belonging no longer had any significance, either political or personal.

For that reason, in step with the degradation of the situation in the country and the dissemination of the ideology directed against Ceausescu and the political bureaucracy, not only the members but also the lower echelons of that bureaucracy started if not opposing, at least resisting the official policies. At the bottom, the party secretaries, who were workers in the first place and were discharging some sort of "a-dollar-a-year" political function, would obviously identify themselves with the workers and not with the political bureaucracy. The local political bureaucracy in turn started to increasingly identify itself with the local interests, thinking of the central leadership as of an often hostile environment factor which had to be adeptly resisted. Although the appointment and keeping in office of the members of that bureaucracy depended only and solely on Ceausescu and its staff department, many of them were ready to side with the local bureaucratic and technocratic structures and develop local or sectorial policies instead of applying the policy devised at the top of the pyramid. Those figures of political bureaucrats, more concerned with the local interests than with the communist party's policy, became the more popular as they acted less in compliance with central guidelines. After the revolution, such activity was considered as "opposition to Ceausescu". Actually, it was only the normal sign of decomposition of the establishment that had reached the stage at which various sectors and especially local administrative zones are ready to become autonomous from the central power because it antagonizes their own interests. The process was not a new one: the history of feudalism and the history of the colonial empires' falling apart are histories of precisely this process, obviously at a different scale.

It was important for the preparation of the Romanian revolution that before it the communist party was no longer a political force. It wasn't even an operational organization any more. That is why it did not function in any way during the revolution, when the true forces that confrunted one another were, on the one hand, the mass of the population, the citizens whom the communist party ignored all along its history and, on the other hand, the state's institutions, the only organizational structure in operation. Even Ceausescu understood it. When he opposed the demonstrations in Timisoara or Bucharest, he opposed them in his capacity as the head of the state and not as the head of the ruling party. During his trial staged after the revolution he acted in the same position as the head of state. The pre-revolution decomposition of the communist party was so complete that it not only failed to play any role prior to and during the revolution, but it did not even show up after the revolution in order to dissolve itself or to allow its members to quit. Which has led to the politically inconsequential paradox that, formally, it counts now as many members as it had before the revolution.

4. The Hopes of the Revolution

The Victorious Revolution

The success of the revolution was mainly due to the fact that the institutions meant to defend the political regime did not function. More precisely, they refused to function, by the pretext that they were institutions of the state and not of the political regime. That phenomenon is to be credited with the victory of the revolution. It consisted of the abrupt – and unexpected for Ceausescu – separation of the administrative bureaucracy from the political regime. Left without a political support precisely since, in order to have no opposition at the party's level, it had relied on the state administration, the political regime did not only collapse, it simply vanished.

The detachment of the institutions making up the system of the state's administrative bureaucracy – the army, police, central and local governments, etc. – from the political regime was a process that advanced during the battle fought for the control of the power, but it became a fact at the moment when the regime endangered the state itself. The administrative bureaucracy does not have to choose between the state and the political regime because the administrative bureaucracy is the state itself. When it was sure that the state was in danger, the administrative bureaucracy sacrificed the political regime. Although, at least at the beginning, everybody was convinced that only its leaders would be sacrificed.

All these processes of dissolution of the support which the political regime generally and Ceausescu particularly needed in order to resist, lasted long. A certain minimal level may have been reached as early as November 1987, when the Brasov workers' demonstration took place. However, it was not able to trigger the revolution, the same as the Timisoara demonstration was unable to start in 1989. The revolution in Romania was not seeking a pretext, because there were pretexts all the time – actually any event could be turned into a pretext for the revolution, including the apprehension of a Reformed priest in a provincial town. It was waiting for an organization and for leaders. It is here that have their place all the small plots and attempts of organization that proceeded more or less coherently but with a relative intensity, in the period prior to the revolution. Ultimately, the revolution started without being organized and it took the concrete form of a big, spontaneous movement of the population. And it was spontaneous, even though there were nuclei of incitation of the population and of keeping its spirits up in the most difficult period, on the night of 21 to 22 December, when it was still possible that the revolution be suppressed by the army.

Actually, what allowed for the revolution to succede was the obvious lack of legitimacy of the political regime. For, the legitimacy of the regime was ensured only and solely by the popular support and, within it, by the workers' support. The regime claimed to be at the people's service and the representative of the industrial workers. When, on the morning of 22 December, the workers left the enterprises to get out in the street and demand Ceausescu's resignation, it was clear for everybody that his legitimacy at the helm of the state as representative of the workers no longer existed. That allowed the state's institutions to detach themselves from the leaders of a regime that had turned illegitimate. Neither the army nor the militia, and not even the "Securitate" were institutions built to fight against the people, if need be, in order to maintain a small group of political leaders in rule. In that respect, Ceausescu's dictatorship differed from other dictatorships in which the repression bodies were not serving the state, but the regime or only its leaders. Such dictatorships can be overthrown only through civil war or military coups. If Ceausescu had availed of a small private army, that could, maybe, have been able to suppress the revolution. But, things being as they were, he was deserted even by his personal guard, which was not personal at all, but a mere service which an institution of the state provided to its legitimate head.

It has been worth enlarging on all this process as it helps understanding what revolution meant for the administrative bureaucracy. From a bureaucratic point of view, to accept the revolution meant to consider the legitimacy and not the legality. That was tantamount to a sudden shift of the subordination from a center of political decision – Ceausescu and the summits of the party and of incumbent government – to another center of political decision: the leaders of the revolution, whoever they were. By backing the revolution, the administrative bureaucracy – people and institutions – remained in power. It remained to be seen at whose service they would place that power.

Triumphant in spite of the absence of leaders and organization, the revolution generated hopes for a change. Most of them have proved to be unrealistic as they were unjustified. But then, on the first day of the ebullience generated by the triumph, optimism and confidence in the future prevailed.

The Expectations

What did people expect and hope from the revolution? Almost everything. In terms of politics, the fall of the "Ceausescu clan", meaning in fact not only his family but the whole bunch of associates, that were expected to yield the place to the competent, correct and congenial leadership preached by the ideology of the revolution. Apart from a wise leadership, the major expectation was for a democracy, not quite sufficiently defined in terms of rules of access but clear in its content, meaning the population's participation in decision making. The population had been practically eliminated from politics by the communist party's bureaucracy and it had no intention at all to remain so any longer. The form of democracy which the revolution imposed immediately was the democracy within institutions and enterprises. The revolution triggered a wave of elections for executives there, some sort of democracy of work collectivities. Although the system was soon eliminated by the country's new political leadership, the population has remained interested and active in politics, from street demonstrations to participation in elections. Only after three or four years of endless disappointment, has the interest in politics of the man in the street started fading away.

A very important package of expectations was pinned to the change of one of the most abhored characteristics of the former society, that could be termed as "social hypocrasy". That name conceals a very rich phenomenology and a way of living after all. Two important components were meeting there. One was associated with the impossibility to speak out opinions, views or truths, other than official ones or than those accepted and approved of by the political control bodies. Formally, there was only one opinion in the communist society – the official one. The communist party's propaganda system was not only forbidding the expression of alternate opinions or of criticism against the official opinion. It was also forcing everybody to repeat or overtly back the official one. That compelled to generalized hypocrisy which had generated in turn subtle forms of disguised opposition, like Ana Blandiana's poem about a tomcat that seemed to impersonate Ceausescu. Another important component was related to the rules of conduct and success in society. There were two such sets of rules, a formal one, that was almost never observed, and another, informal one, that was virtually operating in the open, employed by everyone but never recognized as such, as it was profundly illegal. The former was mimicking the promotion of competence, honesty, etc. The latter was a generalized system of corruption and nepotism which, however, rigorously observed all formal aspects of the former. Nobody, not even Ceausescu's entourage, cherished any illusion about the applicability of the official system which they were actually breaking as light – heartedly as all others did. What was categorically expected from the revolution was the elimination of the compulsory hypocrisy, of the need to always simulate a false reality, and also the change of the mechanism based on corruption, nepotism and the arbitrary use of the power.

Closely associated with it was the belief that the revolution ushered in an era of social justice and equity. Not so much of egalitarianism. On the contrary, the uniformity of egalitarianism was well known and it was therefore rejected by everyone, including those who could not hope for a privileged position if they objectively appraised themselves. Communism promoted privileges and advantages that had nothing to do with the individuality, with the person, but had everything to do with the position held in the bureaucratic structures. Such a system of distribution of the privileges was just bound to generate a genuine aristocracy of the power that had no personal merits. The revolution launched a campaign against that type of privileges, a campaign well sustained by the technocratic ideology relying on personal merits and their recognition through level of education and professional accomplishments. Behind the requirements for the elimination of the function privileges there was however a more profound expectation as well. An essential characteristic of communism is its collectivism. In the structure of values typical for this society, collectivity is always valued higher than the individual and the individual is expected not only to let himself subordinated but also to "melt" in the collectivity.That characteristic of the system was pushed to its extreme by Ceausescu and his propaganda system, so much that Romania seemed to be made only of him (maybe also his wife), as the only individuality, on the one hand, and the formless and anonymous mass of the "people", on the other hand. The revolution was expected to redeem to their right the individual, with his peculiarities and, possibly also the small group of individuals, who would recognize themselves as sharing common characteristics. In other words, people expected a dramatic revigoration of the civil society and the Romanians' mass adhesion to the hundreds of initiatives of the nongovernmental organizations to set up branches in Romania fully proves it. But, above all, the revolution was expected to establish a system of values central to which would be the individual and not the collective abstractions like the working class or the people.

The reconsideration of the individualism was not in the least seen as antagonizing the social justice and equity. Especially in its last years, socialism had been characterized precisely by an extremely tough social inequity. Not only did the individual, taken as such, seem to have no value at all, but the distribution in the society was extremely inequitable. What was the characteristic of the system and explains also the expectations emerged with the revolution is the observation that such an inequity was manifest not so much in the great difference of goods and services the privileged strata availed of by comparison with the disadvantaged ones, although it was significant, as rather in the arbitrariness of the distribution on the one hand, and its profoundly illegal character, on the other hand. The revolution was expected to fight them all. Among other things, that was precisely why the population strongly reacted whent it was first confrunted with a genuinely individualist ideology and in an extreme form at that. In the spring of 1990, the young wing of the National Liberal Party, freshly remade and still groping for a doctrine, started proclaiming some sort of primitive social Darwinism in a form that resembled that of Jack London's characters. The result was a disaster not only from an electoral point of view, but also theoretically. The most remarkable achievement of that attempt was the establishment of the notion of "savage liberalism", which both the population and all political forces agreed to reject.

But, of course, the first thing expected from the revolution was a rise in the living standard and in the quality of life. The technocratic ideology had steadily promoted the idea that one lived poorly in Romania, an otherwise rich country, because it was poorly managed. In the last years, adding to that explanation was also the official explanation that Romania had to make efforts to pay off the foreign debt. When in 1988, Ceausescu announced that Romania had paid off its foreign debt, everybody expected a fast lifting of the restrictions of every kind imposed on the people's consumption, especially on food and energy. It did not happen, and the elimination of those restrictions was one of the strongest claims of the revolution. The greater was therefore the disappointment when, experts this time, estimated that bringing the electricity production, for instance, up to the household and industrial consumption demand would take no less than about five years. That was a first moment of truth, rather cruel, and the beginning of a process of understanding of the fact that shortages in the country were not the result of Ceausescu's absurd thrift but also of a degradation of the whole economy that had not even been suspected by public opinion. And, to a great extent, not even by the technocracy, it too, misled by the forged statistics of the official festivism.

But the revolution expectations were not associated only with increased comsumption, or the remaking of urban lightning. At least just as much they were associated with economic recovery. Everybody hoped for a fast economic recovery, the more so as the developed West too, was expected to support it by the model of the support given to Poland and Hungary. Moreover, the Romanians expected a special prize, given that they made a revolution. Almost nobody thought that the Romanian revolution occured later than all the other ones and that Romania's previous international isolation has deterred many of the interests the West could have in the zone, consequently, of the reasons why it might intervene. Apart from international sopport, the Romanians very much counted on themselves. Let us not forget that the fundamental thesis of the rechnocracy's ideology was that it, the technocracy, was able to do what Ceausescu and the political bureaucracy did not manage. The main argument was its own position as technocracy, its technical competence and the assumption that the main issues that waited for solution were technical in nature. So, nobody doubted that the economic rehabilitation would be fast and spectacular.

None of those expectations was fulfilled. Consequent to the revolution, essential changes have taken place both in the political system and in the economy and social structures, in culture, education, international relations. But these changes were neither foreseen nor hoped for on those first days of the revolution. From this angle, the revolution has remained unfinished in all domains. Its consequences, disappointing as compared with the hopes, have been fast summed up as a balance of discontents. But they need a closer inspection, not in order to be illustrated more, but in order to have their essence understood and, above all, to get an explanation as to why, for all the changes, the new reality operates faultily or not at all. Since the revolution has remained incomplete, we need a critical analysis of the transition.

The Spontaneous Transition

Were all those hopes and expectations really justified? It should be stressed that they relied on nothing but a rather inarticulate everyday ideology, which was more of a mythology than a doctrine, regarding the social reality that had to be changed. In that respect, the expectations were groundless. The only point in their favor was that there had been a revolution.

The revolution had annulled to a great extent the determinations which tha past, meaning the reality, brings into the future. At the climactic moment of the revolution, none of the rules, laws, mechanisms of any kind operated any longer. Any change seemed possible at that time. But, beyond appearances, the revolution ushered in also real possibilities. Some of them could not even be foreseen then. But people intuited that, if not everything at least a great many things could be done. What is sure is that, on those days of victory of the revolution, any direction of change was possible. This is very important and needs emphasis since, as long as the revolution is not finished, this potential of change keeps high.

A revolution annuls rules, institutions and social mechanisms, but it surely does not annul any normal functioning. For instance, it does not annul the laws of nature or those economic mechanisms that do not depend on the form of social organization, like the basic laws of monetary circulation. But, since it has the force to radically influence or change social and economic behaviors, a revolution can change as radically the economy and the society or the political system alike. Therefore, no kind of classical analysis wholly stands when it is about a revolution, since all analyses start from the assumption of stable characteristics of reality, wheras a revolution annuls or has the ability of annulling such a stability.

At the moment of triumph of a revolution, a society has very high degree of liberty. It can take almost any way. Subsequently, restrictions dictated by the internal or international environment can intervene and change the evolution, but, at least in establishing the initial direction of the change, the arbitrariness is virtually complete. The arbitrariness is to be settled politically. This means that the decision on the direction of change belongs to the political leadership of the revolution. Often, such decisions are only too little realistic or are contradicted by subsequent evolutions. Generally, proposing a utopian direction of change is not something rarely met with in revolutions. And even if these directions are afterwards moderated or amended, as it has always happened in hsitory, the prime decision retains remarkable influence and importance.

What characterizes the Romanian revolution is that, in the absence of a previously crystalized political leadership, such decision on the sense of change has never been made explicitly. However, changes did occur. And, as Theodor Stolojan noted on anlaysing his own experience as a prime minister in the post-revolution period, the changes occured at the highest possible speed and pace, at the pace at which new institutions were possible to introduce in order to fill in the void created by the destruction of the old ones. That process has decided fundamentally the characteristics of the transition in post-revolution Romania.

The transition is the period of movement between two stable periods. One is the socialist society which was exited through the revolution. The other may be the one that the revolution has proposed or may be one of which nobody has thought. But, it is sure that the changes that occur after a revolution are bound to lead to another period of stability. Societies abhore instabilities hence also transitions. Always, in periods of transition, there are fundamental institutions that do not operate and important social relations that are labile. Therefore, the societies rapidly develop their institutions and stabilize their social relations. After the December revolution, all institutions and all social relations could have been changed. But, because there was no one to change them, they have changed themselves and have stabilized themselves, because societies simply cannot exist in the absence of institutions and relations. For that reason, the transition in Romania has proceeded spontaneously to a great extent. The revolution ushered in the possibility of change, and even forced it when it destroyed the old institutions and relations and vacated the place for new ones.

These changes did occur, but they were neither foreseen nor controlled. They simply resulted from the behaviors of individuals and social groups, in keeping with the balances of forces among them. A political system has thus come into being. The political system born after the revolution has not been given direction by anyone. The political parties have emerged without the approval of the revolution leaders. On the contrary, they were forced to acknowledge the realities of political parties after the emergence of the National Peasant Party and of the National Liberal Party. Then, for a long time, all Romanian politicians and doctrinaires stated that the best thing for the Romanian political life would be to orbit around two political parties that should take turns at the power, and countless electoral systems and party laws proposed, that were hoped to be conducive to such an ideal system. In actual fact, it has all remained mere words, and Romania is counting now over 150 registered political parties, about a dozen of which are represented in the Parliament and some other ones outside it are involved in the intrigue acting as politics in Romania. The new political system does not resemble the old one, but it has accomplished none of the expectations pinned to the revolution, since it is neither democratic nor able to provide a real political leadership of society. In this respect, the political transition did occur, a change did occur, but it marked the failure of the political revolution.

Things are about the same with the economy. No sign of economic growth, modernization, renewed technologies, restructuring and the like.

But this does not mean that the Romanian economy has not changed essentially. By no means can one speak of a socialist economy any longer, even though most of the production means still wait for privatization. But, these changes have not in the least fulfilled the hopes pinned to the revolution. Maybe the best example in this respect is the private sector. The private sector, which unquestionably is the doing of the revolution, was expected to become the engine of an economic development focussing on productivity, quality and efficiency. It has not achieved any of these. instead of developing the production, of raising the quality and allowing for the accumulations needed by investments in technology, the private sector has simply turned into a mess for some to get rich on account of others. Caritas, the bankrupt get-rich-fast company, and, generally, the pyramid money-spinning schemes that have mushroomed in the freshly "capitalist" economy of Romania, and of the other formerly socialist countries for the matter, are characteristics for the wildcat transition in the economy. Sure, the private sector does not mean only Caritas, but it does not mean something else in the first place either. The wildcat transition, although the reform programs were promising and even meaning something quite different, had led there too, to a so unexpected reality, that we do not even understant it clearly. Anyway, it has meant a failure of the economic revolution.

If the changing Romanian society behaves like a river the embakments of which have been destroyed and which is overflowing completely out of control, obeying only by the law of gravitation, then it is not in the least correct to speak of a "reform". We can surely speak of a change, for it is clear that Romania is changing, but it is an uncontrolled change of which we know neither where it is leading to nor how it proceeds.

But, for the population this is unconceivable and absolutely unacceptable. The population may be ready to accept the costs of transformations and the troubles that go with them and even the mistakes that seem to be dotting the "reform", on condition that it should be convinced that eventually all of them will lead to a foreseeable future, and that future will not be worse than he present, promising instead a sizeable improvement. Communism too, used to promise about the same, and the population is backing now the efforts for getting rid of its characteristics – the privatization, for instance – precisely because the preachers of communism proved to be liar prophets. For the population's point of view, the reduction of the 1989 revolution to the mere replacement of a bunch of liar or uninspired prophets by another bunch of the same kind means an immaterial change and it is questionable whether making a revolution for that purpose was worth the pain. True, the preachers of communism and the rulers of socialist Romania were also accused of ill faith, but that accusation is minor. If it was not communism but only its leaders that were guilty of Romania's economic, social and cultural decline in the eighth and ninth decades – a very popular thesis before and right after the revolution – then all that had to be done was to change the rulers. But, President Ion Iliescu, who accused in 1989 Ceausescu for not having respected the principles of scientific communism, thinks quite different now, four years after that statement, and claims just as strongly that only "the passage to a market economy" can be a solution for Romania, just as, in fact, for all countries of the former communist bloc. What is worrying is that neither Ion Iliescu nor the other political and economic leaders, or the reputed specialists and journalists, the union leaders, all those who repeat the same statement, are relying on anything when they say it and when they ask all the others not only to believe them but also to follow them. Whereto? This is something nobody knows, not even the leaders that, professionally advised by their aides, are putting on a confidence they don't really have.

So, the first big reason of worry is that we are not controlling the change in any way. Neither the population, nor the rulers or even those who consider themselves as being on the Opposition have any clear idea of what, how and why ought to be changed. However, major changes are obviously taking place. After the revolution, we introduced in the social body a host of new elements to which it has to adjust itself somehow: from price liberalization to making over one million jobless, from fast rise in the people's consumption to the abolition or free medical care, etc. All old mechanisms and structures have been seriously affected and some of them dismantled for good. Or, a social body does not settle for voids, a new structure or mechanism always appear in order to replace older, disused or destroyed ones. So, the society does change. But, since we are not in control of the change, we cannot say how it changes.

We don't even have information enough regarding the changes that have already occured or about to occur, many of them as unforeseen side effects of new elements introduced by the reform. Changes do take place, but they are spontaneous. We can say but little about them, for, the most conspicuous are also the most superficial ones. The multi-party system is a reality just as superficial as the freedom of the press. Behind the plurality of the partie there lies the uniqueness of the "re-form": all the "program-like" slogans of the parties sound like carbon copies and they illustrate the same general ideology. Even the change in governance, from a center-right coalition (National Salvation Front – liberals under the Stolojan government) to a center-left coalition (Demo-cratic National Salvation Front with the Romanian National Unity Party, Greater Romania Party and Socialist Labor under the Vacaroiu govern-ment) was made without any important change in the reform policy. After its installation, the Vacaroiu Government did nothing for two years but go on with the reform program of the former Stolojan Government.

As for the real profound changes, the paradox is that one cannot realize to what extent they are really departing from what could be con-sidered as the failure of the old regime. We are so little able to appraise their content, that we cannot say it for sure that we are really departing from the former regime instead of sinking even deeper precisely what was its disfunctional part.

This applies to all domains. The transition has taken place, it has even started to draw to an end, which is proved by the decline in the pace and importance of changes. The structures that have emerged with-out being wanted or planned by somebody, have started to get stabi-lized, entrenched. We have barely awakened from the enthusiasm gen-erated by the revolution and have left behind the political battle about "who should lead Romania in the transition?", that we have found out that the transition has already occured, and the resulting society is not in the least what we have wanted.

The Critical Point of Transition

No matter how bitter the disappointment caused by the failure of the revolution's expectations, they are surely not able to change the reality. As recorded by history, the number of social movements that ended by failing the expectations of those who hopefully supported them, is very big. The most recent experience of the kind for the Romanians is prob-ably the communist revolution. It too, generated hopes and expecta-tions of about the same kind as the December revolution. But now, five years after the revolution, we are reaching a critical moment of the transition. It is not only about sentimental responses like expectations and disappointments. The transition that has proceeded spontaneously is now drawing to an end, leaving behind a certain type of society. And this type of society is disappointing and even disfunctional. And, at least in some respects, it generates dangers, both social and national.

Beyond any other objectives of the transition or of the economic and political reforms proposed and beyond any proposals or programs set forth by political parties, there is a consensus, not only of politicians, but of the population, on two fundamental objectives – stability and change. Stability refers to the very possibility of governing, of maintaining an order in the social, economic and political life, rules that should allow everybody to find their way in reality. Change means keeping the society on the path of changes and, by this, keeping the hope alive for a mending of the things, even if current ideologies, politics and governance will have to be replaced by new ones. There is a real and virtually unanimous consensus of the population as to the need for order and rules. Not necessarily some specific order and some specific rules; the revolution and the four years that followed have shown that all these can be changed. But the very preferences as to what order and rules ought to be introduced or changed are secondary as compared with the base represented by order generally.

It is the same with the change. The necessity of changing the present is a matter of absolute consensus. But the population is divided already into competing camps when it comes to decide how to change this present.

These two big objectives, generalized, espoused by the whole population, are not explicit and they are not exclusively represented by some specific political party. But they wholly explain the population's political bahavior, the elections returns and the evolution of the orientations of public opinion and, ultimately, of their representatives. When the political fight threatened the stability of the country and of the everyday life, the overwhelming majority of the population voted against those who seemed to be promoters of instability, of arbitrariness and insecurity (in 1990, mainly the historic parties), and for those who were adding the change (i.e. the transition) to stability. Throughout the period after 1989, the perception of the Socialist Labor Party as a party opposing stability to the change was the main reason for that party's lack of popularity, in spite of its populism. The elections of 1992 brought before the electorate an opposition far less opposed to stability than in 1989, and its growing political importance is precisely the result of such a change of image, just like the National Salvation Front led by Petre Roman lost most of the votes it had won in 1989 precisely because it became, by attacking Ion Iliescu, the main bearer of destabilization.

After 1992, when stability ceased being threatened, but threat was mounting against the change, the popular support has started shrinking, not only for the ruling Party of Social Democracy of Romania but also for President Iliescu.

The fact that something does not work is not important as long as it does not affect the two big objectives on which the population obviously agrees. But as they are in danger, the preoccupation becomes acute. And it is growing the more so as now both objectives are perceived as being in danger. This is the critical point of the transition which both the population and some politicians start to intuite first of all as a big impasse.

The change is the first that seems to have yielded. Althoug novelties still appear or are heralded, none of them gives the certainty or the hope for essential changes with deep-going effects that can be taken for signs of a further movement of the society.

On the contrary, the society seems to be getting more and more stuck in the present and neither the government nor the opposition seem to have resources any longer to push it out of this immobility. The only major novelty of the PSDR rule – the Law of Speeding up the Privatization – is just a revival of the principle of privatization of 1991: free distribution of 30 per cent of the privatized economy to the population. Other initiatives – the Law of Nationalized Houses, for instance, are confined to proclaiming the status quo. The transition seems to be coming to a halt and, with it, vanish also the hope that the changes that still miss could ever take place and the changes that displease could be mended. For, if the population is still accepting this obviously dissatisfactory reality, it does it only because it thinks of it as only an unpleasant stage on a road leading to a definitely better world than the present one. Stoppage of changes, or at least of the essential changes, is tantamount to the threat that this world "in transition" should become permanent, and this is unacceptable.

Moreover, it is not only the change but also the stability that starts being perceived as being in danger. For two main reasons. First, because the extant order and rules are only partial and here and there they do not operate. The current stability is acceptable only as long as the movement guarantees its completion and improvement on the run. When the movement stops, the guarantee too, stops and the stability is threatened. Even more important is another threat to stability, which takes over with the stoppage of the transition. deprived of motion, the main institutions of the order, political ones first of all, start decomposing and threatening thus the general stability.

At this stage of the transition it is obvious that something has to be done. The need for intervention starts being felt, even though unclearly, at all levels and, somehow, even inside the establishment. The bad news is that, as it appeared from the spontaneous transition of so far, the society is not able to respond, no matter how needed the response is. The political parties are not built to model the transition. They are so impotent in relation to this objective that they cannot even give such a necessity a doctrinary articulation. The two all-mighty bureaucracies, the administrative bureaucracy and the industrial technocracy are, by their structure, not functional in relation to such problems. They might account for a useful instrument of intervention in reality, employed to solve the technical problems of its intervention, if a force apt to define and coordinate the intervention existed. But they cannot become such a force themselves. Moreover, if such taking over of the transition and its modelling would affect the current system of distribution of the power, then the normal tendency of the bureaucracy is to resist the change. The civil society may get excited and aggitated. Actually, it is it that issues most of the signals about the perception of the present impasse and of the need for change. But, the civil society is not ripe enough for it. And, anyway, the change entails the reconstruction of the political level of the society.

The way out of the impasse goes through politics. But politics do not respond and, after five years of waiting, we can conclude that they are not able to. And it is not enough to accept the conclusion. We must also understand why has the political revolution failed.

III. THE FAILURE OF THE POLITICAL REVOLUTION

1.The Power System of the Revolution

The first thing which a revolution dismantles is the political system. It is so constant a feature as sometimes the revolutions are equated with this first consequence. Actually, the change in the political regime is only the beginning of a train of transformations which affects all components of society.

The December 1989 revolution can be recognized as a genuine revolution precisely because it abruptly, brutally and completely abolished the incumbent political regime. It did not only eliminate its main actors – which is actually not essential -, but it also swept all political institutions, both those directly associated with the communist party and those that, formally at least, were autonomous state institutions: the State Council, the Grand National Assembly and the Council of Ministers. For a few days, there were no central authority in Romania. The authority moved to the street and it belonged to anyone who was able to shout loud enough to rally enough passers-by around him. True, on the evening of 22 December, the Director of the Bucharest Technical House, together with several hundred people who entered the Television building announced the setting up of a new body of state power – the National Council of the National Salvation Front -, but, obviously, its authority, just like its legitimacy, relied only on the people's real wish to leave behind as soon as possible the anarchy that threatened to take over in the absence of any authority.

We may wonder that a dozen such institutions were not formed in a dozen other places in Bucharest and across the country, that should then compete among themselves for legitimacy and popular support. But even if such attempts did exist – in Timisoara one day before Ceausescu's fall, or in the building of the communist party's central committee, on the same afternoon of 22 December, they immediately yielded to the authority already publicly announced on TV. And this is extremely significant, just as significant as the fact that nobody challenged the composition of the new institution. The population did not seem very interested in exactly who was and who was not a member in it, but first of all in the existence of the institution itself. For, the real power remained for a long time in the population's hands. And it was ready to follow anyone who gave the impression that he wanted to go some direction.

The Improvised Leadership

For a long time, the new political body survived only because it had no serious opposition to resist. When the opposition did emerge – firmly resolved to replace it – the NCNSF survived precisely because people did not see it clear what the opposition was and what it wanted. And also because it later appeared to be flexible enough when the opposition managed to mobilize a significant popular, media and international support, to simply take it in. It happened when the NCNSF turned into the Provisional National Unity Council. In spite of its ability to survive, the NCNSF can hardly be identified as the center of a revolution. The installation of that new political body, theoretically possessed of absolute power, since it amassed the prerogatives and powers of all political institutions overthrown by the revolution, from Parliament to the political center of the executive and the supreme command of the army, was followed by the most unclear post-revolution period. It lasted from the first days of the triumph of the revolution until after the elections of May 1990.

What was disappointing with the freshly installed NCNSF was that it did not know what to do. Generally, in a revolution, after the dismantlement of the institutions of the former political system there follows a fast period on innovation and construction. The old rules of the political power are eliminated and the new ones are announced and instituted. The new institutions are established as soon as possible, and they start operating, even in an improvised manner, no matter how incomplete the conditions. But, above all, the power starts being exerted in a new way, with different objectives and by different rules. And its main objective and accomplishment is the setting in motion of new mechanisms and institutions in the non-political domains of society, in the economy, administration, everyday life. For, this is precisely what distinguishes a revolution from a mere coup d'etat (with which the December revolution was often compared), the fact that a political force assumes the task to introduce the non-political changes the society needs but cannot introduce by itself. The respective political force can succeed or it can fail, the real changes will be more or less like the initial political project, but in the case of a revolution that followed a normal course, it is sure that it will try to impose the political program of the revolution. But we have already seen that the Romanian revolution was wanting precisely with this part of construction that would follow the victory.

Yet, what characterized the NCNSF is that it was doing nothing of what it was expected to. It did not define a clear direction for the changes. In the evening of 22 December, with the announcement of its composition, the NCNSF issued a 12-point Declaration and Program. On the next days, all the population and all the institutions and organizations still in operation hurried to endorse it, since it was the only document that could give the revolution a sense. But the declaration was far from being a program. Like all "programs" articulated from then on, it was only a list of wishes, most of them had nothing to do with any analysis of reality, other ones – referring to national symbols, etc. – were only a formal way of announcing that the revolution had triumphed. But the most significant was that, after launching the Declaration and Program, the NCNSF did nothing else for the attainment of the objectives announced there. It simply existed, in order to fill the vacuum of power and the absence of institutions brought about by the revolution and to administrate the country's current affairs. So, after an unexpectedly fast and easy success with the overthrow of the previous political regime, the Romanian revolution was marking time in confusion, not knowing which way to go. It was clear that the NCNSF did not know to do with the conquered power, because it did not know what it wanted. The power emerged after the revolution and as its consequence did not have sense. But this is precisely why political institutions are necessary and exist, to give the power a sense and its exercice a meaning. As a political institution, the NCNSF failed completely in discharging that function. The failure, or the infirmity then induced were perpetuated throughout the system of political institutions developed after the 1990 elections. Started victoriously in December 1989, the Romanian revolution remained unaccomplished precisely in the domain where it had to be accomplished the soonest and the fullest, the political domain.

The appearance of this infirmity and its stabilization as a general characteristic of the post-revolution period can be justified by a host of events and successions, some of them unforeseeable, other ones uncontrollable. In brief, it could be explained as a chance result, which would be tantamount to stating that the Romanians were simply unlucky, even when they made a revolution. Yet, on a closer analysis of this train of events, one can distinguish behind the apparent disorder a process that proceeded in a relative coherence and steadiness. It is the process of coming into being of a system of power distribution which, by its own characteristics, is simply non-revolutionary. It is not necessarily opposed to a revolution, it is not a counterrevolution, made in secrecy, as a part of the political opposition and of the intelligentsia like to believe, in order to find some consolation for its failures. But it is neither willing nor able to impose and carry through changes. The coming into being of this new system of power distribution meant the failure of the political revolution and it now means the failure of transition. We will try to analyse this system below.

The Administration of the Power and Romania's Salvation

Since it did not have general objectives and nothing special to pursue in the first place, the NCNSF started setting order in the country and administrating the power so as to ensure a social life as normal as it could. The changes it made in the legislation and institutional structures accounted neither for an innovation nor for a step ahead. They only gave legal and documentary consecration to what the revolution had already achieved in actual life. In that respect, the NCNSF behaved less as political leader of the revolution and rather like its functionary. As if it was waitig for a genuine political actor to take over the power, in full awareness as to what to do with it. Unfortunately, then and now, this has been only a metaphor. There was no such political actor and none has shown up in the meanwhile.

No wonder that the NCNSF was not properly acting its role as a political leader, that it did not have an outlook on the transformations that had to be implemented and of the way on which the country had to be taken to, and that it was hesitating to take steps before itself changed one way or another. It was not a political body, first because it had not been constituted as such. Its over one hundred members were gathered there according to the most varied criteria, but surely not according to political ones. Almost all personalities who had the tinniest public image were incorporated in the NCNSF. Some because were famous as dissidents, as having opposed Ceausescu, popularized as such by Western mass media, like Doina Cornea, Ana Blandiana, Mircea Dinescu or Andrei Plesu. Others were known as dissidents not so much due to the Radio Free Europe programs, but rather through the rumors that were often a substitute for newscasts in Romania. It was the case of Ion Iliescu, Silviu Brucan, Alexandru Barladeanu and other former communist leaders, considered to be reformists or "enlightened". Others ended up in the NCNSF because in the middle of the anonymous crowd they were recognizable figures, often because of their profession that entailed frequence public or TV appearances. It was especially the case of the actors who played a particularly important role in the Romanian revolution, both because they were known to the public, therefore they were listened to, and because they had the ability to be coherent and uninhibited when addressing the crowd. The NCNSF included also all spontaneous leaders of the Bucharest demonstration and, sure, the leading figure of the Timisoara movement, Laszlo Tokes. Finally, other ones became NCNSF members simply because they happened to be in the room when the list was made.

All those people were far from making a political leadership of something. They did not even make up a group, they were just a crowd, picked up at chance, from the bigger crowd outside. They did not share the same views, they belonged to generations with differing experiences and they valued different things. By way of exception, such a combination could have offered a happy complementarity if, beyond all differences, they have shared a common belief or outlook as to what would happen to and in Romania and as to their own role. But that was a far cry from reality. Those one hundred people or so did not have the faintest idea about what was to happen and had but a very faint image of their possibilities to influence the course of the events. Moreover, they did not have a global image of the situation in the country and of the events under way. Besides, they did not know and did not trust one another. So, very soon, the majority took a passive stand, simply following the several leaders who distinguished themselves quickly enough. As for the latter, they started to compete with one another and the competition looked well like a street brawl, because it had no rules.

In the end, the team led by Ion Iliescu won. It was politically more experienced, and Ion Iliescu enjoyed more credibility with the public than any of the other potentiel leaders.But above all, in that period of generalized confusion, he proved a sound common sense that allowed him, even when he made wrong options – as was the appointment of general Militaru as Defence minister – to choose a compromise solution in the end. Those solutions had numerous arguable characteristics and consequences, but they also entailed the big advantage of keeping things under control and of preventing the triggering of irreversible catastrophes. And there were lots of them in sight not only as possible but also as probable.

The winning of the confrontation inside the NCNSF by Ion Iliescu and his supporters greatly decided the fate and orientation of the new political body. Actually, the winner was the middle line, the group that ensured also a certain continuity with the former society and its realities that could not be ignored, and that was firmly resolved to make some changes. On the other hand, for that group and for that policy, the priority number one was not at all the change but the preservation. Not of the old society but of the country.

Right after the revolutions, Romania was faced with two differing but equally acute problems. One was the change. A revolution had taken place, that had proved that the whole country opted for changing not only Ceausescu but the type of policy promoted by them and for changing the institutions on which its implementation rested. That problem has become relatively clear in time and we will enlarge on it here. But there was also another problem which, although no less acute, was often omitted because of the obviously more spectacular appearance of the change. It is about the maintenance of the society, upset by the revolution, in an equilibrum no matter how precareous, and about keeping Romania in its entirety and, as much as possible, in a more advantageous position in the new European and world structure that was coming into being after the falling apart of the communist bloc, the decay of the Soviet Union and the new role which the budding European Community and its member-countries, especially unified Germany, were clearly poised to play.

On an internal plane, the Romanian revolution dismantled all structures and institutions that, communist or not, had the function to keep the society in a coherent form and to make its various sectors cooperate with one another. The devastating effects of the revolution were far bigger than anyone expected in that respect. The social body itself was in danger, because there was no stable authority, because any rule, not only political but also social, could be questioned and any value became at least suspect for the mere reason of having functioned under the former regime as well. One of the most used phrases at that time was "the power vacuum". Actually, there has never been a vacuum of power, just a vacuum oh authoritativeness of the state's central institutions. One of the tasks assumed by the NCNSF led by Ion Iliescu and subsequently by the PNUC, and afterwards by Romania's presidency, was to re-create, little by little, the authoritativeness of these institutions and to administrate at the time when the institutions were unable to do it.

That administration of the country consisted above all of keeping the economy in operation. The NCNSF, together with the newly constituted government had to go on administrating the centralized resources of the economy, to supply the cities and the population, remake the administrative network destroyed by the revolution and maintain the foreign trade in conditions of dramatically shrinking foreign outlets. Second, the NCNSF had to put out the political fires that kept bursting out for some reason or another and that were sometimes not only threatening to overthrow it but were endangering the state itself. The NCNSF and, mainly, President Ion Iliescu discharged those functions with a relative success. Both the economy and the social life were provided a minimum of administration, but that minimum was precisely what was needed for keeping everything from falling apart. Most often, the government yielded to pressures of all kind, from political ones, turning the NCNSF into the PNUC and incorporating at least formally the opposition in the power structures, to the trade union pressures. For instance, after a token resistance, it yielded to the pressure for reducing the workweek to five days and to all requests for pensioning ahead of the legal age, etc. It was, maybe, the most expensive social and economic administration throughout modern Romania's history, but the main objective, to keep the country in a minimum state of stability and control, was attained.

That short-term objective, applicable whenever something happened, was paralleled by a long-term objective that consisted of setting in motion again the authority structure and the normal functioning of the institutions. The "return to normality", which meant to a great extent reducing the possibility of a new political insurrection and remaking a network of rules of power distribution and use, was the main obsession of the group led by Ion Iliescu. That objective was attained by stages. At least three stages could be distinguished. The first was the provisional stabilization of the power, obtained in the end through the setting up of the PNUC and the organization of general elections in May 1990. A second stage was the resumption of the governing after elections and,

especially, after the 13 – 15 June 1990 incidents. And the final objective
was reached with the endorsement of the Constitution and of the organization of new general elections in September 1992.

It took three years to remake the main political and social institutions on the ruins of those destroyed by the revolution. This can give a
general idea about the extraordinary power of destruction of the revolution. On the other hand, the reconstruction was the main objective of
the power installed in December 1989. Under the circumstances, the
change proper was obviously deferred to a secondary plane. Maybe this
is the most difficult to appraise. The governance estabilished after the
revolution was mainly obsessed with eliminating the negative consequences of the revolution, with the fastest remaking of the institutions
and structures without which a state cannot survive, and with avoiding
the furthur degradation of the political and social relations. For that, it
recuperated or accepted the recuperation of many of the "remains", persons and institutions closely associated with the former regime. But the
revolution took place precisely because essential changes were necessary in all sectors, from the political to the economic, social and cultural ones. And in that respect, the priority given to stability and recovery pushed the change to secondary plane or even dropped it when it
seemed to spell danger and stability and recovery.

Essentially, beyond any of the settled or unsettled specific issues,
beyond any potential or real danger avoided, the remaking of internal
stability was tantamount to the building of a new system of distribution
of the power in society. Stabilization eventually meant only the ever
more complete taking over of the authority by the consituted power
system. In the political domain, this the most important achievement of
the post-revolution period. Its characteristics are responsible for the
unfolding of the transition so far and especially from now own. This
system needs to be analyzed, appraised and, above all, changed. If it
does not change, the completion of the December revolution is not possible, either in the political domain, or in the economy or social construction.

The Decomposition of the Power System of the Revolution

In any society, the power is shared among social groups, according
to a more or less explicit or organized system of rules. A revolution
would always disband such a system in order to put other one in its

place. But, even before the new system is installed, legislated and institutionalized, the power is still shared and exercised, that time by the bodies of the revolution. The phrase the most disseminated in the country after 22 December was the vacuum of power. Actually, a vacuum of power exists, even if a vacuum of legitimacy of the power may arise, or a chronical absence of legal institutions to exert it. There was no vacuum of power in the case of the December revolution either.

After Ceausescu's ousting, on 22 December, there were several hours when not even an improvised system of power administration existed. The main cause was the absence of a political leadership of the revolution. There were a few hours, but just a few hours, when the power was simply diffuse. But it does not mean that it was not exerted. There were a few hours before the setting up of the NCNSF, when the suggestions or recommandations made before TV cameras by anyone who happened to be there became decisions that set in motion masses of people or armored divisions. The situation became a little clear with the formation, in the evening, of the new center of political decision. But that was only the center. The next morning, the formation started of an ad-hoc system of power-sharing and administration. That system was generated by the revolution and, what is extremely significant, it engulfed all or almost all the population.

The formation of the NCNSF on 22 December in Bucharest was the signal for the launching all over the country of a tremendous and spontaneous process of political organization. Starting the dat after and until the first days of January, local National Salvation Front Councils were set up both in localities and counties, replacing the former people's councils, but especially in enterprises and institutions, taking over their management. All of them hurried to recognize the authority of the National Council and stated their readiness to apply its policy, when it would announce which is that. The Declaration and Program of the National Council was far from synthetizing a political line, but it was anyway suggesting that it would follow soon.

So, the NCNSF, first emerged as a National Council of a Front that did not exist, found itself abruptly at the head of a huge political establishment perfectly organized and ready to be disciplined. The branches of that organization virtually controlled the whole country, all power centers, irrespective of their size and, unlike the former organizations of the communist party, they enjoyed for the time being authoritativeness and popular support alike. Besides, the local organizations controlled also what the NCNSF controlled only too little, the crowd that was still out in the street, in very big numbers, or was ready to come out if the councils had asked. The NSF Councils were mainly based on work collectivities and elected by them. They represented their members and depended on them since, having no rule of functioning or a mandate issued by some higher echelon, their members could be changed as soon as their activity no longer suited the crowd. They could also be changed whenever some demagogue, supported by a small but noisy group, managed, through persuasion or intimidation, to get the support of the majority. The Councils obviously were an improvisation, born out of the revolution. But they respected its democratic principle, they had power and were ready to use it. And, above all, they got entrenched as bodies of political coordination of the technocracy, for, their main role was to appoint and guide the technical executives of the enterprises and institutions.

That tremendous enrolment of the population in a political organization must not surprise. The population, that participated in the revolution,now wanted to participate in its futherance. However, the NCNSF seemed rather emarassed instead of being pleased with the situation. And, one month later, it made a decision that would decisively influence Romania's subsequent political life and even more than that. It decided to push the whole organization out of the game, by dismantling the newly created Councils or turning over them into something else, trade unions for instance. The Councils in localities or counties were integrated with the administrative system, taking over the prerogatives of the former townhalls. As for those in enterprises, their transformation into trade unions was tried in a first stage, given that they had been elected by work collectivities. As the attempt failed, because new trade unions too had emerged meanwhile, that opposed such an usurpation, in the end they were simply abolished, with the enterprise managers assuming their position as absolute rulers, subordinated only to the relevant minister (or to the central industrial department, where it existed).

Nobody was aware at that time of the extraordinary significance borne by the dismantlement of those ad-hoc political bodies that made up the pyramid on which the NCNSF could have rested, if it could have wanted to promote a specific policy. True, the initiative to dismantle them did not belong solely to the NCNSF. Like almost always, it only yielded to pressure, no matter wherefrom. Or, accusatory voices from among the budding opposition protested against the remaking of the political organizations in enterprises, a form of organization typical of the communist party. They were right in principle. The modern political parties are organizations of citizens, not of workers; their membership rests on territorial principles and, at least formally, they do not interfere with the executive of economic or social organizations. Later on, some political parties, like Christian Democratic National Peasant Party (CDNPP) tried to set up enterprise organizations but, at that time, they thought it in their interest to oppose a structure that would offer the NCNSF a remarkable support. As the main NCNSF leaders were former members of the defunct communist party's political bureaucracy and as they were already under the accusation that they represented nothing but its restoration in disguise, it is probable that, when they did yield to pressures, they wanted simply to get rid of one more trouble. But, at the same time, the NSF Councils embarrassed them because they interfered with order circuits of the power which had just been set in operation, namely the administration and technocracy.

In the end, the councils in enterprises were abolished, and with them was abolished also the only political organization born out of the revolution, that might have taken over the initiative of the changes in its behalf. The only formal framework in existence, which allowed the population to participate in the political life in other way than through street demonstrations and riots, was also abolished. And the NCNSF remained a bodiless head, with narrow views at that. From that moment, its only connection with the population remained the institutionalized bureaucracy and, at times of really serious crisis, the charisma which Ion Iliescu could bring forth on addressing the people directly on TV. There were plenty of such moments and they lasted into June 1990. It is worth mentioning that the response to those appeals was weaker and weaker. Not because Ion Iliescu had grown less popular – the elections proved that the overwhelming majority of the population preferred him instead of anybody else -, and surely not because the revolution-time enthusiasm had cooled down – the mass attendance at polling stations during the elections proved otherwise -, but because the role of improvised crowd spontaneously responding to its political leader was less and less adequate and satisfactory. That could by no means replace the sharing in the administration of the power.

However, the most important consequence of the abolition of the councils did not refer to those who no longer participated in power sharing, but to those who filled the thus created void. The main beneficiary was the technocracy with its administrative extensions. That was a remarkable result. It was then that was settled the true battle for power, in January – February 1990 and not in the elections that followed since May 1990 until October 1992. And it was settled in favor of the main enemy of the communist political bureaucracy: the industrial technocracy.

The first to win was the idea or the principle of a technocratic leadership instead of a political one. That idea was already popular during the revolution, as a reflex of identifying any political leadership with the communist party activists. That idea was espoused by the NCNSF and steadily applied. Once the councils in enterprises abolished and the territorial councils equated with mere bodies of the local administration, the NCNSF itself could be identified rather with a bureaucratic structure, the state's highest administrative institution, than with a political organization. The NCNSF – and subsequently the PNUC – would make laws and coordinate the government. The government itself was even formally apolitical. Just like the governments that would follow, it was a government of technicians. When the political parties emerged, none of its important members joined any of the parties. Not even the prime minister, who decided to participate in elections as an independent candidate, as a technician enjoying popularity but not following any policy.

The decision made in January 1990, to yield the control and exercise of the power to the industrial technocracy jointly with the administrative bureaucracy, carried into effect mainly through the dismantlement of the only political organization of the power-sharing mechanism was a major option that actually decided the fate of the power in the new society. It is very probable that those who made it at that time have never explicitly articulated that option. Just the same, the reasons why they made the decision to abolish the NSF Councils were far more specific and positively different in wording. But the reasons of a decision are not necessarily bound to have a connection with the opinion made through decision. Phrased or not as an option, it existed. It was one of the few really political options made in the period after the revolution. Its effect consisted of the shift of the power from the hands of the politically organized population into the hands of the two bureaucracies – administrative and industrial. The leading body of the revolution thus acted precisely as if it had been the representative of those two important groups of power in the former socialist society. And the victory of the technocracy was complete. It had not only freed itself of a direct political tutelage, but had managed also to get rid of any political subordination.

It was not an accident. It was a direction of change steadily pursued. If not the only one, then one of the few. Its result was the coming into being of a system of power-sharing that lived on through the five years that have passed since the revolution and got stabilized after the 1992 elections. For all the new political system institutionalized as multiparty system, etc. After that, pseudo-political formations were set up, of the kind of Fronts or parties that, by holding in name the power won pursuant to elections, had the mission to allow this bureaucracy to unreservedly exercise it.

The End of Politics

Dramatic about the decision made then by the NCNSF was not so much what it dismantled, but what it built and with what consequences. The first consequence that deserves mention is the end of politics. The other is the emergence and stabilization of a real system of power, diferring from the formal one. Those two consequences taken together are tantamount to the failure of the political revolution.

The "end of politics" sounds rather pathetic, but the notion describes the phenomenon that occured right after the revolution and that was in fact the main source of failure of the political revolution. Since it is beyond doubt that the councils in institutions and enterprises, unable and unwilling to technically coordinate their activity, would have pressed for precise policies, be it only in order to justify their existence. Those policies might have been accepted or not. Yet, they would have been a reference point and would have introduced political matters that would have at least the merit of being closely related to the population's preoccupations. However, the NCNSF cannot take the whole blame for the end of policies within the transition. It can be blamed for having been a political body that did not engage in politics and that severed its ties to a possible political base. After the May 1990 elections, the same characteristic, in differing forms, was reproduced by the political parties.

The 1989 revolution dismantled the communist party's political bureaucracy, but it created a new political superstructure: parties, parliaments, president, etc., as well as a bureaucracy under loose political control, having the role to monitor or arbitrage the use of the power: the Constitutional Court, the Court of Public Accounts, etc. The normal revolutionary process would have meant the transfer of the political power, of the ability – not only of the right to make political decisions of the employment of the national resources – from the hands of the communist party's bureaucracy to the hands of the new political superstructure. Such a move would not have been counter-revolutionary at all. The revolution was not targeted against the mere existence of a political system, no matter which. Neither was it targeted against a political subordination of the industrial technocracy. Like any revolution in history, the December revolution was targeted against a system of power-sharing and use, hence against a certain policy and not against any policy. On the contrary, the expectations of the revolution, diffuse, unclear, imprecisely articulated as they were, but real, absolutely needed the articulation of a policy in order to come true. The failure to replace a political coordination of the power-sharing and use by another political control means failure to accomplish the political revolution and explains its failure.

The initial cause surely was the absence of a policy that should be promoted in the name of the revolution and for its accomplishment. This cause stands to this day. But, meanwhile, things have grown more complicated. Like I said before, a society does not settle for vacuum of power and the absence of a political coordination has simply become a component of the establishment. Even an institutionalized component. Like any power system, the one built after the revolution, in the absence of any political coordination, is complete. The political transition, from one mechanism of power-sharing and use to another, did occur, and rather fast for that matter. Faster than in other domains. The rules exist, the frontiers among various participants in the power are well established, and the relations among them have stabilized. But all these, participants, rules and relations are not recognized formally. Just the opposite, they are dissimulated by a formal institutional structure of the political power which, in actual fact, does not exercise any power, but which exist like some sort of cover, performing the protocol functions on the one hand, and acting as a scape goat on the other hand, when faced with discontents, negative responses or rejection from those subject to the actions of the real power. In the structure "erected" after the revolution in order to replace the political system torn down by it, the role of formal, protocol structure and of scape goat goes to the political parties, to the Parliament and the Presidency. None of them makes real policy, coordinates or controls the use of power and, generally, none of them participates in its administration.

2. Post-revolution Romania's Power System

However, Romania does have a power system, a host of institutions and groups that share the power and administrates it. This rather complex system deserves analysis and understanding not only because, as a rule, it is good to understand the power mechanisms in a society, but also because it is the major producer of a post-revolution spontaneous transition. This system did not take from the onset the form in which it has stabilized today. Moreover, this form is still being adjusted and new features might still appear. Yet, with its most important features, it emerged as early as the spring of 1990. It would get the final form in 1991, with the formation of the Stolojan Government, and it would confirm its stability in the context of any foreseeable political evolutions in 1992. In its current form, the system is built on four levels.

The Naked Emperor

Of all these levels, the greatest importance is attached to the summit. According to a tradition as old as history itself, it used to be concomitantly a political institution and a person – ruler, king or president – who concentrated, at least formally, all or almost all the power. Also traditionally, the person holding this function is the most popular personality as well as the one supposed to be the most competent. It is toward this person that the whole power is shifting all major problems, waiting for decisions to solve them. It is to him that are attributed, when he does not do so himself, all the good things that happen under his rule and most of the evil ones. Generally, it is from this summit that everybody expects that the power be exercised, no matter how arbitrarily.

Such a conception about the political summit of the power pyramid is neither original nor "Balkan", betraying that is, some backwardness in the Romanian political culture resulted from non-European influences in our culture. It fits in a still prevailing paradigm about the construction of the power systems in which the towering figure is the State. According to the ideology that goes with it, the State is an unhistoric entity, above individuals, institutions, rules and any other assets, the survival and prosperity of which is the final objective of the whole population's activity and whose interests prevail over any other, individual or group interests. Behind the religion for this not too new god, there hide the more earthly interests of its priests, of the administration that is. The whole construction – ideology, doctrines, political theory, legislation, institutions and their relations with the society and the population – is characteristic of their type of society in which the power is distributed mainly by the administrative bureaucracy. It is the oldest and most disseminated form of organization of the power in history. In Romania it has been continuous, in varied forms. Not even communism changed it radically. Although the political bureaucracy was distinct from the administrative bureaucracy and tried to subordinate it, its main legitimacy was not political in nature, relying instead on the possibility of taking a shortcut toward the summit of the pyramid. The activists were the direct agents of the pyramid summit, some sort of bailiffs that were seeing to it that the administrative and economic institutions' own interests should not encroach upon the interests of the summit, meaning the state.

After the revolution, the reorganization of the power has not changed either the theory or the essential structure in existence. The big political battles were fought for getting hold of the previously existing structure and not for changing it. The only notable change consisted of restraining the role of the political bureaucracy (neither the NSF activists nor, later on, the Party of Social Democracy of Romania's activists, were able to recuperate within the power system the place previously held by the communist party ones), but that consolidated even more the importance of the pyramid summit. One more factor came in here, the practise, which evinces a tendency of turning into tradition. The conjunctures, President Ion Iliescu's personality, the people's expectations and the behaviors of those near that power summit made the summit be unique, in spite of the existence of the two parallel structures – the administration and the party. The Constitutional provision that the head of state shall not be concomitantly a member of some party certainly has no other role than to legitimate his authority over those who have different political allegiances.

The solution of the only one summit of the power became almost final after two major political events: the conflict between Petre Roman and Ion Iliescu, and the unification of the biggest part of the Opposition within the Democratic Convention. In the former case, the initially bicephalic structure of the power, in which both the president and the prime minister were powerful from an administrative and political viewpoint alike, ended up in a conflict the result of which was the party's and government's subordination to the president. In the latter case, the Opposition simply adjusted itself to the solution resulted from that conflict, building some kind of shadow presidency, meant to replace the real one in the event of electoral victory, but not to change its attributes.

The summit of the pyramid, meaning Romania's President and his aides, has become, according rather to tradition than to the letter of the legislation and theory about the democratic organization of the power, the most important center of political and administrative decision. At least this is how the image created about this center is seen from the level of public opinion and no less even from the level of the administrative and political system. Another, complementary image adds to it, the image of rationality, competence, ability, wisdom and, obviously, of organization and superior means the summit avails of. Both images are however deceptive. In the power system built after the revolution, the decision and the means are not concentrated at the summit, but at the medium level of administrative institutions and industrial bureaucracy. The newness brought by the revolution consisted precisely of freeing this level of higher subordinations. This does not mean that the political suprastructures of the medium level become useless or empty. The change is more subtle. They keep their status and prestige and even a part of the authority. For a change, their initiative and room for manoeuvring are dramatically shrinking and they turn from ruling institutions meant to offer strategic orientations and fundamental directions for evolution, into institutions that legitimate the decisions and policies made at the medium, administrative level. A whole package of causes and favoring factors contribute to a change in the role and function of the political summit of the power system. The most important of them are to be found right inside it.

Although by definition and even more by the image attributed this summit of the pyramid is prevailing political, neither its construction nor its operation make it fit for the role. Since December 1989 to this day it has never availed of the necessary instruments to become a political institution. Above anything else, it does not avail of information. The touch of the summit with the reality, speaking either of the president, or of party leaders or institutions definitely proclaimed to be political, like the Parliament, is more than loose. There is a certain correspondence addressed to them, suffocated by vast casuistry, in which the information of some consequence is impossible to tell from the accidental information or from exaggerations, fantasies and, often, even lies. The visits and personal touch are more often than not, full of formalism or, the other way round, full of subjectivism, having therefore no usable content. At their best, they can offer an incomplete image or isolated cases the representativeness of which is null. Apart from these inadequate sources, the summit does not avail of any mechanism of systematic gathering of information, irrespective of content. Therefore, on order to get informed, the country's rulers have to turn to the press and to the information supplied by normal. Administrative ways.

To the extent to which they are abreast with the media – the Presidency, the Parliament and the Government alike avail of services specializing in newspaper reading the pinpoint especially what the press writes about them -, the members of the summit are just as informed as any citizen of this country and just as aware of what is happening in actual fact. It is some sort of vicious circle that develops here, because much oh what the press writes or conveys is generated right by them, through statements, news conferences or releases. This "dialogue with the media" keeps in fact the whole description of reality at a continuous but inefficient exchange of impressions between the several members of the political summit and their functionaries, on the one hand, and the about fifty or sixty journalists, especially Bucharesters, on the other hand, and the discussion in this small circle makes a notable contribution to the formation of the false package of problems around which the whole "Romanian political life" revolves and in which, after six years, the public has participated with less and less enthusiasm. The visible shrinking of the space meant for politics in the Romanian press is the most significant signal of this lack of interest.

The administrative information, even if gathered by means of an often huge apparatus, is not in the least more useful than the press information. First, because it has a markedly technical character and none of the institutions avails of specialists or of the methodology to draw the political significance and consequences from the technical information. At any rate, beyond such simple sentences as "if the production grows, this does not mean that the economic policy is correct" – which applies to any possible policy -, the inference relies on common sense solely. Besides, it is a wrong assumption, as the biggest production growths in Romania were recorded under the communist regime, and it appears now that, in actual fact, the economic policies of that period were wrong. But, even as a simple description of technical details of the economy and social life, the information is often incomplete. No institution in the country currently avails of the necessary methodology or infrastructure to gather significant and correct information from the economy or society. A classical example in this respect are the data related to the economy; the methodology of gathering data only now starts being devised, with Western expertise, but their gathering and correlation are so incomplete that often the size of the error cannot even be assessed. So, the hidden economy, meaning the economy which is not registered with official statistics, is appraised by various experts, some of them belonging even to institutions that specialize in economic data gathering and processing, at between forty and two hundred per cent of the official economy. The spectacular cases are not necessarily also the gravest ones, but they are telling. When the government released in the summer of 1995 the list of enterprises put out for privatization, it appeared that some of them had already turned private, and in one case a producer of nuclear equipment had been recorded as furniture producer. In brief, at the highest level, the political leaders are overwhelmed by a genuine avalanche of information regarding isolated cases or ununderstandable and most often incorrect technical details, and they are unable to distinguish the real meanings of this mountain of information.

The lack of communication adds to the lack of information. Neither the Presidency nor the Parliament and not even the leaderships of the political parties are institutions devised for communication, although theoretically that ought to be their main activity. The frequent showing off in the press or on TV, as well as the endless chain of "messages" relayed through spokes-persons, have nothing in common with a real communication. The essential weakness in this respect is not the lack of means but the conception underlying their use. According to it, the highest authority in the state is not the population but the <u>State</u>, the superior and dominating entity. The mission of the population is to serve the State, sometimes even against the former's own interests. Therefore, the authorities must rather control and manipulate the population for the State's benefit, instead of being receptive to the population's initiatives, messages and interests. On such basis, the communication with the population is obviously impossible. And not only with the population, but also with any other institution which is formally autonomous and develops its own interests, such as the political parties or the Parliament. The lack of communication between the country's president and the political parties was long blamed on the rigidity of the opposition and on its hard feelings against the president personally. Both features are real, but it has been later on noticed that the relation was not much different also with the parties of the government coalition and even with the PSDR, the party that is under the president's direct authority. The result is that the president's rare political initiatives have permanently remained without any political effect. In 1992, on his inaugural, the speech made by the president was remarkable through the line he suggested for the reform. In the autumn of 1994, he resumed that initiative, proposing a genuine restructuring of the political relations, with the opposition parties included, based on a minimal program acceptable to everybody. In 1995, with the objective in mind to launch a genuine campaign against corruption, he addressed to the ruling party, proposing that the PSDR parliamentarians should quit the so profitable functions as members of Administration Boards and General Assemblies of Share-holders of the state-owned companies. None of those initiatives had any political reverberation. Instead of espousing the president's initiatives, the parties did not even heed them and the PSDR made no exception. On the other hand, it was obvious that all those initiatives were launched without any previous communication precisely with those for whom they were meant.

Adding to all this is the fundamental weakness of the summit in terms of authoritativeness. The conception and habit were inherited from the defunct communist party, that the main relation for which the executives of the institutions at the top are prepared should be the subordination, meaning a purely administrative relation. More than that, of all relations of subordination, the one which those "on top" know how to use as a rule is the simplest and more inefficient of all – the relation in which the authority rests almost exclusively on the possibility of the summit to appoint or demote the subordinates. By content and effects, such a relation is not unlike the relation between the sultan and the rulers of the Romanian Countries during what is known in the country's history as the Phanariot era (18th and early 19th centuries). The sultan used to appoint and dismiss as rules of the Romanian lands wealthy representatives of Greek townsfolk (Phanariots) in the Ottoman empire, who would buy their way to the throne. The word has ever after remained a synonym for "immoral", "corrupt". The fact that it is so old does not make it worse, but it points to its limits. It is mainly useful and efficient when only one thing is expected from the subordinate (the tribute, in the historical case), no matter how it is obtained, since the subordinate has complete autonomy, and the relation is the object of a public contract, so it can be legitimately denounced when its functionality changes. In the context of the Romanian policy, this unique objective has very soon turned into a personal relation. The truthfulness of the appointed person to the one who appointed him has become the main applicable criterion, irrespective of the appointee's competence, good or ill intentions or activity. The generalization of this kind of relation in all structures of a political nature has had two serious consequences. First, it has annulled any chance that the structures do precisely the thing for which they had been created, which is a genuine policy. Just like the feudal barons, the people of the establishment can do whatever crosses their mind, on condition that they back their lord in need. As real policy needs coherence and a coordination based on such a relation cannot ensure it, then policy itself is reduced, for the subordinated echelons, to an endless chain of inter-personal conflicts and rivalries, and for the summit – to the ability of sailing through them, while making sure that the combatants remain truthful to it.

The other serious consequence is that the authoritativeness is based from top to bottom and not the other way round. The two presidents of the Party of Social Democracy of Romania, for instance, are basing their authoritativeness not on the party they are leading, but on their having been appointed by President Ion Iliescu. In turn, a head of county organization or a prefect is a head pending on the relation with the person who appointed him and not because he is accepted by the organization, a.s.o. The final image is very much like the old Indian metaphor of succession of the generations, in which every individual is clinging with a hand to the foot of the individual in front of him, and the last in the file is clinging to a grass stem eaten by a rat. The rat that is eating the root of such a system of political authoritativeness is precisely the contradiction between its pretense as representative of the national interests and the evidence that every one of its components is pursuing either his own interests, or, in the best of cases, the interests of maintaining the system. The explanation of the mechanism with the ruling party as example must not generate the illusion that the mechanism might change simply by changing the party that won the elections. The political opposition operates according to the same rules and, beyond political polemics, it is perfectly integrated with the system.

But even if, by its very construction, the whole mechanism is incapable of making policy, the summit must make political decisions, deferred to it precisely by the impotence of the infrastructure to promote policy. In this respect, the situation of the summit is quite dramatic. Deprived of relevant information, of communication, of authoritativeness and a genuine political infrastructure, the summit has to make decisions on all the political matters which either the bureaucracy, or the population or the conjunctures defer to it. Its only solution is to improvise and, often, to turn for advice and support to genuine informal teams, often participated in by the most unexpected persons or institutions. The political decisions thus usually acquire the character of personal and conjunctural acts. Hence, the unexpected and often contradictory decisions, talks and negotiations that are never publicized and, above all, hence the absence of a political consistency.

With such an infrastructure, the group at the top which settles the political problems remains mostly obscure. Except for a small number of public figures, like President Ion Iliescu for instance, those who participate in endorsing decisions that are often extremely important and consequential, remain unknown. Just as unknown remain the mechanisms guiding the decision-making, and the criteria or real reasons why a certain solution was chosen instead of another one. The sure result of such a situation is the arbitrariness of the decision. Arbitrariness here does not mean that it was a chance decision. It only means that it is not foreseeable. As a rule and assets that govern the mechanisms of these decisions are neither public nor controllable or stable for that matter, they often appear as the result of the rulers' whims.

Only few systems of political leadership can fuel more the speculations about the existence of a Mafia-type group that secretly leads the destinies of a country or of a people. On the other hand, only rarely were such speculations less justified. Far from benefiting from the stability and coherence of rational organizations oriented to a purpose, even of occult, the decisions of the summit are characterized by improvisation and fortuitousness. Even as regards its composition, this summit group is more stable that its own decisions. Sure, the country's president, the president and speaker of the Chambers, the leaders of the political parties – those among them who participate in decision-making – are identifiable political characters. But, around everyone of them, some sort of personal court is growing, made up of counsellors, office workers, confidants, mere admirers or favor peddlers, all of whom are trying to influence at least some of the decisions made, according to reasons and criteria that are political only rarely but are never accounting for components of a policy.

This summit, only partly structured, with a vague and hard to distinguish identity, with an ever more vague responsibility, never possible to define in its entirety, is permanently boiling and changing. Sometimes extending to groups or persons from the most unexpected zones of the administration or of the political stage, at other times getting narrower and eliminating, surprisingly, precisely those who seemed the most thoroughly anchored right in its nucleus, this summit is being sapped by an endless, impersonal intrigue and an endless war against the countercandidates to the leading position, either from the opposition or from the own camp. This group is the one that has been leading the country within the power system constructed after the revolution. Its ties to the country's political structure are loose and, above all, they are not political. The ties to the population are even looser.

And so, the end of politics that was in sight right after the revolution, has become consecrated through institutionalization. It is included precisely in the mechanism of exercising the power, because the political summit of the mechanism is not political, but a substitute for politics, as was soja in the pork salami under Ceausescu. In the current power system, the emperor is stripped precisely of his most important cloth, the political one.

A Government That Does not Govern

The second level is the administration, the core of which is the government's secretariat-general and the bureaucracy of the ministry and government agencies. It is from this level downward that starts the real exercise of the power. The summit of this level is the government, the prime minister and the cabinet members.

As a rule, although ruling the state administration, the government is no part of it. And as a rule, the government is the political superstructure of the administration. This does not apply to the power system built after the revolution. In this system, the ministers make only the summit of the administration, its interface with the group that makes decisions on political matters, although it does not make political decisions. They are not politicians, and more often than not, they are not included in the group entrusted with making political decisions. Likewise, precisely in order to keep their function as peaks of the administration, the government members are, not, as a rule, also peaks of the ruling political parties. The governments that followed one another since December 1989 to this day – except for the period between March and September 1991, which was the climax of the offensive conducted by the Roman Government to take over the control of the political summit of the country's leadership – did not include any important leader of the ruling party or coalition. The government formed after the May 1990 elections included no National Salvation Front leader, except for Bogdan Niculescu-Duvaz. He was appointed to the unimportant office of minister of Youth and Sports, in order to give a minimum of satisfaction to the team of young revolutionaries who led the NSF at that time. After the Roman Government's fall in September 1991, the Stolojan Government was formed on the basis of a coalition of several parties, NSF included (with its two wings, pro-Roman and pro-Iliescu) and the National Liberal Party. For all the fierce battle it had fought that far in order to accede to power, the NLP did not send to the government any important representative. The ministers appointed by it, although to such important posts as the Finance or Justice, were second-class personalities in the party, with no real role in its leadership. Finally, on the formation of the Vacaroiu Government, at a time when the system was already stabilized, none of the members of the newly appointed cabinet had a really important position in the ruling party. Confirming the rule that seems to get entrenched in Romania, the prime minister is not even a member of the ruling party, he has no real political influence, and, generally, does not engage in politics. The government has gone through two reshuffles since, none of them based on political criteria – unless one cares to give the name of politics to the intrigue inside the government coalition and the personal conflicts among its leaders – and the new members of the government were in all cases politically inconsequential figures introduced as technicians. Sure, in all these choices, the main criterion was the loyalty, but it was about a loyalty to persons, to some member or another of the "political" summit, and not to a specific policy.

Although the power starts being effective at the level of the administration, it is still not effective at the government's level. It is not the ministers and it is not the government that concentrate the administrative power. This characteristic applied to all governments that followed after the revolution. In their capacity as governments of technicians, they confined themselves to settling the routine administrative issues and to administrating the country. They confined themselves to being not a body of governance, but a body of administration. The excuse, if one may say so, was explicitly articulated on defining the Stolojan Government. All along the period up to the general elections of 1992, the governments were waiting for the moment when a "normal" political system would come into being on the ruins of the system dismantled by the revolution, in order to take over the helm. Like shown before, that attitude, that has already turned into the major paradigm of the power system, was defined as early as the formation of the NCNSF and of the first government after the revolution. Because of the complexity of the conditions required for the coordination of the change to be assumed, the victorious revolution of December 1989 had to wait until 1992 in order to be continued.

The moment for a turn seemed to have come after the 1992 elections – almost three years after the revolution -, but then it appeared clearly that the absence of a governance, just like the absence of politics were neither accidental nor transitional, that they were simply part of the establishment. In brief, they were the rule. The appointment of the Vacaroiu Government is by far the best illustration of this rule and the almost pure form of action of the system. It also illustrates the utter inexistence of a connection between the formal political system and the real system of power sharing and exercise. During the 1992 elections, a fierce battle was fought for ballots. The more so as the opposition was then united within the Democratic Convention, and the ruling party members were divided between the two competing wings of the former NSF. The electoral battle was won by the Democratic National Salvation Front (now PSDR), thanks to the support it got from President Iliescu. The new winner political party would form the government and govern. All this taken together, the election campaign, the elections participated in by several parties that had similar changes to win, the formation of the government by the party or majority coalition that had won the elections and, then, the governing according to the ideas presented during the election campaign meant what everybody expected, namely the ushering in of normality in Romania, through the building of a normal power system.

Well, it didn't happen. The Vacaroiu Government was formed. And that decision is a perfect illustration of the real power system and not of the formal one, with political parties, parliament and elections. Premier Nicolae Vacaroiu is of course the most representative figure. And the most significant fact is that there is no connection whatsoever between him and the election returns. He was not and is not either, after three years in power, at least a member of any of the parties that make up the majority coalition. He was not engaged in politics before the election and has not been engaged in politics even after he was appointed prime minister. The designation of the Vacaroiu Government actually meant the annulment not only of the 1992 elections, but also of the usefulness of the whole political system created after December 1989. It has also revealed the obscure character of the decisions that act as substitutes for political decisions. Nicolae Vacaroiu's appointment as prime minister could not have been foreseen by anyone. And after that, nobody, not even those who did it, could explain why him. There is no set of criteria conductive to the decision about Nicolae Vacaroiu. He may have – and probably does – a great many personal qualities. In a country with 23 million inhabitants like Romania, there probably are several tens of thousands people very much like Nicolae Vacaroiu, and just as entitled to hold the position as prime minister. For him to be chosen from among these tens of thousands, there had to exist additional criteria. And they were neither political nor democratic. It is not about Nicolae Vacaroiu as a man, but only about those who made decisions regarding him. The decision was made inside that small summit group and through the obscure mechanisms in which in the end nobody knows how comes a decision to be made.

What is important is that the formation of the Vacaroiu Government heralded the stabilization of that power system in which the government does not play a political role. It is a simple interface of the state administration and it does not govern. And, for the things to be even more clear, the same Vacaroiu Government has demonstrated that there is no connection whatsoever between the government's activity and the political "programs" of the parties that voted him in Parliament. To dispel any doubt in this respect, the government presented in the Parliament its own "Government Strategy", a theoretical work on what ought to be done in Romania, if someone decided to do something. The work was articulated by a team of technicians who did not care about the parties' political programs, who made politics the way monsieur Jourdain made prose, without knowing that they were making it. Neither the prime minister, nor the government and the parliamentarians were serious about the "Government Strategy". Once passed in the Parliament, it had no more influence on the activity of either government or political parties.

The avatars of the Vacaroiu Government meant no accident but a real coming to a normal, different though from the one which the revolution had prefigured and the Constitution and new laws had formalized. The government reshuffles that followed have entrenched the rule that there is no rule by which ministers are dismissed or appointed. None of the appointments could be foreseen, at least by the appointees who sometimes learned about the appointment on the very day that it happened, or by the dismissed ones, some of whom learned about their dismissal from the press. So important political decisions as the replacement of a minister, were made based on criteria that remained completely unknown both to the public and the politicians and that ended by consecrating the idea that the government is not political, it does not engage in politcs and does not depend on politics, although it does depend on politicians.

Since it does not make policy, the government's main function is to provide the connection and ground for compromises between the administrative bureaucracy as a whole and the group that makes the political decisions at the summit. The government also has the role to ensure the legitimacy of the administrative authority and to intervene in order to settle the numerous frictions emerging at the second level of articulation of the power system, between the administrative bureaucracy and the industrial technocracy. These functions are important but they do account for the administration of the power.

The immediate consequence of the government's lack of power is the lack of governance. The lack of governance has already been mentioned as part of the most general characteristics of the whole power system – the lack of influence of the leading structures on the evolution of realities, plus the lack of responsibility. The lack of governance must be blamed on the whole power system and on the political one first of all. But, with the government itself, the lack of governance takes far more concrete forms, all of them orbited around the package of central causes consisting, on the one hand, of the fact that the government does not want anything and, on the other hand, of the fact that, assuming that it does want something, it does not know what. So the government confines itself to presiding over the administrative bureaucracy, to justifying its decisions before the public opinion and relaying "up there", when required, the political criteria of settlement of the problems that cannot be solved exclusively according to the algorithms specific to the administration.

It should be stressed that as things are coming more and more to a normal and institutional reconstruction is drawing to an end, the absence of a governance becomes ever more obvious and pressing. The governments' not governing, meaning a floating above reality without doing anything to change it, has characterized all governments after the revolution, in different proportions though. For the first governments, the main priority was, like I said, the construction of the administration's institutions complete with the relevant legislation. The Roman Government was able to take advantage of the over one hundred bills promoted by it in the Parliament, as if governments were some sort of offices to manufacture bills. But, at that time, the absence of the legislation was obvious and it could be claimed to be the main cause of the absence of governance – the instruments were missing, meaning the laws and institutions. The Stolojan Government could claim for a whole year that it did not have the political mandate to govern. Therefore, the real problem of the absence of governance starts precisely with the Vacaroiu Government, with the government created after the 1992 elections although, as shown before, it did not at all result from those elections.

The Vacaroiu Government can no longer claim that it is still waiting for something. It would be little credible now, five years after the revolution. Just like the previous governments, it prepared and promoted in the Parliament a number of bills bigger than the Parliament can debate and pass during its session, but this can no longer be claimed as a cause for the absence of a governance. One the one hand, because the bills promoted have but little connection with the really urgent problems of the economy and of the society, and, on the other hand because most of the laws, and especially the really important ones or those deemed as necessary come into force not during the Parliament's sessions but during its recesses. As it known that the parliament is slow in passing bills and precisely in order to avoid this shifting of the responsibility for not governing to parliamentarians, before every parliamentary recess, the Parliament grants the government's right to rule by ordinance, i.e. to set in motion laws which it urgently needs even before their debate in the Parliament. Every time, the government availed of that prerogative, which has however not brought it one step closer to the governance.

The problem for the incumbent government – irrespective of its composition – is that it simply has nothing else to do. As the transition is drawing to an end, the government seems to have fewer and fewer things to do. One of the things which puzzles the rulers and the opposition alike is the impossibility to criticize essentially the governance of after the September 1992 elections. Its answer always comes in from of a list of things that have been done – presented to advantage so as to sound very impressive -, compared with a list of the things have not been done yet, and that sounds rather unimportant. The more so as most of the things that have not been done yet at least been started.

The current government lists to its credit in the economic field: the curbing of the economic crisis, the growth of exports, the elimination of subsidies, the introduction of the VAT, the curbing of the inflation and of the budget deficit, the conclusion of the accord with the IMF and the resumption of foreign financing, the beginning of the restructuring, the progress – slow, of course, but with speed-up promises – of privatization and the securing of the national currency's internal convertibility. On an external plane, the sum-up sounds even better: the association with the European Union, the admission to the Council of Europe, the regaining of the Most Favored Nation status with the Americans, the association with the NATO through the Partnership for Peace, the reconsideration of Romania's role in the Balkans and in East Europe. So, the government may wonder: "What is it that we have not done?" and the opposition and its critics, the too caught in the same power system, find themselves unable to reproach anything that matters on it. The most they can do is to refer to the so-called "pace of the reform", an empty phrase used as main element of the demagogy about reformists and conservatives. Beyond it, the opposition can only refer to details, some of them extremely unconvincing. This situation has contributed a lot to the change in the opposition's attitude, that shift from de-legitimizing the incumbent rulers to probing for possibilities to cooperate with them in governance. Which proves that there are no opinions of the opposition that can not be reconciled with the rulers' ones.

To the rulers – and not only to them – the difficulty is that, by solving or advancing with the settlement of almost all problems posed by the reform, they do not have other ones to pursue, on the settlement of which the change for the better of the Romanian society should depend. In brief, this big issue of the government, no matter whether the opposition is co-opted or not in the governance, is that it does not know what to do next, more precisely, that it no longer has anything to do. The incumbent governance, opposition and all, seems to have been exhausted without having been able to change the Romanian society for the better. Instead, they both have ended by getting more or less purposeful, or either one of them.

We shall see later what ought to do a government that governs. But what can be said already now is that, above anything else, it ought to engage in politics. This means to define its sectorial policies within an explicit global policy, and to start implementing them. Policies and especially sectorial policies are being realized also in the current power system, even though they are never articulated in an explicit manner. It is only that their application and control do not belong to the government as they do not belong to the small group of persons at the summit of the power system either, but to the other two levels of the power system: the administration and the industrial technocracy.

The first is the administration, for which the government operates as a factor of legitimation and as a scapegoat, but not as an authority.

The Power of the Administration and the Administration of the Power

After the revolution, there has been much talk of the administration, mainly in critical terms. The administration has been considered as a remarkable force, if not even the most important, of the opposition to the change, and the phrase "stagnant bureaucracy" made a career thanks to the easiness with which it allowed the politicians to find a scapegoat for their own failures. The administrative bureaucracy has never been very popular in Romania, so it was not difficult to accredit the idea that it was because of it that change was going in the wrong direction or was not going at all. But there has been also a more serious phenomenon that has made of the bureaucracy the target of attacks. It is about the conflict between generations, which has prevailed in the clashes of the post-revolution period. We will enlarge on it later, since it has meant more than an attack on the administrative bureaucracy. But, as it is dominated by the older generation, the attack of the young intellectuals, to whom the revolution has opened the road to functions and the appetite for making up a new elite of the power, was focused for a while on them. In the end, the conflict was settled for the benefit of the older generation and of the pre-revolution leaders of the administration. The naive intellectuals of the period of "revolutionary romanticism" remained with the consolation of being able to further their own failures on the administrative bureaucracy.

In actual fact, things have not been and are not that simple. It is true that the post-revolution administrative system is more like a carbon copy of the pre-revolution administrative system. It is not fair to label this system as communist. The communists too, had taken it over from the previous regime which, without having invented it, had adjusted the system inherited from the Phanariot feudalism to the requirements of a modern society. In brief, the administrative system of Romania now is the system it has almost always had. It is nobody's fault that the revolution did not manage to change it. But it definitely is a failure. The fact that the administrative system has managed to reproduce itself is only partially its merit. To a great extent, it is the merit of the new power emerged after the revolution. On 23 December, right after the setting up of the new body of the revolutionary political power, one of the first steps taken by the NCNSF was to command the administration, ministries and the other central institutions to continue their activity. The new government set up immediately after that, did the same, basing its activity on the functioning even if approximate, of the former administration. The result was the re-re-creation of the pre-revolution administrative system and, in this way, of the whole mechanism of ruling the society and of social control which the revolution had annihilated.

Such a change was not fortuitous. It was the result of the implicit ideology that underlined the Romanian revolution of 1989, equally espoused also by the mass of demonstrators and by the new political leaders. Its basic thesis was that the Romanian society could be changed by replacing the old and "evil" rulers with new and "good" rulers. Even the passage to a multy-party political system, where the selection of the new rulers is made periodically, based on free elections, does not mean a change in the system of ruling the society, but only a change in the system of electing the rulers. Complying with that ideology, the leaders of the revolution replaced the administrative functionaries but they abstained from replacing the administration. Above all, they did not change the outlook on its role and functionality, which, in fact, meant the reproduction of the former bureaucracy, with a different staff this time. Later, when it appeared that the new and young people, for all their scientific titles, were incapable of finding their way in the intricate web of administrative relations and circuits, old functionaries started being used again. That was a source of reproaches regarding the restoration, but it made the administration more efficient.

The power of a bureaucracy – and the administration is one of the best articulated bureaucracies – resides precisely in the fact that it is not the people that matter, but the structures and rules of activity. No administration has ever been reformed through the replacement only of its staff. Not even its mere restructuring, the continuous changing of the relations of subordination and of the organizational branching has had any effect. The Romanian revolution has tried them all, so we are possessed of this experience. In the summer of 1990 all economic ministries were dismantled and a Ministry of Industries was set up instead, with the hope that such a reorganization would free for good the industrial technocracy in enterprises of the administrative control, for the simple reason that there no longer were functionaries enough in the ministries to take care of it. The subsequent dismantlement of the central industrial departments was one more step on the same line. Both steps have remained without a real effect on the relations between the technocracy and administration. If a change at their level still occurred, it was not due to those administrative pseudo-reforms, but to the modification of the relations with the industrial technocracy.

The transition took over and reproduced the pre-revolution administration, which it introduced in the new power system created after the revolution. The take over did not mean that it retained a part, in some places the bigger part, of the staff, or that it retained the institutions, many of them indispensable for any modern society, the take over meant that it reproduced the functions of the administration in the power system. The administration has the same functions in the power system built after the revolution as it had under the former system. It was other characteristics and relations that changed.

The key to the whole system in the relation with the population. The administration can be employed in two ways. It can be employed in order to provide services to the population. From waste collection to medical care, education, public transport or public order. And in this case the administration avails of power, because it controls the resources needed for performing the services that are its duty. But, it does not control the population, being rather subject to the population's control. Such an administrative system has never existed in Romania, and the less so under the socialist regime. The current power system in turn, employs the administration as an instrument to administer, manage and control the population. Consequently, the administration provides services, but it provides them to its control center, no matter which. In such a power system, the population is not considered to be the main beneficiary of the exercise of power, but its main object. And, surely, as one of the major sources to manage.

For the administration, this makes a great difference. It is building its structure and mechanisms contingent upon the definition between it and the population. In a situation like our present one, the administration organizes its functioning from bottom to top. What really matters, what sets the criteria of professionalism and proper functioning, which represent criteria of rewarding and promoting the functionaries and, generally, operates as a general requirement along the administrative system, is the meeting of the needs of the higher level. The lower level is regarded as the instrument or resource of which it avails for this purpose. All administrative institutions change not only their way of functioning, but also their sense as compared with the initial or formal one. Formally, the sense remains to provide services to the population. But even these services are regarded rather as a way of taking in resources from the population in order to meet the needs of a higher level. In this way, it was possible to regard the education, for instance, under the former regime, first of all as a means to form an occupational structure defined by the communist party's policy – through that "Procrustes' bed" of industrial high schools -, and in the current regime as a simple resource of cutting down budget expenditures. In this respect, there is no essential difference between the old regime and the present one as to the functions and way of employment of the administration. The revolution did not manage to essentially change the role of the administration and, for that reason, it did not manage to essentially change the system of power sharing. The administration keeps being used as a mechanism to dominate the population instead of as a mechanism to serve the population.

The most significant in this respect is that this apparently paradoxical process, by which the administration has got more and more consolidated in the years after the revolution, although the services it offers to the population are lesser and lesser in terms of quantity and quality alike. This degradation proceeds simultaneously at the levels of local and central administration. But some significant differences exist. The degradation of the urban and communal services, the main task of the local governments, has not been very notable in the years after the revolution, not could it be, given that they already recorded a degradation almost beyond any limit before 1989. The faulty energy and water supply, the lack of hygiene specific to the big cities, the insufficient transport, the house shortage, etc., all these had reached the upper limit under Ceausescu. The only new characteristic, emerged after the revolution, is the mounting crime, blamed, for propaganda purposes, on the growing individual freedoms, but actually caused by a complex of factors one of which is that of all institutions of the administration, the revolution has shaken the most precisely the police, because of its political function held under the former regime. One of the priorities of the revolution was, of course, to restructurate this institution of the police, but such a radical measure would not fit in the moderate views of the NCNSF and of the governments that followed, which, like shown before, were concerned with using whatever they could from the old regime in order to maintain the national and social stability. The restructuring of the Romanian police is still a target to be reached. However, the disfunction of the local administration has been perceived above all as an inability to improve an inherited situation, while the disfunction of the central administration shows in the degradation of services or activities at a national level.

The first of them is obviously the economic, but here we have an evolution. After the central administration, through the agency of the new government, assumed right after the revolution the task to administrate "more wisely" the national economy – without achieving anything in this respect -, the governments that followed one another after the 1990 elections and until the 1992 elections adopted an attitude of "withdrawal from the economy", considering that it has to be freed of the administration's control and, generally, of any central management. The process was gradual and incomplete, but these governments have publicly adopted the position of interfering as little as possible with the economy and have promoted a legislation that greatly enlarges the autonomy of the state enterprises, while reducing the government's responsibilities for their economic performance. Just the opposite, the Vacaroiu Government was formed against the background of strong ideological and practical pressures for the government – meaning administrative – intervention to be resumed in the economy which meant mainly a return to some of the government subsidies given to state enterprises, that had been cut or threatened to be cut (actually they have never been desisted completely). But, in spite of the opposition's statements about the tendencies to return to the old system of command economy, an essential change had already occurred and, for all the appearances, the situation was not at all what it had been before 1989. The main difference consisted in the dominant position of the industrial technocracy and the extremely shaky, almost inexistent position in the power system of the political institutions.

However, the most important degradation of the results of administrative activity has not occurred in the economy, but in the services provided to the population and society, from education, health care, social security and assistance to fighting unemployment, environmental protection and national security.

There are numerous explanations in this respect and, like I said, one of the new characteristics of the current regime is its growing ability to explain and communicate these explanations to the population and to the international bodies. But the main cause which does not show in these explanations is that the improvement of these services and, generally, of any service meant for the population, simply do not make an objective of the administration. It is not built for this but for taking in from the population all necessary resources for reaching its real purpose, meaning to provide services to the power level to which it is subordinated. Under the circumstances, the administrative system is oriented to two fundamental activities: to collect resources and to maintain the stability or social peace, i.e. to maintain the population under control.

The collection of resources proceeds in several ways but, in a relatively primitive administration as the one inherited from the previous regime, the direct ways have special priority. The most direct of all is the tax and rate system. In a complicated society, as the modern societies are, the tax and rate system is one of the most important means of implementing certain policies, either economic or social. This rests on the reality that any rate or tax has numerous consequences, both economic and social, at least some of them being foreseeable. And it is actually in this system that resides the key of any governing. For, a governance consists essentially of the redistribution of a bigger or smaller part of the society's resources, not in keeping with the objectives and interests of those who have generated these resources, but in the pursuit of objectives set by the society's rulers – the elite or the group that controls the power system. The power itself means precisely the possibility first to collect this part of the social resources and then to use it for its own purposes. But, of course, the rates and taxes represent only one of the ways to absorb resources after their generation. Another, just as important mechanism is the modelling of the consumption and the simplest way here is to limit it. I will mention here one more mechanism, the administration's taking over directly the control and distribution of the essential resources, such as the land or mineral deposits or some imported staples.

The Romanian power system too, is built mainly if not solely for this same purpose. Within the power system, the administration has first the function to trace the resources and suck them in. Then, to distribute a part of them for the above-mentioned services meant for the population. And eventually, to provide to the policies established at a national level to necessary resources for their implementation. Two essential moments can be distinguished in this process. One is the selection of the adsorbed resources. The other is the selection of the destination of the thus collected resources and of the relations among various destination. Such a selective and modelling manipulation of the rates and taxes is impossible for the current power system. The main reason is not the often claimed inability to understand and anticipate the economic and social consequences. One of the reasons is the very limited size of these resources as compared with the specified necessities. But even more important is the option as to the priorities. And for the current power system it could be defined like this: the priority of providing services to be population and society must be considered as having the lowest degree in relation to the other priorities. This is the golden rule of the Romanian administration after the revolution. It has not been proclaimed in as many words, but the administration obeys by it almost unhesitating, the more so as it is accustomed to it. True, this same rule had guided the functioning of the administration also under the former regime. It had then to take in the resources and control the population in order to implement the objectives set by the political bureaucracy. Now, the same functions are performed in order to satisfy the industrial technocracy.

Secured social stability is obviously necessary in order to allow for the collection and redistribution of the resources.. The administration is this time as well the main instrument. And here occurs a process which is very telling of the way how the relations between the administration and the population have stabilized in the period after the revolution. For, in this respect, the administration is subject to pressures that come from two main directions. One is the trade unions. But, the trade unions do not mean the population, they mean the employees who, one way or another, are ultimately encompassed in the bureaucratic system, be it administrative or technocratic. The other direction is the population itself, less organized, less coherent and far less dangerous. At least so far, the administration has chosen the strategy of yielding all the time to the unions' pressures, and then to annul their victories through monetary and fiscal policies, and of never yielding to the population almost regardless of its requests.

The administration has eventually constructed also a true ideology of its own power and of repressing the claim movements, by the deceptive name of "state of law". Although the ideological substantiation is more sophisticated, its essence consists of the statement that the population must obey by the administrative decisions and rules. The existence of administrative mechanisms for challenging them is a mere formality. Even more interesting is the fact that the three levels of the power system that exercise the real power do not deem it necessary to observe themselves the rules and decisions. I do not mean the cases of graft or frequent illegality that remain unpunished and that can be simply blamed on disfunctions of the juridiciary, on transition, etc. It is about instances of disregard of the rules, like the formation of thee Vacaroiu Government or the "Reform Strategy" of the government being ignored.

Adding to this ideology of the "state of law", to legitimate the administrative power over the population, is another, more subtle, more credible and definitely more dangerous ideology. It is the ideology of "national interests and objectives". And it is complex and has been steadily developed, for various reasons and in support of extremely diverse interests ever since 1848. Its basic thesis is that the national interests prevail over the individual interests and that the latter can and even must be sacrificed without hesitation for the attainment of a national interest. Nobody has ever challenged this thesis throughout Romania's modern and contemporary thesis, and it has been accepted by the population itself all along. The cause of credibility of this ideology must be sought in the historic difficulties of formation of the national Romanian state and in the real dangers it had to cope with in its short history. Or, this never challenged basis has been employed to create legitimacy for the most varied instances. The secret of all inventions of this kind consists of the concentration not on national interests – which as a rule remain obscure –, but on the institution that is entitled to act in their name. During the communist regime, this institution was the communist party. In the post-revolution regime this institution no longer is a political party, first because no political party can identify itself with the state any longer. For a change, the administration, especially the central one, can. Of course, it cannot define the national interests. It can only define its own objectives, and these are trivial. But it can present instead any decision referring to the furtherance of the domination on the population and of the adsorption of the biggest possible amount of resources from it, as decisions made for meeting national interests. The other way round, any challenging or opposition to them can be and are presented as opposing the national interests, therefore as blamable.

Of course, national interests do exist, and we will enlarge on them later. Their most characteristic approach in the post-revolution period is that, although they make one of the most commonplace cliches of the political and administrative discourse, so far, none of the actors of the power – either participant or would-be participant in governance – has made any serious effort to single out and define them. The national interests keep being unknown, which favors their replacement by group interests, by interests of some institutions or even, more rarely but more seriously, of persons. But, beyond this substitution, the thesis of national interests' prevalence over the individual ones takes over and maintains, as a principle of the state-individual relation, the state's superiority over the individual. The state, consequently the administration, keeps being perceived as a distinct entity that transcends the individuals making it, either taken separately or as a whole. This requisite is vital for maintaining the function of control over the population which the administration assumes as its main social function. At the other end of the relation, the population's role is to be a simple resource – or source of resources – for the administration.

Two disjunct domains are thus established. On the one hand, there is the state, the main function of which is to watch over and meet the national interests, and which considers itself – and is considered – entitled to act for this purpose without caring too much about the interests of the individuals and of the population. On the other hand, there are the interests of the population and of the individuals comprised in it, that have as space of manifestation what is left after the interests and objectives of the state, meaning the central administration, are satisfied. The "national interests" ideology and the system of values substationing it are only the base of the central administration bureaucracy's dominance over the society. From budgets and legislation to institutional structures, the administration and the society alike are built to comply with this principle. As it is a generalized ideology, nobody challenges it. It has not crossed the mind of anyone, political parties, trade unions, non-governmental organizations or individuals, that the most important national interest is to satisfy the interests of the population and of the individuals, from economic and security interests to cultural or educational ones.

In the end, it appears that the administration, in spite of the power it exercises on the population and of its control of important resources, is only an element in the system of power sharing. The decisions on the way how the resources are redistributed and how the power is used do not belong to the administration. Under the communist regime, they belonged to the communist party's political bureaucracy. In the current power system resulted from the transition, they belong, in a far more complex way, to the industrial technocracy.

The Population or the Lack of Power

A third level is the industrial technocracy. We will enlarge below on its role in the power system and on the road covered to reach it. At the last level of the system, where the power is adsorbed but not allocated, there is the population. Not the workers, not the farmers, not the wage-earners, but the population, the citizens, characterized not by occupation, not by income and property, not by cultural level, age, sex or nationality, but by the mere position of being – to quote Ceausescu – simple citizens. In the political system built after the revolution this is tantamount to being voters. In the power system, it is tantamount to being deprived of power.

There are at least three characteristics which the population shares by itself, in relation to the other levels of the power system. It is the only level at which it is the object of the power and not a participant in it. Also, it is the only level of power which is not structured in any way and does not avail of an organization of its own. Third, it is the only one that reacts to the other levels.

There are numerous structures that can be distinguished at the population's level, by employing the most varied criteria, from demographic to economic or cultural ones. However, none of these structures is a power structure. In relation to the power, the population is a huge, formless mass. Moreover, it is forced not to get structured. We have already seen how the "politicians" of the first level opposed a spontaneous political structuring of the population immediately after the revolution. Just the same, the administration opposes the structuring of the population at a community level. The real battle for the autonomy of the local authorities is not being fought between the local governments and the central one. Sure, there is also such a battle, but it is not essential, because it has a political substratum. It simply happened that the local and general elections, both held in 1992, were won by opposing political groupings. Consequently, while the central administration is controlled by the politicians of the government coalition, the politicians at the head of the local governments are mostly representatives of the opposition. The core of the conflict is therefore not administrative in nature, although the slogans shouted in the battle obviously refer to democracy, local autonomy, etc. Like all political battles, this one too, will end with a compromise in principle and will continue indefinitely in fact, at a larger or smaller scale, contingent upon the evolution of the local balances of forces. There is in this period of "settlement" of power relations also a confrontation between the center and the periphery, between the central administrative institutions that fight for greater control over their subsidiaries in counties and localities and the latter's striving to get more autonomy in decision-making and, implicitly, greater control over the local resources. Old new. It happened the same under the former regime. Numerous local leaders, who held important functions in the communist party's hierarchy anyway, developed a fine image of themselves with the population for having represented rather the local interests than those of the central bureaucracy. The competition between the Capital and counties and, in counties, among localities, is internal from the administrative bureaucracy's viewpoint and it too, is bound to end in a compromise, as the two components, the central and local administration, belong in the end to the same level of the power.

The real battle for the power is being waged between the population and the administration. Between the administration that is striving to strengthen its control over the population, making it as efficient as possible on the one hand, and as free of a counterweight as possible on the other hand, and the population, unstructured, unorganized, for which the opportunity has however emerged of taking over the control of a part of the administration, the local one, through the agency of politicians that can be sanctioned by the population. The population has lost the battle so far. First, because in the current system, the parties' support to the politicians that run in local elections is more important than the direct support of the population. The local elections keep being a mere reflex of the political fight at a national level. And the political parties, whether in the opposition or ruling, are backing the current power system. Second, because the politicians nominated by parties are their party's representatives on a local plane and not the population's representatives in relation to the administrative structures. Consequently, they are rapidly integrated in the power system as administrative leaders, in a way very similar to the way how the government was integrated as a mere summit deprived of authority of the central administrative pyramid.

Under the circumstances, the population has nothing left but the effort to evade the control and the power. It is a strategy which the population has applied for centuries. Because it cannot oppose the administration, because it does not have objectives, organization, ideological base and means, the population has always chosen the solution of circumventing, eluding, evading, which can take any form, from the simple fiscal shelter and unsympathetic behavior toward the administration, to smuggling, profiteering, delinquency and, above all, this hidden, underground economy, parallel and often parasitic to the official one, that has developed so much after the revolution.

After the revolution, the population's lack of power has got stabilized as a characteristic of the establishment only relatively late. An evolution has taken place here, characterized by a quite special starting point and by an obvious and steady tendency. The starting point was the concentration of the power during the revolution precisely at the level of the population. In a first stage, the population controlled directly the power, which the big and anonymous groups of people distrustfully entrusted to improvised leaders whose inititatives used to be endorsed or rejected on the spot. That form of primitive democracy is obviously inadequate in a modern society and especially in a numerous population. It succumbed rapidly and the street very soon remained with only an inconsequential role in modelling the decisions, no matter how picturesque and irritating that role is, as it happened with the University Square story. Very soon, starting right from December 1989, the street ceased being the place of manifestation of the population and it remained only the ground of the political parties' manoeuver groups. However, for a period long enough after the revolution, that lasted even after the May 1990 elections, the population remained the main factor that legitimated the access to power. It is not about the formal criterion of the election returns, but about the population's active and intense participation in the country's political life.

This is important because the only way in which the population can participate in the power sharing system as holder of the power and not only as its object, is politics. But the population does not articulate political themes, objectives and strategies. All it has been able to do was to get integrated, in good faith and sometimes even passionately, in the themes, objectives and strategies articulated by the political parties and personalities it agreed with. As they belonged to the battle for holding the key places at the top of the power system, the population has got integrated in that fight. In the beginning it did so very enthusiastically, identifying itself with the politicians' interests. But, as the life in Romania was growing more and more complex and, because of the economic crisis, increasingly difficult, and the transition, which the political parties had long stopped caring about, was continued at random, the population started to withdraw more and more from the political battle. It was increasingly obvious that the parties' objectives were not the electorate's objectives too, despite the political demagogy wasted by the politicians of all camps. For a while, until after the 1992 elections, some of the themes put forth in the political battle continued to stir the affective participation at least of some categories of the electorate. In Transylvania, the nationalist speeches and the permanent threat with the danger spelt at it, normally had the effect of the finger that scratches a real wound. Other themes were just as sensible. For both industrial workers and farmers, the ghost of denationalization, through the redemption of the nationalized property to the former owners, continues to be a choice not only undesirable but also unacceptable. Finally, for all the population that was getting impoverished – and this means the majority of the population -, the emergence of a thin layer of rich, as result of corruption of the administration and industrial technocracy, seemed an unfair situation that had to be fought against.

But, after the 1992 elections, it became obvious that the political system was not only getting integrated with the stabilized power system, but it also supporting it, by giving it precisely the legitimacy which the political parties has elicited from the population. Consequently, the population has started no longer to respond to these themes either, no matter how well shown to advantage by the politicians. Not because the subjects as such, or the assets associated with them, have lost something of their topical or acute nature, but because the mere existence of the debated realities is no longer a simple heritage from the past, but a product of the post-revolution society, and the parties and politicians are its main supporters and beneficiaries.

So, the population has started to turn its back to the political life, once it got convinced that the participation in the political life does not entail also a participation in power. Watching the mere replacement of some politicians by others in the state's leading offices, as well as the consecutive replacement of some functionaries by other functionaries in the leading functions of the administration or of the economy would not stir more interest than watching a sport competition. It was clear that any change of the kind would have but minor or no consequence on the real problem the people had to cope with in the everyday life. And, above all, that it would not affect in any way the further functioning of the system.

The population's drawing back from the political life is a process that has continuously proceeded since December 1989 into this day and there are signs that it will continue, unless the relation between the political system and the power system undergoes a significant change. In December 1989, the revolution suddenly brought the whole population to the condition of political activism, as politics is the only way in which the population, having no structure and no organization, can get structured and organized to share in the power. But this sharing has steadily declined ever since. The establishment of the power system relying on the cooperation between the administration and the industrial technocracy has decisively influenced the parties' evolution and has ruled out the possibility of organizing the population as a political factor. The subsequent development of the parties into mere camps of supporters of certain candidates to the power functions and the population's involvement in this sterile fight left any political activism without a content. After the endorsement of the Constitution and the concentration, pursuant to the 1992 elections, of the political battle in the Parliament halls, the political battle itself has turned into a mere boring and uninteresting TV show. The population's attitude has slowly turned from profound affective involvement during the revolution, to disappointment and then to contempt.

The population's withdrawal from the political life is the most visible aspect of a process that is tantamount to the population's withdrawal from the public life. The statement is a little unusual, but it is characteristic of the stage of the power relations at which the population is not only deprived of power, but it becomes aware of its access to power and of its lack of means to press for access. The population's withdrawal from the public life does not come as a novelty. It characterized the whole previous regime, especially its last decade, when not only the population but even the members of the communist party simply refused to take an interest in politics, since they had no role in it. But the population's present withdrawal from politics has a more complex significance. It does not mean only that the population has realized that its role is reduced only to legitimizing the access to power of people whom it has no way to influence afterwards. Adding to this is the loss of confidence in the possibility to change the reality through political activity and decision.

3. The Failure of the Political Transition

The mission of the political transition was to change the power system. The pre-revolution system relied on the dominance of the political bureaucracy over the administrative bureaucracy and the latter's complete control over the population and over the working class, through the agency of the industrial technocracy. Such a system, typically pre-industrial, could be created and kept in operation only through the elimination – economic and even physical – of the Romanian bourgeoisie emerged in the inter-bellum period, and with the support of the class of industrial workers. The system was challenged and ultimately dismantled by the industrial technocracy, that developed parallel to the working class and was increasingly important, as industry became prevalent in the social system of production. All this story is rather commonplace in the evolution of the societies as a result of industrialization. In socialist Romania the industrial technocracy simply took over the role played by the bourgeoisie in the post-feudal societies of the 18th and 19th centuries.

However, the technocracy is no bourgeoisie and the power system created by it is not the one created by the bourgeoisie in Western Europe. Besides, we no longer live at the end of the Middle Ages, but at the end of the 20th century. So, although the power system has changed pursuant to the revolution, we have every right to wonder whether it has changed the way we expected it to and even whether it has changed the way it ought to.

Power without Democracy

An option comes in here, a choice which is out of place in the scientific analysis because it has something to do with politics. When we say that the power system ought to be of some specific sort, we start from certain assets and choices which we consider as compulsory. Such a starting point applies to a great many aspects of the society, but it does not apply to the power system. The cause is that a power system is fundamental in a society. All components of the society, including the assets and options at the people's disposal are modelled in keeping with the system. That is why it is very important that we should be aware of the power system we are creating because, in this period of transition, there is the chance, extremely rare in history, to build the power system which most of a society's people want. The fact that the Romanian revolution quite strongly affirmed that most of the country's people want a democratic power system seems to me a sound argument

And this is not the only one. Another argument, even stronger than invoking the revolution, is the necessity of development. Romania has to develop, and for this a democratic power system is essential. In Romania's case this is an exceptional situation because there usually is no direct relation between democracy and development. True, development is a must of democracy which, as a power system, is expensive and sometimes even wasteful. Democracy is also conditioned by the technical possibilities of communication and by a limit level of political knowledge and correct information about the problems on which decisions have to be made. But Romania has long gone past that minimal level of economic and technological development required by democracy.

It is just as true that democracy does not condition the development. Moreover, in certain cases the authoritarian regimes are more efficient in mobilizing resources for development, than the democratic ones. Romania developed rapidly between 1950 and 1980, at an accumulation rate that topped even Japan's in some periods. And that performance was possible only under an authoritarian regime, apt to mobilize all resources for the benefit of development, keeping the consumption at an unnaturally low level. That the development and the resources were oriented in a direction that ultimately proved to be wrong is a different story and part of the criticism of the socialist system. This last amendment can cast the token of a doubt on the ability of a regime in which the power is distributed to only one command center to ensure efficient economic and social development. Therefore, we could bring forth the example of Japan, a country that has been ruled for half century after World War Two, not only by the same political party, but especially by the same combination between administration and industrial technocracy that is coming into being now in Romania as well. And it has been ruled in an authoritarian manner, yet in far more subtle and more efficient forms than those employed by the communist party in Romania.

Even though the development is not conditioned by the existence of a democratic regime, we find ourselves now in the exceptional situation in which we desperately need such a political system if we want to trigger and maintain the specific processes of development. The transition, political, economic and social alike, has come to an equilibrium when the power system has got stabilized and when everyone of those who have the least control of some resources have occupied a place in the system which they are unwilling or unable to change. With this stabilization, the radical changes in society have come to an end. Sure, there will come more changes, but they are already foreseeable, fitting in the distinguishable tendencies of the structures and relations that have come into being. This foreseeable changes no longer affect the power system, although they still might affect many of the personalities that incarnate it now. But, these foreseeable changes do not bring development. Their tendency is to produce and stabilize the typical structures of underdevelopment instead.

To ensure the development, Romania's main issue is not the economic growth, but the keeping of a high pace of changes, in the economy and in society alike. And none of the participants in the power is interested any longer in a further change of realities. Their objective now is the reproduction of the extant relations. The only category which is a potential promoter of the change is the population. Not the working class, not some other occupational or income category, but the citizens, the city people above all. First, because they are the worst hit by the economic crisis and will benefit the least from the resumption of the economic growth. Second because they are the only ones who do not share in the power. Not even by alliance with some elite.

The population can put serious pressure for change only if it has access the power one way or another. It is not about the formal access, about the participation in voting once in four years, in order to decide which one of the groupings inside the administration or technocracy will replace the other in the functions at the top of their state, without changing by this anything in the power system. It is about remaking the extant power system so that at least a part of the resources should be controlled by the population and for the use of the other resources the population should be the factor of appraisal.

Such a situation, no matter how rare, bears the name of democracy. There is only one way for the population to have access to the direct or indirect control of the resources, and this is the political democracy, both at a local level and at national one. The political democracy would mean the political control of the power system formed of the administrative bureaucracy and the technocracy.

No matter how little appealing are these two bureaucracies, and their lack of appeal is to a great extent a groundless superstition, they are indispensable. Of all systems of social organization none is as efficient as the bureaucratic one. But is not only efficient, it is the only one that can be controlled from an established center and through stable mechanisms or institutions. Bureaucracy is the only way of administrating the power which allows for complete control over the population. But it is at the same time the only way of administrating the power that allows the population to control its use through politics. It depends on how you use it. And, of course, on the power system.

Or, the current power system is obviously undemocratic. It cannot ensure the population's control over the system, because it relies precisely on controlling the population, by subordinating it as completely as can to the administration. Moreover, it cannot accept at least the political control of the administration. The administration is controlled by the technocracy. In order to preserve its supremacy, the technocracy cannot accept a political control over the administration. It happened under the former regime and the technocracy protested against it.

But the existence of a token control is necessary. Any country needs a political system. Even if it does not really rule, the political system is useful for the legitimation of the decisions made by the holders of the power and for the development of the environment they need in order to secure their implementation. It also necessary in order to make sure that nobody, no genuine political force likely to aspire after a ruling position, comes into being in order to fill in the vacancy. Therefore, the technocracy has supported the formation of the political parties and of the parliamentary regime and is supporting their functioning according to the present characteristics. On the other hand, the parties never come at a real leadership. The way it can be used to maintain a system that is authoritarian in its essence, the multi-party system can equally be employed to maintain a system deprived of politics. And this gives us the key to the whole post-revolution evolution.

The Power without Politics

What characterized the transition all these years has been its spontaneous nature. It seems at least unrealistic to speak of the spontaneity of the transition as long as the new legislation counts the new regulations by the hundreds and they cover all domains and aspects of the society, from economy and education to the frontier crossing regime and the radio programs. But, one has to distinguish among the superficial aspects of the transition and the profound ones. Just as one must tell the difference between recording a social reality in terms of legislation and changing that reality by introducing the legislation. Last but not least, one must not yield to the most disseminated superstition of any administration in this world, and especially of the Romanian one, meaning that once a regulation issued, the reality will change to fit its content and the legislators' intentions. The changes purposefully introduced along the transition were confined to merely changing the Romanian institutions after the pattern of the Western institutions. When, as expected, they functioned in a quite different way, in keeping with the reality around them, the solution endorsed has always been to operate further changes with the institutions. The restructurings and reorganizations have been the favorite preoccupation of the administration and governments all these five years and they are tending to become an autonomous activity, an objective in itself, not very connected with the reality. Meanwhile, the wildcat transition keeps changing social structures and relations, major economic orientations, basic cultural models and important social institutions like the family or the communities.

The spontaneous character of the transition is responsible for a great many characteristics of the current Romanian society. Among other things, it is responsible for the current power system. There is a direct connection between them. The power system has resulted also because the transition has proceeded spontaneously instead of being controlled and oriented toward a project of society politically defined. Once formed, it further needs a spontaneous transition in order to get stabilized and to reproduce itself and especially in order to be able to change the society in such a way as it should be the normal power system in the society.

The requisite for this is the absence of a global policy and the instability of the sectorial policies. The connection between the power system and the spontaneous character of the transition should be understood well, as the latter is determined by the former. A power system that relies on two mainstays – the industrial technocracy and the administrative bureaucracy does not make of Romania an exception. But we must be aware of the consequences. The industrial technocracy and the administrative bureaucracy are constitutive elements of any modern power system. It holds the medium level of the system. In the more rare case in which they want to control the society, they have to eliminate the extremes from the power, i.e. the basis consisting of the population, and the summit, represented by politicians. What makes the task of the technocracy and administration more easy is that both can be eliminated from the game with only one move – emptying the political life of any content. The analysis of the modern societies provides two extreme examples in this, both illustrating the situation of developed countries – Japan and Sweden.

Japan can be considered as a typical case of success of a power system based on a combination of industrial technocracy and state administration. They have been mutually supportive all along the period after World War Two and the Japanese technocracy is now the most powerful in the world, while the administration keeps playing an important role in maintaining the cohesion of the system and the control of the two "ends" – the population and the politicians. The role of the later in the power system is immaterial for a change. Sweden illustrates the opposite case. Sweden is a small country, lying in a northern corner of Europe, with a disproportionately powerful industrial technocracy: Swedish companies have been among the biggest in the world for almost a century, capable to take in or to adjust themselves to all economic and technological changes of the last fifty years. At the same time, because from energy production and transport to education and urbanism, most of the infrastructure is state-controlled, Sweden also has an extremely powerful administration, due to the amount of resources it controls. But Sweden has always had an independent population, with a very high level of education, civic included, and politically organized on a wide scale as early as the last century. The Swedish power system is dominated by the population, through the agency of the political parties. In Japan, the medium level of the system has managed to eliminate the extremes, taking over the rule of the society. In Sweden, the population and the parties politically control the technocracy and the administration. In Romania, after the revolution, the technocracy and the administration have started their ascent to power, by eliminating the population's first attempts of political organization and depriving the political life of content. The result and requisite of such a process is the spontaneous transition, meaning a transition whose evolution cannot be influenced from identifiable decision centers.

But if such decision centers exist, how can the technocracy hold the power, even by combination with the administration? To understand this, we must elaborate further on the technocracy. The talk about it so far included a very strong personification. Because we have called by only one name a big number of people who have similar characteristics and hold a decisive place in the society's production system: they manage the industrial processes of production, and because we have often spoken of them as if they were a single social actor, the impression may have been created that the industrial technocracy is similar to an organization. It seems to have one will, the awareness of its own group interests, the ability to single out the solutions that are beneficial to it, and to impose their application. As such an organization does not exist formally, we can suspect that there is a genuine plot, with secret accords and underground actions to influence the organizations or personalities on which, at least apparently, depend the options advantageous for the industrial technocracy. Nothing more wrong than the image of such a "plot of managers", no matter how tempting at a time when almost everybody is looking for such underground determinations, precisely because at the surface nothing seems to be rational and steady. To speak of the industrial technocracy as if it were only one social and political actor is just a convenient way of explaining more easily that a host of behaviors with no connection among themselves, can lead to a common result as foreseeable as if it had been intentioned and coordinated by a decision center.

We will use this way of expression again, but it must be clear that such a decision center does not exist. In actual fact, the people belonging to the industrial technocracy do not keep special links among themselves, and when such links do exist, they can be just as friendly, tense or conflicting as inside any other group of people. In spite of the economic and technical connections that exist among the enterprises of some industrial branch or that cooperate in manufacturing the same product, their managers have not come to form, like the trade unions, organizations of their own, and the communication among them is quite loose, when it is not full of inter-personal competition or tensions. And there are lots of tensions, which is proved by the confrontations among the competing formations that propose the organization of the industrial technocracy and their poor efficiency in ensuring unitary attitudes, to say nothing of their policies.

The Romanian technocracy has not reached a real level of organization – comparable with that of the Japanese technocracy, for instance, and for the time being it does not need it. The decisions which the technocrats make, by exercising their power, do not refer to the economy as a whole, or to industrial branches. Every small technocratic grouping takes care only and solely of its own, bigger or smaller, enterprise, of its own relations and problems. To settle them, it needs either more resources, which it claims from the society, or changes in the legislation, or any other administrative actions or decisions. These requests of the small groups of technocrats are relayed to other enterprises, to banks and commerce, to the administration, population, political parties and parliamentarians and even abroad, to their business partners. When a big number of such requests have a common content, that can be generalized, the idea slowly emerges of promoting a new law or changing some of the already operating ones. Sometimes, when the meeting of the request entails several administrative decisions connected among them, there is an industrial pseudo-policy at work, and that is where the political parties come in, taking it over as a banner and ensuring its legitimacy with the public opinion. Two telling examples are enough.

The first is the most important step taken by the second Roman Government which, presented as the gist of the economic reform, consecrated the respective government as reformist for the rest of its career. The measure was the price liberalization starting with the autumn of 1991. As is known, the measure was justified from a political-ideological point of view. The price liberalization, which was recommended insistently by the World Bank and the IMF alike, was presented as an essential step toward the market economy. As its result, the administratively controlled prices, a characteristic of communism which we wanted to leave behind, would be left at the producers' will, that would adjust them in keeping with the market, according to the golden rule of the demand and supply. If the demand outgrew the supply, the prices too would rise; if, on the contrary, the demand dropped below the level of the supply, the prices too, would drop in order to stimulate the demand. Simple and convincing. We expected to set one foot in capitalism, by setting in motion what was pompously called "the objective mechanisms of the market". However, a tremendous debate started on that major administrative measure, participated in by the political parties and the trade unions and public opinion alike, for the first time but definitely dividing the participants into "reformists" and "conservatives". It took President Iliescu to intervene in the debate with the whole weight of his popularity, in order to convince the "conservatives" to accept the measure and the population to bear with it, since it was of course the population that had to pay for the costs. He also had to use all his authoritativeness to cool the "reformers" down a little and make them accept a stage-wise price thaw, so that the shock on the population's living standard should be smaller in the beginning. It was then that was launched in the Romanian political debate the theme that would hold the central place, the theme of the "pace of the reform". The two camps were formed: one for a "shock reform", opposed by the other that was for a "gradual reform". The phrases would be from then on used as political labels. And they still are.

Well, behind that huge debate there was a far more commonplace reality. The industrial technocracy was pressing for the price rises with all industrial products. No congress of the technocracy or undeground plots had taken place. The enterprise managers and chief accountants had had no secret meetings in order to agree on how to corrupt the politicians and rulers to sustain the measure, and they had not articulated a plan for its ideological presentation. They were simply faced with the same fundamental problem: in almost all industrial enterprises the production expenditures were bigger than the incomes made from the sale of the production. All along the period after the revolution, the salaries and extras added to them had been raised, sometimes even doubled, whereas the work time had been shortened, with the introduction of the shorter work-week, and longer rest holidays, and consequent to strikes. Industrial discipline had dramatically declined after the revolution and a big part of the production, finished goods or components or even raw materials, would be simply stolen, sometimes right by the enterprise's workers and at other times by the executives themselves.

The trade in stolen goods mounted with some products, to international levels. To round off the image, we should also mention the technocracy's managerial clumsiness. All of them dramatically affected the labor productivity, hence the financial results of the enterprises.

In the autumn of 1990, the Romanian industry as a whole, was spending more that it was producing, so the solution that suggested itself was the allocation of more resources, a part taken over from other industrial branches and a part from the population. The mechanism was simple: to raise the prices of industrial goods. And the necessary decision for that was presented and considered as indispensable. Which was not true. At least theoretically, two alternative solutions were also possible.

One was to subsidise the whole industry. There were, there have always been in the Romanian industrial system, enterprises, even whole industrial branches subsidised either directly from the budget, as in the case of the mining industry, or indirectly, through soft credits or investment funds. So, it was yesterday's news. The method had been successfully applied throughout the former regime, in order to keep the administrative control of the resources that would have otherwise fallen under the direct control of the technocracy. Such a solution would have been tantamount to the making of the industrial technocracy's subordination to the administration generally and to the government particularly, if all indispensable aid would have been managed by the government through the administration.

The other solution would have been even more radical and absolutely more like the market economy. It would have meant to take firm measures to increase labor productivity, cut down production expenditures, strengthen labor discipline and restructure some of the enterprises, maybe most of them. The starting point for such a solution would have been the acceptance of the idea that the decline in productivity that followed after the revolution was greatly to be blamed precisely on the industrial technocracy, on its inability to secure precisely what it had promised when the old regime was overthrown, meaning an intelligent management of industrial resources and capacities. It would have meant the admission of the necessity to restructure the current technocracy, as a prerequisite for any other restructuring. Beyond such processes of an ideological nature, it would have also meant a political control over the technocracy, relying on a policy of industrial development with the stress shifted from technology to management.

So, we have three alternate solutions, two of which would have led directly to lessening the power of the industrial technocracy, through the taking over of the control on it either by the administration or by some political structure. The third solution would have only consecrated the dominance of the technocracy both on the administration and on politicians. It was it that was endorsed, proving the technocracy's capacity to eliminate the alternatives that do not favor it and to impose those that consecrate its authority over the resources.

The second example is provided by the so-called "financial blockages", that have started becoming a routine mechanism of adjustment of the national economy. The mechanism by which the industrial technocracy imposes decisions at a national level without needing any national coordination, through the mere repetition of the same behavior, becomes even more obvious. The financial blockage emerges when a number of enterprises are no longer able to pay their suppliers. In turn, the suppliers have to pay their own suppliers but, of course, they don't do it, because they do not have the means. This chain-insolvency inexorable spreads all over the economy, while nobody seems to care too much about it. It has become almost economic routine and it is regarded as such. Even the government has joined in this "financial blockage" play, delaying the payments to its suppliers or forcing the local governments to delay the payments by delaying the release of the funds meant for them. This adds to the financial blockage but curbs the government expenditures and, consequently, the budget deficit.

This process cannot go on indefinitely. There comes a moment when the economy is simply unable to function any longer, since, because of both money and credit shortage, nobody is able to make the necessary payments. Here too, there are several solutions, some of which disadvantage the industrial technocracy, and the most radical ones directly affect its power. A radical solution would be the strengthening of the financial and contract discipline, introducing bankruptcy and revamping the enterprises that become unable to settle the debts, and curbing the financial blockage. The banks might come in here, by denying the credits. But they do not do it, fearing social reactions. And the trade unions are the main instrument of transferring the task of settlement of the "financial blockage" to the government, meaning to the society. The government undertakes the "financial deblocking", meaning that it pumps new resources into the industrial system, but not in order to better it. It helps its reproduction in the current form, deficiencies and all. In five years, the Romanian industry has come to a financial blockage three times and the situation has been settled as many times by the society's taking over the costs.

The industrial technocracy has not needed a decision center to impose decisions obviously to its advantage in none of these cases. But, every time, the solution was chosen to favor the industrial technocracy, the reproduction of its dominant position in the process of industrial production, although the process is as expensive as it is bad, and maintaining it unchanged is the main cause of deterioration of the living standard and of the formation of the structures specific to underdevelopment.

Precisely because it does not avail of a decision center of its own, the industrial technocracy has to work for preventing such a center from emerging somewhere else, especially at a political level. A center of political coordination would automatically lead to the imposition of industrial policies on the technocracy. The absence of such a center favors the spontaneous transition. And the spontaneous transition favors the technocracy.

But how comes that, as it holds the power, the technocracy does not act toward raising the efficiency, productivity and remunerativeness of its own enterprises? The most widely disseminated belief is that the technocracy is absolutely interested in the success of the enterprises it manages. In this general form, the assumption is correct. But, it has been taken for granted that the "enterprises' success" means their increased efficiency and profitability. This assumption is wrong. Under the communist regime, the profitability and efficiency were never an objective of the industrial activity, in spite of the frequent reference to them in the official speeches and in the communist party's programs. Any measure to promote them would be rapidly stifled precisely by those who applied it, because its effects contradicted the political objectives of the regime. After the revolution, freed of political pressure, the enterprises, the technocracy that is, have defined their success not by efficiency and profitability, but by mere reproduction. The industrial technocracy has no need to promote the efficiency and profitability, because its own positions do not depend on them. Their power does not depend on the results of production, but on its mere existence, on the existence of the enterprise, of its workers, of the resources earmarked to keep the equipment and installations in operation, of the place it holds within the production system and from which results the size of the social pressure it can exercise.

In order to reproduce all these, there must not exist any kind of policy. Neither industrial nor even social. The former would impose directly and immediately on industrial objectives the promoters of which would subordinate the technocracy. The social policies would set criteria of importance and would force the industrial activities to become functional in relation to them. In other words, they would force the industrial system not only to exist but also to let itself used for purposes that are not defined by itself. The industrial technocracy has not conspired in order to eliminate the politically coordinated transition for the benefit of a wildcat transition. But, through its simple social behavior, it backed the spontaneous character of the transition and opposed, ideologically and politically, any attempted control on itself. It has promoted the formation of the current power system whose main beneficiary it is.

A congenial conjuncture has undoubtedly been the inability of the political system to take over the leadership of the society, especially because it has not been able to generate genuine political parties.

IV. THE ORIGINAL PARTIES
– THE OPPOSITION

In such a system of power sharing, the political parties have no role, therefore no genuine power. The wording "genuine power" is not very correct, but it should be stressed here in order to be distinguished from another, far more conspicuous aspect, which is often mistaken by the public opinion for the power. Since the politicians, actually the national and local leaderships of the major political parties and, especially, their parliamentarians, benefit from numerous small privileges and personal advantages. They can vary from preferential pay rises and free public transport to the access to the petty influence peddling performed through the administration or technocracy, which can sometimes be extremely lucrative. These personal privileges though have no connection with the power and they must not be mistaken for it. The power refers to the capacity of deciding on the orientation and use of the resources in society. But the privileges can mean – and it is happening in Romania after the revolution – the payment given to these politicians in name in order to accept not to share in the power. They participate instead in the power ceremonialism, which means the long train of negotiations, meetings, talks, etc., which end by blessing the decisions made in the genuine power centers. They also participate in the power etiquette which, although annoying sometimes, still has its share of comfort. For, apart from wreath laying, parliamentary addresses and official meetings, it also means service car, body guard, preferential access to administrative services, trips abroad, etc.

1. The Stage of "Original Democracy"

The system of distribution of the political power that has come into being in Romania after the revolution does not need political parties to operate. On the contrary, the political parties can be, in certain circumstances, a serious inconvenience. The assumption that there was a plot meant to eliminate the political parties from the power is incorrect. And it is pointless to consider that the bureaucracy, the technocracy and the small group at the summit of the system, that hold the decision-making functions in the state, have conspired together in order to keep all these five years the parties in the humiliating but gilded position of as decorous garlands on the edifice of the real power. An explanation based on the hypothesis of a plot would please both the public, that usually enjoys the plot stories, and the politicians, who might use it in their polemic with the political opponents. It would be even more convenient, because it is infinitely more easy to eliminate a plot than to turn the current groups of politicians into genuine political parties, apt to exercise the power. But, it would definitely be false. In actual fact, the main causes for the political parties' not participating in the power system must be sought above all just inside the political parties.

When, in December 1989, the NCNSF started organizing the power system based on the pyramid structure of the administrative bureaucracy of the former regime, it had no political parties at hand to introduce in the system. And it did not need them. Nor did the population need them, as it hurried to try and change the NSF into a political party, an initiative with which the National Council was very cautious. That unfortunate statement by Ion Iliescu regarding the "original democracy" that would no longer need political parties, is still remembered. It has been frequently resorted to in order to prove that Ion Iliescu longs for authoritarianism, given that he opposed the sine qua non of any democracy, meaning the plurality of political parties.

The thesis of "original democracy" was furiously attacked by the political opposition and mocked at by international mass media, but between December 1989 and May 1990, Romania really traversed a period of original democracy. Several features that characterized that originality got stabilized in that period and continued to be definitional for the Romanian political system even when it took more normal forms.

First, the fight at a political level was fought in order to establish who would lead the country and not how and whereto would it be led. On the very first days after the revolution, when the dissidents coming from the cultural elite started challenging the dissidents coming from the former political bureaucracy, the theme of the dispute was not that they were bad leaders and had another objectives than those of the revolution. The reason of the challenge was simply that people like Ion Iliescu, Silviu Brucan, Alexandru Barladeanu, Dan Martian a.s.o., were not entitled to lead because they had been part of the former nomenklatura and that it was only fair and moral that those who had once enjoyed the privileges of the leadership should step aside and make room for others.

The country's leading offices and the power generally were not considered as a functionality but as a reward, and those who had never had access to it felt more entitled to get it than those who had already had it.

This theme referring to "who has the right to rule the country" has become not only the main theme, but the only really important one of the political debate after the revolution. It was around it that the political parties were formed, the electoral campaigns proceeded and all subsequent political intrigues were conducted. It was not a battle for power. It was a battle for the privileges that go with the holding and exercise of the power. For the protocol that goes with the high functions in the state, from cars, secretaries and body guards to appearances on TV, official meetings and participation in ceremonies. For the privilege of getting numberless small favors from the people around, whether subordinates or merely persons fascinated by the function or high title conferred, and for the "power" to dispense small favors to friends and relatives, such as homes, jobs, a profitable business or a special treatment in the relations with the administrative institutions. It was a mean competition indeed, and nobody realized it better than the population. The population's attitude toward politics has remained the same and has clearly been determined by the perception of this reality, no matter how embellished by flowery speeches.

Another characteristic of that period was the endorsement of the solution that, as long as the stake was only the sharing of the power privileges and not the power itself, the conflicts would be defused by ensuring the participation in them of reasonable enemies. In a way, this principle operated right from the beginning, from the setting up of the NCNSF, which took in everybody who claimed it or who simply happened to be around. The consecration of the solution though was the setting up of the PNUC.

The Illusion of the "National Consensus"

The PNUC would definitely hold a top place in a hierarchy of originalities of the democracy. It assumed the role of parliament of the extant political parties, where they could agree among themselves on how to rule the country. Although it was formed as a result of the opposition's pressures against Ion Iliescu and the grouping represented by him, the PNUC meant in fact his great victory. It was the very incarnation of the doctrine dearest to him: the national consensus. In broad lines, this doctrine theorizes the government of the society by the technocracy through the agency of a powerful and centralized administrative bureaucracy. It obviously has never been presented as such and it is very likely that not even Ion Iliescu is fully aware of it.

National consensus means that, beyond a group or personal interests, beyond any options, there is a unique solution, the best one, the solution imposed by reality if, assisted by technicians and specialists, one comes to know it well enough. This basic solution is just as inflexible and inexorable as the laws of gravitation. In order to stress its absolute character, it is considered as representing the national interest and, nobody can rise against the national interest, a consensus emerges about it. In front of the solution that promotes the national interest, the politicians can only bow, accepting it, while operating small and unimportant amendments. They may reflect group or even personal interests which, as a rule, are diverging, but legitimate after all, considering the diversity of the "human nature" and of the society. They can be settled by compromise, by bargain. By no means can they affect the basic solution. When the compromise is achieved, the complete national consensus is reached and the solution can be applied to everybody's satisfaction.

The foundation of this doctrine consists of two assumptions, never stated explicitly, both of which are wrong. One states that all, or at least the most important problems of the transition and of the society's development, are of a technical nature and they can therefore be settled by correct scientific approaches. This assumption is not shared only by the Romanian industrial technocracy. The experts of the World Bank or of the International Monetary Fund have no other, more fundamental belief when they articulate recipes of macro-economic stabilization for Romania and the other East-European countries, than that the problems of an economy are always technical in nature and their models and equations always find the technically correct solution for these problems. If the result is not always up to expectations, this is happening because, sometimes, the wrong equations were employed, or, most often, because the politicians, afraid of losing their popularity and the elections, were not firm enough in their application. The whole army of foreign advisers come in Romania to give technical assistance and the billions of dollars spent on them by the developed states and their international organizations, exist thanks to the same belief in this assumption about the technical character of the solutions to the problems of the transition.

Unfortunately, the assumption is wrong. I say unfortunately because if it were true, any problem would be ultimately settled well and for the benefit of everyone. All one would have to do is to find the team of people clever and trained enough to articulate the solution. But this is not a problem, for, like I said, there are billions of dollars and thousands of first-class experts the West is keeping at Romania's disposal. The assumption is wrong, because all, absolutely all major problems of the transition are problems of distribution of the resources and of their use, meaning of sharing and using power in society. And there is no scientific solution here. Only groups of people, interested in taking over and control the power. It does not matter that some of them are generous and want to use the conquered power for the benefit of the whole people or of all citizens. Most of the power and therefore of the resources will always be used to remake the power system. This means first of all to give back the control of resources to that specific group and not to another one. It also means to change the whole economy and all social structures, so that the society should not function unless that group (elite, social class, the name does not matter) is being continuously reproduced as the group in power.

Such mechanisms are extremely complex, but we will see them immediately at work. What is important here is that underlying the solutions to the essential problems of the transition are options, choices of directions, arbitrary from the experts' viewpoint. Irrespective of their form, they directly or indirectly answer the question "Who will hold the power and for whose benefit will it be used?" There are no technical answers to such a question. The few foreign experts who were aware of this reality, before setting to work, asked the common question, surprising though for the Romanian authorities: "What do you want to achieve in the respective domain?" When they were answered that it was their job to tell us what we wanted to achieve, they shrugged, and made major political decisions for us. After that, the solutions were not applied because their options obviously did not match the options of those whom they had come to advise.

The other fundamental assumption is that everybody has something to gain from a compromise. This assumption can be given also a patriotic and democratic form and it can be associated with a specific attitude. It can be stated that Romania is a country big and rich enough for everybody to have a place under the sun and the right to sustain his or her interests, no matter what. The associated attitude is indulgence, "tolerance" in a language that has also a political undertone, and not only as the human rights jurisdiction. But this language is essentially inherited from the philosophy of the century of "lights" and it too, is rooted in the wrong assumption that human behavior is prevailing rational and that, through reason, universal concord can be reached. It is true that men are rational beings but what the promoters of the Enlightenment did not know was that when group interests are at stake, men can develop justificatory reasonings that can be perfectly valid and perfectly contradictory, because they have opposite starting points. Irrespective of form and origin, the assumption that a compromise is always possible and beneficial is obviously false. True, there are compromises that benefit everybody, but at least as numerous are the compromises that are detrimental to everybody, and those from which nobody gains anything.

The thesis that a compromise is always possible has also another consequence, which is more expensive than any badly concluded compromise. It says that an option for one direction or another can be postponed any time. Consequently, the major political decisions may be made or not made, or, if a decision that propels things to a certain direction is made today, tomorrow it can be changed or associated light-heartedly with another one that propels to a quite different direction. This is the source of all the confusion, contradictions and generalized carelessness that characterized the post-revolution Romanian transition.

Ion Iliescu has sustained and applied this doctrine of the national consensus throughout his activity as president, successively, of the NCNSF, PNUC and, later on, of Romania. He has always tried to impose it as a general rule of political behavior, influencing in this direction as much as can, all the actors of the Romanian political stage. The PNUC was the ideal institutional framework for such an experiment, since the PNUC brought together the leaders of all extant political parties, and Ion Iliescu, in his capacity as its president, was chairing over the debates. He proved he had a real talent for leading the participants' inconsequent and endless discussions toward the endorsement of solutions in which everybody had the feeling of having participated. And he managed to obtain, if not a national consensus, at least the consensus of the PNUC members on the solutions elaborated by the technicians of the administration he was leading. The showing on TV of the PNUC debates presided over and dominated by Ion Iliescu tremendously contributed to the growth of his popularity and to his winning the presidential elections of May 1990 without a real competition.

But, to dominate the PNUC settings was one thing and getting a national consensus was something else. The main reason why all PNUC members or at least their majority agreed on the proposed law-decrees, was that all participants considered the PNUC to be just an intermediate, short-term stage, so they did not attach much importance to what was being decided there. Anyway, everything was going to look different after the elections, pending on who would win. And on the main political question of the parties, meaning who was actually holding the leading functions of the state, the PNUC did not even mean a compromise, let aside a consensus. For the time being, they were held by Ion Iliescu himself and his people. On the formation of the PNUC that reality had to be accepted since otherwise the NCNSF would not have allowed its turning into that "parliament of the parties", and the parties leaders would have got nothing. But, the fact that they had no choice did not make them reach a consensus with those who were holding the functions. And Ion Iliescu would discover how terribly wrong he had been in the case of the non-stop demonstration in the University Square, that would put an end to any illusion about a national consensus, about the "pater patriae" who, putting any petty passion and interest behind, wisely decide on the country's laws for the benefit of all and one.

When the PNUC members were told in full sitting that a group of young people occupied the University Square in Bucharest, blocking the traffic and demonstrating against communism generally and Ion Iliescu particularly, for some of the participants in the sitting the news was not new. They were in a position to know that was happening in the University Square even better than those who had hurried to inform the President, because had participated in the organization and starting of the demonstration. They also knew that the demonstration and anything that had to do with it would be extensively covered by mass media, international in particular. Hearing about the University Square, Ion Iliescu let out the word "tramps" ("hooligans") referring to demonstrators, that went around the world and that was afterwards assumed as a title not only by students but also by great international personalities like Eugene Ionesco.

Many wondered how was it possible that an experienced politician like the president should blunder like that. Lack of information and irritation, they said, which may have been true but not enough. He had had his moments of irritation and poor information before, but he had never goofed. Actually, it was about an erroneous appraisal not of the University Square but of the PNUC, and the main source of the error was the doctrine of the "consensus", and the idea that consensus was a fact in the PNUC. On letting out such an insulting word about the University Square protesters in front of his PNUC colleagues, President Ion Iliescu counted on their solidarity, since the University Square was challenging the extant power format and was attacking directly the idea of a consensus relying on compromise, embodied in the PNUC itself. Things proved to be quite different. No consensus existed and it appeared that, when the question arises as to who should take over the leading functions of the political system – the real problem of the parties born out the revolution -, the compromises are neither possible nor favored. The PNUC rapidly split into a camp supporting the University Square and another one that was against it, and the illusions of the national consensus died away.

Ion Iliescu's effort to apply the doctrine of a national consensus was however not limited to leading the PNUC toward compromises. In February-March 1990, he launched the other essential component of the model – the elaboration of the "scientific" solution of the post-revolution transition. The Romanian Academy reorganized the former Central Institute of Economics into nine research institutes that were instructed to articulate the plan of the economic reform in Romania. By April 1990, over one thousand researchers from all domains and of all specialities put together a ten-volume project which was considered by Ion Iliescu as some kind of fundamental text of the economic and social reform.

I do not know whether someone has read through this text. I think nobody has, because nobody has really needed it. Anyway, it was born dead and, although Romania's government sent a delegation to discuss the main ideas of the project with experts in famous universities and institutes in the United States, it has never had any real influence on the post-revolution governance's economic measures or policies. Nor could it. The text did not contain any economic or social policy, just as it did not shape out any reform. It provided a relative description of the extant situation, listed desiderata that were everybody's, and analysed a part of the possibilities to better the extant system, which was obviously the former socialist system. The main authors of the project were partisans of what was called "the third way", some sort of cross-breed between capitalism and socialism, but they did not have a clear outlook on that either, and there was no way for them to have. The time had been not enough, analyses were not enough, data were scarce and the data that were available were most likely wrong or forged, according to the habit of the former regime. And, above all, there was no political orientation whatsoever, and the people had done the only possible thing under the circumstances. Every author had relied on his own political orientation, implicit as it was, and, since at least several hundred people had made a significant contribution to that text, it betrayed a remarkable lack of unity.

Ion Iliescu was probably the only political figure who took it for granted and continued to make public reference to it even three years after it was buried for good in June 1990, with the Roman Government's taking over and with the appointment of Adrian Severin to manage the economic reform in Romania. But, through the very fact of its existence, such a text was filling every formal conditions to keep the illusion about finding solutions to the problems of the transition by scientific ways. All, or almost all important personalities of the economic and social sciences had been mobilized for its articulation. It was the biggest scientific team ever brought together in Romania to work on a joint project. The final result was a compromise among the various scientists' differing viewpoints and, since they had managed to agree, it was believed to be able to generate at long last the much aspired for national consensus. In actual fact, the compromise that had been reached was not satisfactory to any of the authors and no economist has ever referred to that document again. But President Ion Iliescu was convinced, or at least he made that impression, that the economic and social reform was really shaped according to that text. In 1993, as he wanted to emphasize the continuity of the reform under the four governments that followed after the revolution, he used that first project as an argument. To his mind, it was that project that all the governments had strived to translate into life, irrespective of their political color and make. He could hardly be more mistaken. The project had never functioned and the unity of the reform was just another illusion.

The Formation of the Idea of Political Elite

Even if it did not function at all as a place of national consensus, the PNUC however functioned as a way of negotiating, if not the power, at least the privileges of the power. Which proved to be efficient. True, that would not lead to compromises as to the real policies to be followed, but nobody cared about politics. What they were after was the possibility to use the legitimacy the opposition could give the power before international eyes. Because the opposition was more credible abroad than the NSF, or the PSDR or Ion Iliescu. On the other hand, they wanted to ease the pressure of the mass media campaign unfolded by the opposition and sustained by most of the publications.

That recipe was tested from the onset, through the appointment of personalities who were obviously unfriendly towards the NCNSF leaders, in honorary or even important offices, as was the case of some ambassadors, among whom Alexandru Paleologu became famous, because he was kept in office even after he announced that because of the difference of political views he no longer considered himself as representing to France Romanian's government but the University Square "tramps" ("hooligans"). As the Western governments, the French one included, although inclined to be sympathetic toward and maybe even to unofficially support the University Square demonstrators, were however not ready to enter into diplomatic relations with them, Alexandru Paleologu's situation as an ambassador that was no longer representing any government notably deteriorated, but the President did not replace him until the new Roman Government was installed in June 1990.

However, the incident with the Paris embassy proved that the method of dispensing honours in order to tame the opposition or to let it disgrace itself worked. Consequently, numerous attempts followed, to attract the opposition into the same kind of honorary cooperation. In the spring of 1991, a government reshuffle brought to the cabinet a minister who was a member of the National Liberal Party but no understanding had been striken with the Liberals. In the summer of 1991, several members of the Young Liberals were co-opted as state secretaries, the most important of them being the new secretary of Tourism, a prosperous businessman and one of the leading figures of that opposition party. In September 1991, the Stolojan Government, formed after the Roman Government was overthrown by the miners' riot, was already a coalition government, participated in also by the most important party of the then Opposition – the National Liberal Party.

Meanwhile, other characters of the opposition, especially of the intellectual opposition, got functions, hence privileges as well. Economists, writers, journalists etc. were appointed to diplomatic offices or as executives of certain institutions, which made them abandon, at least partly, the political game or the steady campaign for de-legitimating the power. Still, the most important project of the kind was concocted after the May 1992 elections. President Ion Iliescu obviously presented it in terms of a national consensus, but was only about a compromise in sharing the privileges of the power, of the PNUC kind. The idea was to arrange a DNSF governance together with the democratic Convention, in the beginning, and subsequently only with the CDNPP, the main force of the DC and of the whole opposition.

In October 1992, negotiations were conducted with the Democratic Convention, for the formation, if not of a joint government, at least of a majority coalition. The DNSF, that availed of but a small majority in the Parliament, by coalition with the "national party" (Greater Romania Party, Romanian National Unity Party and Socialist Labor Party), was ready to give up those alliances for a far more comfortable majority which could be ensured by the alliance with the opposition. And its offer consisted of extremely important positions, such as those of speaker of the Chamber of Deputies and cabinet members. The success of such an understanding would have made one wonder what had been the point of the elections, after all, but that was no concern either to winners or to the opposition. The fact that the Democratic Convention turned down any collaboration, especially upon the insistence of Petre Roman's party, now a part of the opposition, was not due to a divergence of views of the governance, but only to the belief that a government made by the DNSF had no chance to survive more than a few months. So, it decided to wait for the whole rule to fall in its arms, without having to share it with the DNSF.

The failure of the negotiations on a joint governing by the opposition and the majority party did not discourage completely the attempts to use further the tactics of sharing out privileges and functions. Sharing the power was out of question, because it was not the DNSF, as a political party, that held the power. The power was held by the industrial technocracy, to which a great many representatives of the opposition were just as strongly linked as the DNSF leaders. But the DNSF did have the possibility to share functions and it offered to share them. The new attempt was made with the CDNPP, which was offered the prospect of a joint governing. The plan failed because there was a group of hard-liners in each of the parties, who were not willing to collaborate with the former enemies.

Unable to buy whole parties from the opposition, the DNSF confined itself to buying personalities through the same tested way of appointing to diplomatic offices some of the less inconvenient personalities from among the opposition. The main target for such a procedure became the NSF which, after having·lost the elections, was going through a grave crisis of identity and leadership.

All that process must not be regarded as a mere political corruption. Actually, the politicians of all parties had started to gradually espouse the idea that, no matter what party they belonged to, they represented the country's new political elite. Among other things, it meant that its representatives would always remain at the leadership of the political system, just changing places among themselves, in keeping with the election returns. The idea of permanence in the country's political leadership, accompanied by a rotation in ministerial functions in every three-four years and an urbane political battle, fought like a duel between gentlemen, was seductive for everybody. To show that it too, agreed to the idea, the ruling party was ready to dispense posts, functions and honors to the opposition as well, which was tired of waiting, asking in exchange that the attacks be extenuated and the de-legitimation of the system be given up. The opposition started to join in the game only late, after the 1992 elections, at a stage that can be called "parliamentary democracy".

A third characteristic, born as early as the first period of the revolution, and developed along the five years that followed, was the elimination of the population from the political game. In this respect, it was not only agreed upon by the political parties, but it was a specific requirement of the technocracy. Like I said, the population is either an executant in the productive process or an object of the administration in the civil society. By no means can it have access to the real power. Consequently, the population had to be kept away from the political system, since an ambitious party, that should represent it and that should want to impose its options and politics, is the only instrument by which the population can influence the power. Specifically, the elimination of the population from politics up to the stage at which, disappointed, it eliminates itself, is being achieved by two concerted fundamental methods. One is to make all major political decisions based on an intricate system of secret intrigues conducted in an informal and rarefied circle of knowers. The other is to eliminate the responsibility of those appointed to offices toward the population and to transfer their appraisal to complicated institutions that should be as dependent as possible on the group in which the main intrigues are conducted.

Or, the responsibility toward the population is the main if not the only way of ensuring political democracy. The power system built along the five years has however transferred the responsibility of those elected or appointed to political or administrative functions, from the population to the parties' or administration's own instances. They are controlled by political leaders, so they are in the fortunate position of being answerable to their own conscience alone, a problem which they have so far successfully solved.

The transfer was not simple and it took a rather long time. The starting point was the population's complete (total) control over the politicians, conquered in the revolution. The population could not only legitimate or de-legitimate a political action or personality, but there not even existed a way of intervening in politics, other than to be at the head of a crowd of people. Until the 1990 elections, in which the balances of forces ultimately depended on the crowd that could be gathered in order to counter the crowd gathered by the opponents, both camps were to the greatest extent under the population's control and subject to the pressures of their leaders, irrespective of their being union leaders or former revolutionaries or simply credible local personalities.

In a first stage, most of the real political battles between parties were fought at the level of local organizations. They proved to be the more important in the case of the parties that belonged to the same camp. The real battle between the NLP and its various fractions was fought for their conquest, just like the underground battle the NLP and the opposition rallied in the Democratic Convention. The main cause of the NLP's having lost the electorate's support in the September 1992 elections was not so much the clumsiness of its electoral campaign and the unfortunate idea of nominating the king as candidate for the republic's presidency, as rather the loss of the support of the local organizations, that were more inclined toward the cooperation with the Democratic Convention that the party's leadership. Just the same, the battle between the NSF (Democratic Party) and DNSF (Party of Social Democracy of Romania), was fought – and it is still being fought – not only and especially for winning the public opinion, but rather for winning over the county and town organizations.

But, as the power system consolidated, the pressure put by the population or trade unions for the replacement of those who were holding an administrative function was less than efficient. As far as the politicians were concerned, their ability to control and manipulate the so-called "collective leadership bodies" of the parties was growing. Formally, all political parties are led, at all echelons, by bodies of the kind of councils, standing delegations, conferences or congresses, etc., that theoretically have the task to endorse decision. In actual fact, they are only used as means to legitimate the decisions made in far more rarefied, often informal circles. And their main mission is to confirm the victory of one or another of the opposite groups inside a political party over their rivals.

Such a situation was closely associated with the formation of the idea of political elite. The elite considered itself as independent and free of the obligation to ask for the common people's opinion or to account to them. That category included the population and the voters, first of all, but also the rank and file of the political parties and even their lower-echelon leaders. Eventually, in the case of the big parties, with a big number of parliamentarians, that elite did not even include all parliamentarians. The beginning was made by the NSF which, after the first elections, did not only avail of a big number of parliamentarians, but had also managed to create a big gap between parliamentarians and the government that was unwilling to share the power with them. In the case of the opposition parties, the bearer of the elitist doctrine was the cultural elite which, after having tried to take over the power itself, ended by melting into the general movement of the opposition rallied under the name of Democratic Convention. Consequently, the elite was willing to make decisions by itself, but this meant only that its motivations were increasingly depending on the inter-personal intrigues conducted in an extremely small and exclusivist circle.

2. The Stage of "Original Parties"

The features of the "original democracy" and the formation of the power system in which the parties do not participate, but whose privileges are shared in by their leaders, can be explained by the inexistence of the political parties, in the beginning, or by the lack of political experience for the next period. But, even after the parties availed of both experience and organization, they made no real attempt to change the power system. And that because from the "original democracy" of the first stage the passage was made to a stage which we could call of "original parties".

Analyzing ideologically the problem of the victory of capitalism and of the democratic world over the communist authoritarian world, the West hurried to forcefully export to the East-European countries its own traditional political system that relied on a plurality of political parties resting on a continuum stretching all the way from the Right to the Left. On the other hand, the former socialist countries had nothing better to do than borrow the Western system. The result is not great in any of the East-European countries.

First, the building of the political parties has proved to be a difficult job. Sure, it was not difficult for groups of people to get together and call themselves a "political party", endorsing, in the absence of a doctrine, at least a label recognized in the Western world – Liberal, Christian-Democrat, Social-Democrat were the most disseminated – and benefit thus from legitimacy and Western support that was often far greater than that they had at home. But, these "parties" most often remained at the stage of small groups with no real audience.

In all elections organized in the East-European countries, most of the ballots did not go so much to the parties as to ad-hoc political organizations, like forums, trade unions, fronts, convention, etc., which were political formations that did not respect the traditional European model or represented so strange alliances as, according to Western criteria, they were "unnatural", as is the Democratic Forum in Hungary or the Democratic Convention in Romania. In other words, in a contradictory bid to imitate the Western political system and still bear a significant message addressed to internal realities, the "parties" of East-Europe have adopted this strange mix of forms, more often than not completely free of a doctrinary message or of what could be termed as "alternate project of society".

Beyond the look as an abortive mutant of the Western political system, the disappointing reality of the newly created political systems in East Europe is that they do not work. Since the reform proceeds in all theses countries "from top to bottom" – the population accepts or bears with it, but it is not the main promoter of the reform, which is controlled by the small government elites – the diffuse, unstable and disoriented political system of these countries is rather an obstacle in the path of the economic and social reforms. Consequently, the heads of the executive are increasingly employing more or less disguised forms of authoritarianism, like Yeltsin in Russia, Wallesa in Poland, Gontz in Hungary or Iliescu in Romania. At the same time, the political inefficiency and the precariousness of the construction start to show up. Barely constituted, the new "democratic" parties of East Europe start falling apart. The inner conflicts, dispersal, restructuring, remade alliances, etc., all of them are signs that the political systems are more or less intensely seeking in all these countries a more adequate form for a content which they do not know yet, but which they "feel" to be somewhat different from what they have managed to import from the West. At least for Romania, this is caused by the fact that the parties are building themselves into a power system with which they do not know what to do and which does not need them in order to operate.

The Political Parties and the Democracy

The political parties emerged right after the revolution. A few days only after the victory of the revolution small leaflets already started being circulated in Bucharest, which announced the formation of the National Peasant Party. It was a "local" initiative of people who were subsequently rejected by the National Peasant Party formed under Corneliu Coposu's leadership. The idea of formation of political parties and, above all, of reviving those that had dominated the Romanian political life in the inter-bellum period, was not very popular in January and February 1990. On the other hand, it was not at all clear what form the political system ought to be given. The prevailing opinion current was that the political system that ensured the democracy – democracy was a reality which the Romanians wanted to keep, after they had won it with so much difficulty – was the system that relied on the competition among several parties. The idea was not born in Romania but, just like most of the ideas about how ought to look the post-revolution Romanian institutional system, whether it was about political institutions or economic and social institutions, was promoted, sometimes with rather high pressure, from the outside.

Anyway, at home there existed the Romanians' absolutely legitimate wish to rebuild the country to the pattern and model of the developed countries in Western Europe. So, in the period right after the revolution, the word the most used in public debates was "model". It was not at all clear what to did it mean to apply the "Swedish model" or the "French model", or even the "Japanese" model of society, but Romania was looking for a reference term to appreciate the transformations achieved and it had obviously to be looked for in the countries that had scored the biggest successes in ensuring a high level of development of the country and better quality of life of its citizens.

In that period, Romania did not avail of the ability to analyze the relation between the various components of a developed Western society, such as the institutional system or even the political system, on the one hand, and the results scored in development, on the other hand. In turn, the Western countries did not volunteer such analyses. In principle, they offered as models their respective reality and, as a general model, their common features. The principle was that everything that existed in a society contributed to obtaining its development level. Consequently, if it wanted to become a developed country with a high living standard, Romania had to reproduce all institutions and systems of the "model" society. The same belief applied to the construction of the political system, Romania wanted to become a democratic country. For that, the Romanians convinced themselves that it was necessary and enough to build political parties.

In fact, the political parties are a product of democracy and not its cause. Once the political decision is communicated to the population, the political parties show up in order to mediate among the groups of population that have differing options and the administration that has to execute the decisions. But in post-revolution Romania everybody was convinced that one can obtain political democracy by building parties. In the beginning, democracy was simply mistaken for the struggle among parties in order to place their leaders in leading offices. Then, when people got it that democracy was far more than that, they hoped that the parties' fight would end by generating democracy, like some sort of side effect. At the current stage, like in a Hegelian qualitative spiral, the content of democracy is deliberately confined to the parties' fight for the control of the leading functions in the state and of small privileges they entail.

Meanwhile, after a first period of distrust in political parties, an absolutely fierce party building started. Not only the legislation was made in such a way as to allow for the very easy setting up of a political party, but the state took it upon itself to give material support to their functioning, so that a political party soon became a source of incomes for those who decided to use it for other purposes than political. It took five years since the revolution for the Romanians to get convinced that by their mere existence the political parties do not bring any democracy, being able instead to establish a far more subtle dictatorship than the previous one. For, although the power is exercised just as arbitrarily, this arbitrariness is far more efficiently dissimulated and it is also legitimated by the electorate's vote. One of the causes why the reality could develop in this way belongs to the very mode of construction of the political parties.

What prevented the political parties from acceding to real power is a package of instability they all shared and that, mainly, rests on two big feeble points of these ad-hoc organizations. First, little audience with the population. Actually, before the splitting of the NSF – which in the beginning was not even a party, but precisely some sort of generalized reaction against small parties – the political parties were attached more importance on an international plane than at home. The 1990 elections proved that a very big number of parties can have a very small electoral audience. The other infirmity explains the former to a great extent. The Romanian political parties had no policy. They did not represent anyone and any interest except, of course, for the interests of their own main leaders. But their interests either, were not political, referring instead to those privileges to which the winning of the political play would have entitled them.

Like when we distinguished between the real power and the access to personal privileges associated with the holding of state functions, here too, we must make distinction. Any political party will say it wants certain things and will produce some sheets of paper entitled "Program". Unfortunately, those things and that "Program" do not define a policy.

More exactly, any political party in post-revolution Romania will answer in two ways the question "what are you after". Neither one of the answers justifies it as a political party and allows its access to power.

Above all, any political party will state it wants democracy, freedom, welfare for all citizens, economic growth, cultural development and so on. This long string of slogans and other ones of the kind, which all parties employ, and which in the end express the wishes of all citizens, have nothing to do with politics or with the power. They do not define a certain mode of power sharing or the way it is genuine to be used. They do not define a government and, generally, they have nothing to do with the government. No decision can result from them. And, for the Romanian political parties, for all parties, there is nothing left behind these slogans. The parties simply do not have political objectives.

It is not the fault of the slogans. Any political party uses in the relations with the electorate and with its own supporters a certain demagogy which includes all these general slogans. But, in the case of the genuine political parties, demagogy has the mission to legitimate and communicate specific political objectives. In the case of the parties emerged after the revolution, demagogy does not conceal any major political objective. But, like any demagogy, it too, tries to legitimate something, namely individual and group objectives and interests of the politicians.

It is to this that is addressed the second set of answers a political party gives when it has to explain what it wants or when, after winning the elections, it is in a position to impose decisions on the administrative bureaucracy and on the technocrats. It is absolutely normal for politicians too, to have personal interests. Also, it is absolutely normal for the members of a political party to have also group interests. But what is not normal or possible is to turn the personal and group interests of a party's politicians into that party's only objectives. But this is how the Romanian political parties emerged and that is why they still exist.

After 1989, a political party would always be built around a small group of people who, for one reason or another, considered themselves entitled to take over the country's political leadership. Not because they wanted to impose certain changes on the economy or foreign policy, on social relations or any other domain. In the latter case, the legitimation of the access to leadership is justified by the purposes the party pursues.

In the case of the party founders in our country, the legitimation of the claims on the country's leadership is justified not by what they want, but by what they are. Either because they are among those who had led Romania also before the power was conquered by the communist party, therefore they think it is only fair that they should be reinstated in power. Or because they are among those who had suffered the most under the former regime, or because they are those who opposed it the most or even led the crowd during the revolution. They are some who think they are entitled to rule the country because they are young, and clever and cultivated and conversant with western realities, which we anyway want to imitate, while other ones think it is they that are entitled, because they are experienced and know how the bureaucratic mechanism operate.

Generally, it is not difficult to make up some justification in order to claim the country's rule and find a number of people to back it. Which is proved by the fact that no less than 160 political parties were set up in Romania over 1990-1992 and about a hundred of them are still in existence, most of them with no activity whatsoever. What matters though, is not so much their claim or the rule, as the fact that they justify it by what they are. For that reason, they have no chance of becoming real political parties. A real political party justifies its claim by what it wants and by the support it expects to get from the segment of population that wants the same. It is the difference between being something and doing something. As, by their construction, the political parties in Romania cannot go past the former stage, they are doomed to remain some sort of groups of supporters of claimants to the crown, which takes us some two centuries back, in politics, and annuls any chance of democracy.

The "Historic" Parties

The so-called "historic parties" are maybe the most complete illustration of the situation. The historic parties, meaning the Christian Democratic National Peasant Party, National Liberal Party, and Romanian Social-Democratic Party, are in fact only one political party, that had split pursuant to disagreements among their leaders and, to a certain extent, also to differing priority links abroad. But they share the same fundamental legitimacy of the access to the rule of the state. The historic parties claim the country's rule as heirs claim the heritage. They consider themselves to be the heirs of the parties that dominated the inter-bellum Romanian political life. This does not mean too much in itself, therefore, they have adopted and promoted some sort of dialectal-romantic ideology of the good and the evil, in form of the "good" society and "evil" society. Under the previous regime, the inter-bellum society used to be considered as "evil", while the communist society was "good". Now, since socialism was overthrown, and has suddenly become the "evil" society, it seems natural to them to deem the formerly "evil" society as being "good", consequently its former rulers or their descendants should be redeemed to their rights. "Romantic" in all this history is the way of idealizing the past because the present is dissatisfactory. It is precisely what the Romanticists did: dissatisfied with the 19th century bourgeois society they used to idealize the Middle Ages.

Useless to say that the claim to be heirs of a political system that disappeared half a century ago is either naive or a propaganda procedure. The political problems of the present time are quite different from the past ones and the use of the heritage of those times is doubtful to say the least. As a matter of fact, apart from having taken over the names and some of the second-line young politicians of those times, there is no tangible connection between today's "historic ones" and the then parties. The National Peasant Party, for instance, was formed through the merger of the National Party of Transylvania, a party of the Romanian ethnic group, anti-Hungarian in its essence, with the Peasant Party of Romania, a party of land-owner peasants and rural intelligentsia, which made of it a party powerfully associated with the Orthodox faith. On the contrary, the Christian Democratic National Peasant Party is allied with the party of the Hungarian ethnic group in Romania, it has but a very small audience with the peasants and is probably the only Orthodox party in a Catholic international political organization. The Romanian Social Democratic Party was and has remained an inconsequential party in the Romanian political life. But the similarity stops here. In the inter-war period, it was a party of wage-earning intellegentsia and it claimed to be a party of workers. Now, it has no appeal with any of them. Finally, the National Liberal Party was the party of urban bourgeoisie, upper and petty, which dominated the Romanian political life for almost a century. Unless to recall that, one month after the revolution, when the NLP was revived through the agency of former members of the old party, there was no bourgeoisie in Romania. As a matter of fact, to the extent to which it was represented in the party, the new budding Romanian bourgeoisie soon came at odds with the old descendants of the NLP and caused the main split within it. The splitting of the LP-Young wing meant precisely the conflict between the newest successful Romanian enterprises, Dinu Patriciu and Viorel Catarama, and their colleagues, the old "politicians" specialized in political intrigue. Not only the age but also the interests kept them apart. Whereas the new businessmen wanted the power, in order to be able to develop an environment congenial for the rising entrepreneur, the "old ones" (aged and outdated alike) only wanted the access to the honours and privileges of the state functions and were ready for almost any compromise for that.

On top of it all, the three parties, that had been irreconcilable enemies for thirty years, now got allied against a common enemy – Ion Iliescu. It was obviously a matter of persons not of politics. Like I said, none of the parties emerged after the revolution promoted any policy, and the "historic ones" were no exception. The only real thing was their adversity against the former communist leaders, and that was because they wanted to take their place. The fact that a person's political biography or beliefs were no inconvenient to the historic parties is proved not only by the acceptance to their membership of numerous former members or leaders of the communist party, but especially by their failed attempt to enrol among themselves even Ion Iliescu. The combination, even more grotesque than the cheerful reception extended to Miron Cosma at the CDNPP Congress in September 1991, the man who was just leading the miners' riot against Petre Roman and Ion Iliescu, was tried before the 1990 elections. The newly built National Peasant Party proposed Ion Iliescu then to run for Romania's president on behalf of that historic party. Had Ion Iliescu accepted, maybe Romania's post-revolution history would have been different. Ion Iliescu was not only a politician but a man of his beliefs, so he politely turned down their offer and ran in behalf of an artificially party which he made himself later.

The interest of the party leaders to become the country's political leaders was strictly personal, as long as they did not add to that interest some political objective. This does not necessarily mean that they are ambitious or vain. Once they entered the game, they are prisoners of their group of supporters the more so as, having no objectives of their own group, they have to sustain or represent their objectives. In turn, the supporters have their own personal interests which, in the absence of real political objectives, are confined to taking advantage of the political position of the leader they sustain. But with the important parties, like the "historic" ones, group interests add to these simple interests, that can mobilize only a small number of persons. Such a combination of personal and group interests is not a must. At least not with the political parties that have emerged after the revolution. A big number of such parties remained with this first group and vanished from the political arena.

As for the historic parties, they have added to the personal interests of their politicians on top the group interests of an important number of members and supporters. The historic parties brought together the people who, before communists' advent, had enjoyed privileges, advantages or positions of relative power in the then Romanian society, no matter whether they relied on wealth, status or prestige. The interest of everyone of those people was personal but common. It consisted of the attempt to remake as much as possible the situation in existence before the communist revolution. Sure, a statistic of the historic parties' members and supporters will show that not all and not even most of them, are former men of property or descendants of former men of property. But the political leadership of the parties, their "core" is. And it is precisely the leading core that has turned rapidly the common personal interest into a political objective of the country – the Restoration, the remaking of the economic structures, those related to property first of all, social and political structures of inter-bellum Romania.

But, not even such an objective, political as it refers to the distribution of the national resources, cannot substantiate a genuine policy of the transition, even if the group of the interested ones is relatively numerous. Because the problem of a society's political leadership is not to distribute the national pie, even though after the revolution and because of it the redistribution has become possible and turned into the main concern of numberless groups and organizations, some of them politically represented, other ones, like the religious cults or the trade unions, not represented. Even if a group of people plans to take over the political power and then to share among themselves an important part of the national wealth, and get united for this into an organization which participates in elections and calls itself a political party, this mere fact does not have make them represent a genuine political leadership. They do not have any answer to the fundamental question of the power, which is: "for the attainment of which objectives are the society's resources used?". And, for that reason, they do not represent a genuine political party.

If a coalition or historical parties had won the elections, it would not have ruled longer than the NSF or the current coalition resulted from the 1992 elections. Sure, it would have replaced in the functions of political leadership the representatives or supporters of the current parties of the parliamentary majority. It would have probably started to share a bigger or smaller slice of the national wealth among themselves and their supporters, using as a criterion the denationalization, the remaking of the property structure in existence before 1948. It is possible that they would have staged also a political revenge against those who persecuted them all along those forty years, a possibility that scared the incumbent holders of the power even more that the redistribution of the property. After that, they would have had simply nothing else to do, apart from harmlessly parasitizing the real power centers. None of these objectives which the "historic ones" and their allies might attain is enough to give the power in Romania a sense. Consequently, it would not be able to counter the use of the power by the industrial technocracy and administrative bureaucracy, its true holders.

That is why the historic political parties are not genuine parties and the holding by them of the country's political leadership would not mean the creation of a genuine political leadership, even if the group interest of the party's political core is generalized up to its articulation in general principles of organization of the society. For the historic parties' leaders and doctrinaires such a process of theorization and generalization was difficult and very soon they needed more support in the ideological and propaganda substantiation of their own objectives.

Under the circumstances, no wonder that the humanist elite appeared as the natural ally of the "historic ones". There were a number of reasons pushing to it. First, the humanist elite was the main ideologist of the "return to the past" or, according to a later but perfectly acceptable formula to characterize in few words the whole political doctrine of the opposition, "back to capitalism". Second, it was also the main standard-bearer of the attack on neo-communism of the new political leadership from a basis a little closer to the present than the end of World War Two. Last but not least, it dominated the domestic press and the relations with the international mass media. So, it was a valuable acquisition, being the only one able to offer the little ideology the "historic ones" needed in order to survive politically. In turn, the "historic" parties represented for the humanist elite a necessary extension, as they could offer a logistic basis which the elite was unable to organize on its own and, above all, a daily political and propaganda activity precisely in the milieux with which the elite had no communication.

With the assistance of the humanist elite, the "historic" parties have come at a certain ideologization of the personal and group interests of their leaders, With that, they have come to acquire if not political content, at least political appearance. But, almost as much mattered in the establishment of a political profile of the "historic ones" the propaganda efforts of the NSF and its allies.

The Restoration, as a Political Identity of the Opposition

In their fight against Ion Iliescu and his team, the historic parties and the humanist elite developed a strategy say "personalized". What they attacked was not the policy promoted by the NSF. First, such an attack was difficult if not impossible altogether. Until the May 1990 elections, the NSF had no policy and it confined itself to administrating the country. After the 1990 elections, the policy conducted by the new government was contradictory and confusing, the measures that might have been viewed as liberal were countered by measures labelled as "conservative". Besides, even more aggressive criticism than the opposition's developed soon right inside the NSF or to its left. Finally, the opposition was unable to efficiently criticize the NSF policies, because that would have required a comparison with its own policies and they did not exist. When Petre Roman, in his capacity as freshly appointed prime minister, presented to the Parliament his draft program of government, the NLP and CDNPP leaders stated that it could just as well have been their own program. The "resemblance" was not due to any identity of views on economic and social issues, but simply to the fact that the opposition did not have even the fundamental options. The leaders of the opposition "recognized" in the Roman program their own program precisely because they did not have one, and the formulae which they had just heard sounded familiar and acceptable to them.

Unable to attack policies, the historic parties and their allies focussed the attacks on persons. The theme central to their electoral strategy was not of the kind: "this party, the NSF, promotes undesirable or wrong policies", but of the kind: "these people, Iliescu, Roman and their likes are not good leaders". The reasons why they were not good were personal characteristics, starting with their biography – they had belonged to the communist nomenklatura, had learned in Moscow, were old – and ending with the opposition's greatest complaint, that they were the same, which they thought to be unfair. They endorsed this strategy for many reasons, but two must have been prevalent. First, such a description of the enemies was precisely the reverse of the way how they pictured themselves: the people who had been oppressed under the former regime, who had always opposed it, hence who were entitled to pick the fruit of the revolution. Moreover, they were the bearers of democracy, reformism, etc., through the same personal characteristics: either because they had engaged in politics in the inter-bellum period, or because, like Ion Ratiu and Radu Campeanu, Ion Iliescu's main opponents in the first two years of the revolution, they had lived in the West during the communist regime. The unspoken requisite of all the arguments was that the leading functions in the state were a reward and not a functionality. And, from the opposition's viewpoint, the political battle focussed on replacing in offices several key personalities, the most important of which was Ion Iliescu.

The other reason resulted from the opposition's close links with the foreign countries and their dependence on the image built by the international mass media. Focusing on politicians instead of politics is the mass media usual way of approach. First, for technical reasons: you can more easily write or show on TV picture stories about politicians. Besides, in some Western political systems, especially the American one, personalities matter far more than policies and even than parties. But, such an approach is understandable and convincing for the readers or the western papers more than for the Romanian electorate. And the opposition in Romania, the main asset of which was a greater legitimacy with the West than the rulers, had to stick to the West's cliches.

For Ion Iliescu and his supporters such a strategy was not possible. Not because they would not have resorted to personal attacks, the biographies or even the look or clothing fancies of their opponents: Corneliu Coposu's bony figure and Ion Ratiu's butterfly bow made a career in publicistics, and so did the former's connection with the Securitate. But all this was neither enough nor fitting in the utopian image of the president regarding the national consensus, that had to be obtained around a policy and not around a person or group of persons. In his outlook, the electoral campaign ought to consist of the presentation by parties of their own government programs and their criticism of the rivals' programs. After an electoral campaign conducted in this way, the voters would have nothing else to do than vote, after wise pondering, the one that would fit best their own aspirations. Of course, the reality was quite different, the main reason being that neither the NSF in 1990 nor the DNSF in 1992 availed of government programs, unless we consider the Romanian Academy's famous reform program which, apart from President Ion Iliescu, nobody ever mentioned again. So, unable to base their legitimacy on their leaders' personal characteristics, the rulers had to base it on some policy. The difficulty was that they did not have a policy. Then, they resorted to the solution of criticizing the policy of the opposition, for which purpose they created a political identity of the opposition.

In the political and propaganda fight that has proceeded ever since 1990, both camps endorsed a prevailingly negative strategy of convincing the electorate that the rival represented an even greater evil, each of them striving to build a convincing identity of that "evil". For the historic ones, the "evil" was precisely Ion Iliescu and his entourage, with their personal biographies, cliches of thought and speech ("the wooden tongue") and connections. At the opposite end, the NSF's method was to build for the historic ones a political identity with the "restoration" as starting point.

Like I said, the "historic" parties and humanist elite alike did court the idea of restoration. However, to them it was rather nostalgia than a political program. The personal interests of their most active and influential politicians urged them to take seriously into consideration the nullification of certain legislative and political measures of the communist regime and the remaking of some of the ownership and status structures which the 1946-1948 revolution had destroyed. But, as they were mere rewards or compensations with a personal character, all these would not generate in the end a coherent policy and would not question the real structures of the power. The "historic ones" did not mean the restoration, although they very much looked like it. It is hard to tell how they would have behaved once installed in power, when they did not have any starting point to build their own identity on, other than the resemblance with the restoration of the inter-bellum period. The NSF turned that resemblance into the political identity of the opposition.

The identity built for them by the NSF developed the idea of restoration up to its ultimate logical consequences: restoration was presented as meaning the remaking not only of some properties, etc., but also of the power and status structures in the economy and in the society. It attributed to the "historic ones" the objective of remaking the big land estates, of destroying the industry created during the socialist era and, above all, of destroying the Romanian industrial technocracy through its total subordination to the foreign capital. Under the slogan "We don't sell our country!", the NSF mobilized the workers in support of maintaining in power the autochthonous industrial technocracy, turning them not against the big foreign or multinational companies but precisely against the historic parties.

The creation of such a political identity for the historic parties' opposition has been a success. They offered themselves numerous arguments in support of such an image. They insisted to look for legitimacy especially in the realities of the past period, presented as the true "golden era" of Romania. Then, not knowing what they really wanted, they were not sure that it was precisely that. Having no political identity, but needing one, there were enough members of those parties' political leaderships ready to endorse the one built by their political rivals. And, apart from the fight against the NSF, the historical parties knew also the fight between their various components, and the legitimation sought in the inter-bellum period was favoring the group of aged leaders not in the fight against the people in power but against the ambitious young people in their own party. That ambiguity inside the historic parties was responsible for the splitting of the NLP, from which departed the group that surely did not expect to gain something from the restoration and was therefore not willing to accept such an identity. The Liberal Party-Young Wing was the group of the new entrepreneurs, the new businessmen who did not want the national pie to be shared by historic criteria but by post-revolution success criteria.

Even the electoral behavior of the historic parties strengthened their association with a policy of the restoration. One of the most frequently used tactics to attract supporters was to promise an immediate material advantage. The tactics had been much used in the inter-bellum period but it obviously did not fit the current period. A typical example was the CDNPP's attempt to attract the peasants. In the period right after the revolution, the NSF extended the individual plot due to the members of the cooperative farms formed under socialism. The CDNPP pressed for more, demanding that the land be distributed to peasants. For the moment, the measure had but little effect, as the peasants gave their votes in mass numbers to the NSF, but then the NSF took upon itself the task of the land reform, redeeming to the peasants the land they had had in the beginning and retaining as state property only the State Agricultural Enterprises that had resulted mainly from the nationalization of the inter-bellum big land estates. Then, the CDNPP decided to win the peasants over by promising even more land, through the sharing out of the SAE land. They have never explained how did they expect to allot the land and it is doubtful that they have ever given the idea more than a propaganda-oriented thought, for that was a technical problem extremely complicated, considering that the respective tracts of land are not evenly distributed in the country's territory. The NSF immediately interpreted the proposal as an attempt to remake the old estates and the big landlords as an important social class of the country. The CDNPP protested saying it was not its real intention, but it did it unconvincingly.

The fact that a policy of the restoration could not be popular in Romania is no wonder and needs no big explanation. Those that would have had something to lose from such a policy were far more numerous than those that would have gained. Even more important was the fact that the everyday image, not theorized but general, of how ought to look Romania after the revolution, has been formed based on the information and illusion born from the touch with the realities of the developed countries in Western Europe. That was a picture that had nothing in common with an idyllic, pastoral society, which was the utmost promise of the restoration policy. The idea of a return to a rural, agricultural society, which Ceausescu too, had fancied, and which had made him even more unpopular, could not get support in a society in full effort of industrialization and urbanization. Therefore, the president's vague slogans about Swedish or Japanese model were more acceptable than the just as vague slogans of the historic parties about inter-bellum Romania.

Finally, one of the main arguments of identifications of the "historic" parties with the policy of restoration was their pro-monarchy stand.

The Problem of Monarchy

As a matter of fact, the historic parties have not only sustained the restoration of the monarchy in Romania, but they have created this line of problems with all their implications. The idea to settle the political problems of the transition and to establish a political regime which by no means can relapse into communism through the restoration of the monarchy does not belong to them. It was born in Western Europe even before the 1989 revolution, as a result of several conjunctures. First, there was of course a pressure put by the survivors or descendants of the former royal houses of East Europe. They had connections, friends and for mass media they entailed the advantage of interesting the Western public because of their titles and life styles. They were mainly short of money and political influence and these could be attracted only to the extent to which they would manage to make more important factors take an interest in the success of their own cause.

Until the revolution, all those former monarchs arose only a limited interest. In the propaganda effort made by the Western allies against the communist regimes in the last years when no detail had to be neglected and every helping hand was welcome, they applied also to some former sovereigns. Romania's former king, Mihai, spoke on Radio Free Europe against Ceausescu's policy of systematization of the Romanian villages. It is difficult to assess now whether the revival of the interest in the former monarch was meant first of all to stir the Romanian public opinion against Ceausescu or, on the contrary, to build a favorable image for the king Mihai. Anyway, it was a far way to the restoration of the monarchy, a way which the former ruling House could not travel all by itself. It needed support.

The support extended after the victory of the 1989 revolution was hesitant and partial. The overthrow of communism generated nostalgias not only in the East but also in the West and the generalized confusion that emerged against the background of the West having been taken by surprise and completely unprepared to handle the integration of the former socialist states, gave these nostalgias a serious chance not to succeed but at least to be felt rather profoundly. The remaking of the East-European monarchies in Romania, Bulgaria, Serbia and possibly even in Russia, were considered by some Western power centers – not necessarily governmental ones – as an at least noteworthy variant. Adding to that was also the lack of real information about the population's opinions, wishes and behaviors toward the new rulers as well as toward the former monarchs. And the advantages were not negligible. The restoration of the monarchy was considered as a safe political guarantee against any attempt to return to a communist regime, at least from the inside, and in 1990-1991 there were fears in that respect for some countries like Romania, Bulgaria and the former Soviet Union. Then, royalty could have been a solution to end the social unrests and ethnic conflicts that threatened to turn the formerly socialist states into a huge zone of endemic conflict in the middle of Europe. We should also consider the fact that these monarchies could not be restored without Western support and in a negotiation on this matter the former monarchs, in their capacity as would-be kings, were not in a position to turn down any request. There was also the success of the Spanish experiment to consider, in which the restoration of the monarchy after the fall of the Franco's regime meant precisely these things: social peace and bringing the political fights on a legal and democratic ground. The prevailing orientation to the left of the dominant political forces in these countries was obviously no inconvenience, as the Western monarchies already had a rich experience in the collaboration with the socialist or social-democratic governments.

No really important institution or organization, political or involved in politics in the West directly supported the restoration of the monarchy in Romania, for instance. Which proves that none believed too much in the success of such a variant. But they did support it indirectly, sometimes in such roundabout ways as they generated diplomatic scandals or even internal political scandals, as was the case of king Mihai's Danish diplomatic passport. The West's reserves regarding the monarchic solution were prompted by the uncertainties regarding the real support the monarchs enjoyed in their own countries. In that respect Romania was both a typical case and an experiment.

Irrespective of the support given from outside, the main battle was to be fought in the country. In the end it was not even a battle. The problem of the monarchy was from the beginning to the end a false problem, employed by all politicians in order to settle their own conflicts or to stress the polemic among them. What the partisans of the monarchy did not have in order to turn the royal restoration into a major and real problem of the transition was first of all a social base. The Spanish model had no chance of functioning in Romania, first of all because the royalty in Spain had no resemblance with the royalty in Romania. In Spain, the monarchy had been the most important institution of a whole gentile social class, powerful both politically, economically and financially, which not even Franco's regime was able to destroy. In Romania, such a nobility did not exist. The political elite had been a mere extension of the administrative elite. The Romanian kings were bourgeois kings, some sort of hereditary presidents of the state, with functions mainly of external representation. When they did try to get actively involved in the domestic policy, like Carol II did, they soon came at odds with the main political forces, the ancestors of today's historical parties.

When, in the second half of the past century, the young Romanian state tried to gain a place in international politics, on which its own fate tremendously depended, the European policies mainly consisted of the policies of the European royal Houses. The political objectives and interests were profoundly influenced by the family interests of the royal Houses, and a state that was not present in the rarefied club of crowned heads, all of them interconnected by intricate kinships, had no chance of having its say heard and interests minded. That was precisely the reason for bringing to Romania a European royal house and that was the function it successfully fulfilled all along the period until the end of World War One.

The 20th century Europe that was born on the ruins left by the first world conflagration however did not look like the 20th century one. Not only because the monarchies had collapsed in Prussia, Austro-Hungary, Russia, Spain and Portugal (later on in the last two, but against the same background of restructuring of the European political systems), but also because the national policies were now prevailing completely over the transitional policies entailed by the European international dynasties. Under the circumstances, the function of the Romanian king in the international arena shrinked dramatically. The political objectives of the Romanian state had even lesser chances, if any, to be accomplished. The reason that they were also the personal objectives of a man with relations among Europe's monarchs and nobility. So, the Romanian king had to choose between becoming a simple decorous institution and engaging in politics. Carol II opted for the latter whereas king Mihai was the historic embodiment of the former, both during Antonescu's dictatorship and in the few years he remained in power after the war.

The restoration of the monarchy in Romania is faced with the same choices and it is from here that comes also the absence of a real social base and its prevalent character as a pseudo-solution. If it chooses to be a simple decorous institution, its use is hard to justify, but even more difficult it is to justify the effort made for its restoration. If it decides to make policy, then the royalty cannot be considered as a warrantor of social peace and of the rules of political confrontations. As for the ideal variant, meaning a monarch to represent the national interests not so much on an external plane, as in the relations with the parties, politicians and administrative institutions, permanently seeing to their observance and amending the excesses detrimental to them, the king was surely one of the persons the least recommended to play the role. On the one hand, throughout the propaganda campaign about the restoration of the monarchy, he made no attempt to define the national interests and, on the other hand, this role entails the existence of a social and political consensus about these interests. And, no matter how utopian the idea of national consensus, its association with the restoration of the monarchy makes it even more utopian. In actual fact, without wanting it but also without being able to avoid it, the king joined in the political game of the historic parties that were ready to use him but not to serve him.

The historic parties and their allies used the king's main weakness which was that although he wanted or was pushed to act for the restoration of the monarchy, he had no real social base. None of the main social categories in the country would identify its interest with turning the republic into a kingdom. Neither the peasantry, nor the workers or the industrial technocrats were tied to the monarchy in any way and it was not functional as regarded their group interests. The new social class of enterprisers might have backed the monarchy as a guarantee that there would be no return to communism, but such an evolution was unlikely anyway. Besides, it would have led to important changes in the superstructure of the bureaucracy with which they had already reached a way of coexisting. Finally, for the administrative bureaucracy, that would have meant the emergence of a new command layer with which it had no connections and the unforeseeable nature of which made it unwanted. All along the period after the revolution, beyond the statement of general principles, the king did not announce anything about his intentions for the event that he would return to the state's rule. Under the circumstances, the main supporters of the monarchy were the small group of courtiers and former or would-be high royal functionaries, plus the little larger group of those who hoped that, with the king's advent, they would be able to recover something of their former estates or status or both. Even that group was not enough to ensure a real social base for the king, but it was enough, in the absence of any royal program, for their wishes to be taken for his real program and to confirm the fears that a restoration of the monarchy meant far more than the simple remaking of the royal institution.

For that reason, before the historical parties espoused the theme, the restoration of the monarchy was not a political problem. The response to it was rather confusion than fear or adversity. The historic parties did not make it more real but brought it to the focus of the political debate.

We should stress it from the beginning that the leaders of the historic parties were by no means ardent supporters of the monarchy. They did not recognize the king's political authority and that is precisely why they did not come forth with any program and did not endorse any clear and concrete political opinion. But they felt a threat or competition coming from the group of advisers and intimates of the royal family with whom they very soon came to be at odds. Therefore, all along the period when they showed to be more or less close to the monarchy, the leaders of the historic parties were double dealing. In the spring of 1990, when the monarchic idea was very unpopular, they avoided taking a clear pro-monarchic stand, pushing to the front line small monarchist parties that had no audience with the public. When they supported the pro-monarchic propaganda and the idea proper of restoring the monarchy they did it first as a component of the process of glorification of inter-bellum Romania and of their comeback to rule and as a means to win over the monarchists' votes. And, in secret negotiations and talks, they regarded it as a negotiable matter. After the 1990 elections, they endorsed the monarchist thesis very openly, but they used it again in an ambiguous form, that should not make their commitment final.

They backed the monarchy, they refused to vote the Constitution – the first article of which proclaimed Romania's as a republic -, but they also refused to tie their fate to the king's, so, in the 1992 presidential elections they participated with a candidate who in the end declared himself a republican. After the 1992 elections, it became obvious that what the political parties wanted to obtain by backing the restoration of the monarchy was simply a matter of negotiation. The historic parties were ready to capitalize on the advantages that would go with the support of the royalist party, from funds to mass media support and the small part of the electorate represented by monarchists, but they were not ready to assume the costs that went with it.

The restoration of the monarchy in Romania has not for a moment enjoyed wide audience, but both the king and his supporters did very little to increase the audience. They were the first to tackle the problem in a naive and clumsy manner. They did not have real information about the country and the social and electoral base they could count on. They did not even have a concrete plan of action. They wasted five long years on harassment with the Romanian administration about entry visas. The analysis of the actions taken makes one think the idea of their plans was something like a Hollywood script. They expected the king's presence in the country to make the people rise and, by some kind of reverse revolution (history has not recorded yet revolutions aimed at reinstating kings instead of overthrowing them) proclaim the king again. It was not at all clear what procedure was needed to restore the royalty, so they drew inspiration from the December revolution. Therefore, the whole monarchist camp focussed efforts on making the king's return to the country possible. It was not clear what he would do once back in the country. That was obvious with every one of his two visits to Romania.

The first visit was a real adventure, as if copied from a novel. The king arrived incognito, late in the evening, on board of a private plane that radioed to the Romanian authorities the information that it was carrying a team of journalists. He disclosed his true identity at the frontier and the frontier guards, impressed with his title, with the personalities that went to welcome him, and having no instructions, let him in. From the airport, he drove in a small file of cars to Curtea de Arges. Hard to tell what he expected to do there. Rumors with rulers and journalists had it that high church officials were ready to crown him in the local cathedral that had historic resonance. If true, that would be one more proof of the lack of seriousness with which the royal family itself addressed its own problem, because such an archaic procedure, employed during the quarrels for rule in the 14th -16th centuries, was totally ineffectual at the end of the 20th century. Nowhere in the world, not even in post-revolution Romania, are heads of state designated by the church and installed through a mere religious service any longer. Anyway, the king did not reach Curtea de Arges. Meanwhile, the authorities took action fast. After a short pursuit, the king was caught up by police cars, escorted back to the airport, put back on the plane that had brought him in and expelled from the country.

One year later he came again. Legally this time, with a visa very courageously granted by the Stolojan Government which now, true, included also Liberals, an historic party that formally backed the monarchy. The king came on Easter and enjoyed a tremendous public success. Hundreds of thousands of Bucharesters went to see him, to hear him, and accompanied him all along his Bucharest itinerary. It was not a political demonstration in support of the monarchy, it was simply a show. If there was something to be done, one could not think of a more propitious moment. However, neither the king nor his supporters started anything and it was clear that they had nothing to do. The first part of the scenario had been fulfilled even beyond any expectation. The king was in the country, the crowd was rallied and it was sympathetic. The groups of supporters were there and ensured the required enthusiasm. The political leaders of the opposition were by the king's side, impressed with the reception extended to him by the population. Yet, nothing happened, and that confirmed the rulers' cool calculation on issuing him an entry visa without letting themselves impressed by the emotion of some of the politicians of the governance. No matter how impressed the political leaders, there was no way of taking the least smallest toward the power. So, after a several-day trip to northern Moldova, the king returned to Switzerland and resumed the efforts to get another entry visa.

For all its public success, the royal visit on the spring of 1992 was a failure. It revealed the terrible impasse of the king. He could be popular in Romania if he had accepted the role of an "ex", a mere historic evidence, which everybody was curious to see and proud to know. But he could not join in politics without turning against him most of the people who had come to salute him in 1992, nor could he prevent the political parties from turning his person into a favorite theme of dispute. The more attempts to bring the king to the country, in December 1993, on the national holiday, and in the autumn of 1994, when he was again sent back right from the airport, had no other effect than enliven parliamentary speeches.

Except for the few real monarchists, who were so either out of belief or out of interest, the problem of the monarchy was only a means of fighting the usual political fight for the control of political authority. The real objectives of the historic parties and their allies were quite different from the restoration of royalty, and as the time was passing, the divergence was growing. The debate on the monarchy and on supporting it was useful to the opposition in several respects. It would win over the royal house's diplomatic and mass media influence, which was not much but it was useful as it was. Then the king was and still is used for the purpose of opposing to Ion Iliescu a personality the more credible as he is not at all involved in the everyday Romanian politics. The monarchic idea was used also in order to give ideological support to the historic parties' legitimacy and to show to advantage the "golden age" of inter-bellum Romania. Finally, the monarchy was used also as an element of negotiation in the talks conducted after 1992 about a possible participation of the historic parties in a joint governance with the PSDR. But after that it was only a means of harassing the rulers.

The rulers regarded the possibility that the monarchy be reinstated more seriously than the opposition did. First, because they really worried about such a possibility. One of the immediate consequences would have been their replacement in the leadership of the central structures by the opposition, irrespective of the election returns. But the main reason was that the opposition's support to the reinstatement of the monarchy was obviously to their advantage, as it was giving them a political meaning that they would have otherwise missed – it made them republicans. It allowed them to disguise the battle for political privileges in the form of the traditional confrontation between republicans and royalists, characteristic of the European political history in the last two centuries. It gave them the opportunity to show off as democrats and progressives, which were the historic attributes of the republicans, and to paint the opposition in the dark colors of the conservative or reactionary policies, Finally, it gave them numerous opportunities for an endless rethoric and for the assertion of the parliamentarians inclined to demagogy which the ruling parties were not short of. For the ideologists of the governance the opposition's support to the restoration of the monarchy was a serious argument in favor of their darling thesis – the country's defence against a retrograde restoration whose standard-bearers were the "historic ones" and their allies. Consequently, the rulers paid at least as much attention as the opposition to the debate on monarchy. In that superficial battle, the king was a character that suited the propaganda of both camps.

After the endorsement of the Constitution, after the king's visit in the spring of 1992 and after the elections the same year, the problem of monarchy should have disappeared from the Romanian political arena.

But things did not go that way, and the fact that it has remained one of the most debated problems that has generated so many false political events is a proof of the Romanian political parties' inability to find for themselves a political identity by sticking to reality. As we shall see later, the "parliamentary democracy", the third stage in the evolution of the Romanian political system, has turned this inability into a mechanism of survival.

The question whether Romania will remain a republic or become a kingdom is, in principle, a major one. But it becomes a political problem only when the society is really divided about it and at least a part of the power system is interested in changing the current situation. It is not Romania's case. For the present and for a foreseeable future, the problem of the monarchy should be considered one of the problems of the Romanian political scholasticism meant to fuel the "democratic" demagogy.

The Originality of the Hungarian Democratic Union of Romania

Whereas the alliance between the historic parties and the humanist elite proved to be natural, less natural appears to be their alliance with the Hungarian Democratic Union of Romania. The HDUR emerged right after the revolution, as an organization meant to represent the ethnic Hungarian group in the relations with the Romanian state. But, much before the May 1990 elections, it started acting as a unitary party of that group. Formally, the HDUR is a coalition of political parties which apolitical organizations too, are associated. As a political alliance, it is apparently one of the most weird, because it associates parties that theoretically ought to be found in differing camps, as they have differing objectives, such as the Liberals and Socialists. In actual fact, the difference between these parties and groups are minor and, just like the Romanian parties, they are simple delimitations among the entourages of the various leaders of the Hungarian minority. Sure, there are dissensions and rivalries among them, but their objectives do not go beyond winning the fight for the leadership of the organization. This fight is relatively silent and proceeds inside, without however affecting the unity of the organization in its relations with the Romanian state. They define the originality of the HDUR. For, to the organization and, implicitly, to every one of its components, the Hungarian minority's political objectives have absolute priority over any other objective of the component parties or organizations.

This ensures the HDUR's unity, but does not make it politically more clear than any of the parties of the Romanian political forces. Just the opposite since, whereas the Romanian political parties know clearly at least one thing, namely that they want to occupy the leading functions of the Romanian state, such an objective is forbidden to the HDUR. It cannot set itself such an objective, first because, as it represents a clearly defined minority, it has no way to win the elections. On the other hand, by confining itself exclusively to getting rights for the Hungarian minority, the HDUR has no objectives for the Romanian society as a whole. The foundation of the whole activity of the HDUR is precisely the idea that the Hungarian minority is a reality independent from the Romanian reality.

The HDUR itself can exist only starting from such a requisite. Therefore, its efforts are mainly oriented toward the creation of such a reality, of the Hungarian minority as some sort of enclave, with well delimited and even better guarded frontiers, in order to keep the Hungarian populace at bay from Romania's realities. It is not impossible and it would not be such a great novelty. In almost all societies, religious, cultural and sometimes ethnic groups use to isolate themselves in the middle of a society, maintaining rules, behaviors, customs of their own, which separate them from the whole of the community. Endogamy and mother tongue are the most disseminated, but of course they can be associated with other ones. The problem for the HDUR is that the formation and maintenance of these rules are not political activities or objectives and they do not result from the minority's interaction inside the respective group or minority and they wholly depend on the action inside it and on the acceptance by Hungarians of behaviors of self-isolation. As a political organization of the Hungarians, the HDUR is automatically oriented to the outside, to the relations with the Romanian state and is handicapped by the fact that it cannot adopt the only objective of a political organization – to rule the state. Therefore, it just has to make up other objectives for itself, but here too, the possibilities are extremely limited. After having fought for the recognition of the national minorities' rights before the endorsement of the Constitution, once it endorsed and once Romania has signed the relevant international documents, the HDUR has seen its political objectives turn simultaneously unclear and ambiguous. But that has facilitated its alliance with the historic parties and with the humanist elite.

If one eliminates the false assumptions, hypocrisy and demagogy from the debate created with and around the HDUR, one very soon comes to clearly single out its paradox and "originality". First, the HDUR is in a position to choose between political objectives, on the one hand, and cultural or humanitarian objectives, on the other hand. The setting up of a university with tuition in Hungarian, for instance, is a cultural or educative objective. Moreover, it actually is an internal objective of the Hungarian minority. Nothing prevents the Hungarian community in Romania from setting up a university for itself, wherever it wants to. This too, would be one more original feature, because it is not a disseminated institution, not even with the Hungarian communities in other countries, but it is by no means unacceptable. Not even the getting of subsidies from the Romanian state for the maintenance of such a university is political objective and an adequate pressure by Hungarian cultural or civic organizations would be normal and even successful in the end. Therefore, the HDUR no longer can endorse such actions as objectives of its political activity and a way to legitimate its existence. It must turn this problem into a political one, associated with the relations between Hungarians and the Romanian state. There is only one way of doing it and we shall see it immediately, but the HDUR simply cannot afford to use it directly, so it makes up problems that at least seem to be political.

With the university, for instance, the main issue is not its existence proper, not its financing, but the building. Sure, if vested in the abundant rhetoric created in the debate on the Bolyai University, then the problem gets a certain air of respectability and allows for the participants to invest an important affective capital. But, divested of all this, it remains the problem of doubtful significance of having or not having a Hungarian university based in the old buildings of the Austro-Hungarian university in Cluj. Other problems have an even more doubtful political significance, created rather by the rhetoric of debate than by their possible consequences. But the HDUR simply has to stick to this ambiguity, because it is its only way of creating at least the impression of a political significance. For this reason, its policy revolves around problems of the kind of the university building, the Cluj statues, the street and locality name signs, etc. The situation is the more grotesque as neither the HDUR representatives nor the Romanian politicians engaged in polemics seem to have a sense of proportions or humor.

In the relations between a minority, either ethnic, religious or cultural, linguistic, etc., and a state, there can be only two political objectives. One is the integration in the society, the other is the separation from it. The political integration, that does not entail linguistic or social integration, is being achieved through the elimination of the political discriminations – consecrated as such by legislative or administrative means -, in the relations between the minority and the majority. Discriminations of a social or cultural nature are not eliminated because it is not possible. For instance, the legislative or administrative ban on mixed marriages is eliminated, but the social discrimination cannot be eliminated by political measures, because one cannot pass a law to make a certain number of mixed marriages compulsory. The political integration has been the outspoken objective of the HDUR in its relations with the Romanian state until the endorsement of the adequate legislation and especially until the endorsement of the Constitution. We should however mention that whereas, formally, in its relations with the Romanian state the HDUR promoted the political integration, in its practice inside the Hungarian community it supported and even promoted the consolidation of the social discriminations. The result was a process of self-enclavization of the Hungarian community in Romania, that would have befitted rather the other political objective.

This is separation. Political separation is not like social or cultural separation either. Like any political objective, it directly refers to resources and entails a certain redistribution of these resources. Political integration meant the acceptance by the majority of the minority's access to the resources from which it had been politically barred that far. Barring the access of a minority or majority to resources by means other than political in nature, for instance by economic or social means, is still a political problem, but it transcends the ethnic or linguistic minorities and belongs to the whole society. Anyway, it entails the integration as an initial stage. Poverty in Romania, for instance, is not a problem of the Hungarians or of the Romanians, it is a problem of the society as a whole. It is a political problem, but the participation in its settlement is tantamount to the integration in the Romanian society, which the HDUR cannot accept unless it wants to see its various components join adverse camps. The other way round, the political separation means the restriction of the access to well delimited resources, only for that specific minority. Here, the territory is essential. The base for political separation is surely social and cultural self-enclavization, the rejection of the majority by the minority, but all these necessary conditions taken together are not enough. One more step is necessary and this step is the option for separation, that can take any concrete form, from simple community autonomy to political independence and it necessarily requires the delimitation of the space of authority of the new power. This space of authority has absolute need to have also a territorial delimitation, as the political power is closely connected with the territory.

So, the HDUR is currently in a very ambiguous position. The only genuinely political objective it can endorse is to become the new political power in a space which should be determined also from a territorial point of view. As this space cannot be Romania, for the HDUR proposes to lead politically only and solely the Hungarian minority and only and solely for its benefit, then it has to come and delimit a territory where it should be recognized as the dominant political authority. On the other hand, it cannot admit it has such an objective and cannot adopt it openly as a purpose of its political program. Therefore, it has to generate purposefully the ambiguity and confusion around its objectives and stick to such minor and obviously false problems as the street signs, etc. This ambiguity is not entirely the HDUR's own doing. Partly, it was induced by the just as ambiguous policy of the Hungarian government in the last years of Ceausescu's rule and in the first years after the revolution.

One of the problems of these governments was to ensure their own popularity. It is the same with any government, but it is more acute with governments that promote reforms affecting important categories of the population. That is why all governments in the East-European countries in transition have employed or counted on nationalist ideologies. Beyond the gain of popularity of the governance, here too, there was a more profound need. At a time when all systems of values were falling apart, and the previously stable realities were reversed, nationalism ensured a minimum of identity and of community of interests to the changing society.

An almost "natural" form of the Hungarian nationalism is the remaking of "Great Hungary", the redemption of the territories lost after the end of World War One, with the falling apart of the Austro-Hungarian Empire and the formation of the new East-European republics. As long as it was still a party to the Warsaw Treaty and Yugoslavia was still the United States' darling in east Europe, Hungary could not take very openly a claim stand to this effect. Ceausescu's opposition to Gorbachev's reforms allowed it to adopt, for the first time after World War Two, a more nationalist attitude, under the pretext of criticizing Ceausescu's tough communism in Romania and showing concern about the fate of the Hungarians in Romania. After the success of the revolutions in the East and the dissolution of the Soviet sphere of influence, when everything seemed possible, the remaking of "Great Hungary" was taken seriously at least from a propaganda viewpoint. Hungarian officials made spectacular statements about the Trianon Peace Treaty, and the Hungarian government strengthened its ties with the Hungarian minorities in the neighbour countries, intervening directly in the policy pursued by them. The HDUR was no exception. It cannot even be accused of having modelled its statements, stands and political actions in keeping with Budapest's policies. But it also suffered the consequences, as the relatively abrupt and only rarely justified turns in Budapest's policy meant serious trouble for it both in its relations with the Romanian politicians and inside it. Every change of policy in Budapest made one or another of the HDUR leadership groups gain or lose ground. The ambiguity and confusion of the HDUR relations with the Romanian state were paralleled by internal ambiguity and confusion.

The HDUR's relations with the government in Budapest induced one more "originality". On the one hand, it could not show itself or let others regard it as a mere political instrument of the government in Budapest. Its credibility would have been seriously impaired and it would have even run the risk of being declared an illegal organization. No state in the world accepts political organizations controlled by another state in its own territory. On the other hand, it could not deny or sever the ties with Budapest, regarded as the "world" center of the Hungarians and, anyway, as the capital of the motherland. Keeping a balance between the two hypostases is not only a delicate operation, as the frontiers between autonomy, cooperation and subordination are here extremely vague, but also one that generates confusion. Ultimately, the result of this endless series of compromises that made the HDUR political ballet and that was not even conducive to a well defined objective, was the overlapping of the formal structure of the organization, by an-

other structure, rather informal – but no less known inside -, that divided its leaders and their supporters into radicals and moderates and
added to the inner conflicts and disagreements also the conflicts and
disagreements with the leaders in Budapest.

The HDUR's originality does not stop here. Its second objective is
to be really recognized as a political force by those whom it wants to
represent, meaning the Hungarians in Romania. But, the Hungarians
are not all alike, unless they are compared with the non-Hungarians, in
our case with the Romanians. As soon as this element of the reference
disappears, they differ among themselves. Some are rich, others are
poor. Some live and work in the country-side, others do city jobs, others are intellectuals, etc., and these groups have differing political interests. That is why, the Hungarian community in Romania has generated
parties that differ in terms of orientation and doctrine. This diversity of
interests is secondary only as long as the common problem, acknowledged as primary, is the problem of the relations with the Romanians.
Therefore, the HDUR, in order to exist, needs this problem to exist, not
to be settled. Therefore, the HDUR is not only not stating openly the
only real political objective it can endorse, but does not even have something prepared for the event of attaining such an objective. In this respect, it is very much like the past-century British general who, they
said, apart from a smashing defeat, found nothing more frightful than a
decisive victory. The ideal situation to it is the current one, this continued small was of statements, nerves and details, with more or less convincing reverberation on an international plane, that has no end or finality, but that secures the unreserved support of the Hungarians in the
country and some Western sympathy and also a doubtful mission, yet a
safe place in the Romanian political system.

Maybe the best illustration of this ambiguity is the post-revolution
history of the Szekler and Hungarian communities in eastern
Transylvania. It had been a zone where the Hungarians made the majority of the population. During the communist regime, the authorities encouraged the implantation in the zone of Romanian ethnics, moderately
developing the local industry and employing the system of assignation
to job of higher-school leaders in order to stabilize in the area a Romanian intelligentsia. At the same time, the representatives of the administrative authorities used to be appointed mainly from among Romanians. During the revolution, the challenging of the authorities by the

majority Hungarian population combined a political and an ethnic motivation. The population lynched Romanian militiamen and mayors and it is hard to tell now whether the reasons were first of all political or ethnic. Anyway, the revolution was followed by a process of rejection of the Romanian ethnics, against the background of the Hungarian community's tendency of self-enclavization. Most of the Romanian were forced to move from that region to zones with a Romanian majority. That process was backed by the HDUR, but when, giving proof after all, of consistency, the Szekler communities in eastern Transylvania wanted to proclaim their "administrative autonomy", the HDUR did not back that initiative that might have triggered strong reactions with the authorities and with the Romanian population.

But after that followed the "prefects' scandal", in which the HDUR took a quite opposite stand. The government appointed Romanian nationals as prefects and the HDUR protested, demanding prefects of Hungarian nationality. It is not at all clear what meaning did the HDUR attach to the fact. It was exactly the kind of problem that suited in the best by its ambiguity, emotional touch and lack of real importance. On the one hand, it allowed it to associate the Hungarian minority's issue with the administrative act and refer it to the minorities' rights theme. On the other hand, it could hope that the success would be taken as a step ahead in the Hungarians' self-isolation from Romanians. Finally, not even a success would have changed the situation, since the prefects, as appointed representatives of the central government, were directly and totally subordinated to it. In the end, the central government concluded that the prefects' appointment was its exclusive prerogative and no longer negotiated it with the HDUR, after having improvised for a while all kind of hybrid solutions that would bring one Romanian and one Hungarian at the head of the local government. After occasioning numberless speeches, articles and intimations at home and abroad, the conflict died, and the HDUR ended by adding to its program a point about "local autonomy", of which not even its own leaders know whether it means the autonomy of the local administration from the central administration, a principle sanctioned by the Constitution and partly applied through the local administration reform in 1992, or the Hungarians' autonomy in relation to the Romanian state.

Under the circumstances, the alliance with the historic parties entailed an immediate tactical advantage for the HDUR. It could show to everybody, at home and abroad, that what it was after was not unacceptable for the Romanians generally, but only for some of them, meaning those in power. It did not matter to the HDUR who was in power, as their eternally position could not change. But it suited it that the rulers were a grouping which the opposition was ready to challenge totally and which did not have a good image in the Western mass media. That made their own challenge the more credible.

For the "historic" parties and their allies, the alliance with the HDUR meant first of all winning over the votes of the one million or so Hungarians in Romania and, of course, the Hungarian parliamentarians' support to their own political actions. That went with the assets. As for liabilities, it meant the dramatic decline in their credibility in Transylvania where, as a reaction to the HUDR, Romanian nationalist political parties had been set up, the most important of them being the Romanian National Unity Party, and that would collect most of the ballots of the Romanians in the region. In the political relations, that also meant that, no matter how much the RNUP courted the idea of opposing Ion Iliescu and the parties supporting him – in the 1992 elections the RNUP has its own presidential candidate, elected from among its leaders –, it could by no means join the opposition led by the "historic ones", given that the HDUR was in the same camp.

The originality of the alliance between the "historic" parties and the HDUR consisted of the fact that it was not at all political. The cooperation between them only meant being together against the rulers, for the main reason, as good for either of them, that those were the people in power. As a matter of fact, the historic parties did not back any of the HDUR objectives and some of them, real or suspected, they even rejected aloud. A part of the humanist elite was more cosmopolitan and supported the thesis that, at a time of globalization and European integration, specific to the end of the century, the frontiers between states tended to lose some of their importance and the prospect was that they should disappear altogether in a foreseeable future, an ideological theme that suited also the HDUR, except that they meant only the western frontier. Another part of the humanist elite was however profoundly nationalist and not at all satisfied with the alliance with the HDUR. Likewise, inside the historic parties there was, and periodically prevailed, a more nationalist "wing", originating especially in Transylvania. In turn, the HDUR did not interfere with the historic parties' political problems. It was not interested in the restoration of the monarchy, for instance, about which the historic parties were making so much fuss, but which it did not consider to be a problem of the Hungarians. It was only natural, given that the restoration of the monarchy would not have changed at all its own situation. It was not very much interested in the redemption of the properties either, unless it was about the Catholic church, one of its main supporters. In elections, in spite of the alliances, the HDUR participated alone, thus limiting its support to the historic parties and categorically refusing to get melted into some grouping of the opposition.

The alliance between the historic parties and the HDUR was heavily used by the ruling parties in order to make the electorate in Transylvania – and in other parts – turn its back on the historic parties. They presented the problem in the extremely peremptory form of Transylvania's fate. As long as the HDUR was tied to the policy of the Budapest government and the latter was promoting the idea of nullification of the peace treaties concluded after World War One whereby Transylvania had joined Romania, that land was in danger and so was the national Romanian state. The danger seemed the more real as in 1940 the Hungarian diplomacy had managed to snatch a part of the Romanian territory, appending it to Horthy's Hungary. It is hard to estimate how real that danger was, not only in Bucharest, but also in Budapest. The dismemberment of Yugoslavia and Czechoslovakia, Romania's international isolation, especially in Europe, the privileged position Hungary seemed to have in the policy with East Europe and the HDUR's political activism on an internal plane, were elements that justified the worry. Only after the Yugoslav war proved to be easier to start than to stop, and Romania's political and social stability became a component of the Western strategies in the region, the danger can be considered as having considerably decreased.

In the end, the HDUR had become an ingredient the more necessary in the current Romanian political system as it too, ceased making policy. Apart from contributing, by its mere existence, to the creation of one of the main false problems of the Romanian politics, its parliamentarians participate along with the others, in the endless intrigues and schemes that make the Romanian political life, the climax of which was reached in the period which we will call "parliamentary democracy".

V. THE ORIGINAL PARTIES
– THE RULERS

The "originality" of the political parties of the opposition mainly results from the fact that they do not come up with variants of alternate policies for Romania. They do not participate in the power system and do not seem willing to. In the best of cases, they simply mistake the system of privileges that goes with the functions of represention in the state for the power, meaning for the control and use of the national resources. The only objectives they set themselves, for whose attainment they willingly fight, are those associated with the access of a small group of leaders to the functions of political leadership of the state, although these functions are themselves only loosely or not at all associated with the real system of power. This surely does not mean that the political leaders of the opposition are naive, greedy and vain and, by no means, that they are the first to be blamed for the political situation of their parties. It would be extremely simple, because the mere changing of the leaders would result in the automatic change of the parties, of their role and functions and, possibly, would change the whole system of exercising the power in the society. In actual fact, the defect resides in the way how the political parties were formed, as mere groupings that were after ruling the state, in their not being connected with the electorate, as a social base and not as simple as a simple voting machine, and, especially, in the absence of an option for an in-depth change of the society. Ultimately, these are the only defining features of a genuine policy. The limitation of the options to the mode of distribution of a bigger or smaller part of the national wealth or of the results of the economic activities makes them unable to project a genuine change of the country.

The most profound "originality" of the opposition political parties consists of their organic incapability of articulating and promoting transition policies. In this way, a big part of the political system is dramatically cut off from the economic and social reality and, by way of consequence, also from the real system of the power. But things are not at all different with the political party whose leaders, having won the elections twice, have held those much coveted leading functions in the state during the five years that have elapsed since the revolution.

1. The Glory and Decline of the NSF

It was first called National Salvation Front (NSF), subsequently, after the Roman group broke away taking over with the name also most of its organizational structures and logistic support, it was called Democratic National Salvation Front (DNSF), and now its name is the Party of Social Democracy of Romania (PSDR). One can speculate on the fact that even the evolution of the party's name discloses its lack of political objectives. The switch from NSF to DNSF refers to relations inside the party and not to some political objective. The group that split off from the NSF to make the DNSF accused Petre Roman of the absence of democracy inside the party that barred the dissenters from decision-making. It was an involuntary emphasis on the reality that the divorce was actually caused by inner disagreements and not by a disagreement on the party's political orientations which did not matter for most of the dissenters. When, after winning the elections, the DNSF changed its name again, with the main purpose of calling itself a "party" instead of a "front", it found the label it wanted the most for itself – Social-Democrat – had already been taken by someone else. The idea of reversed words (in Romanian: from "social-democratic" into "democratie-sociala") with the noun placed before the adjective, is just a play of words and has no special doctrinary significance. For, if the modern social-democracy had come to associate its name with the policies of a welfare state, this is the result of its whole political and doctrinary activity after World War Two and not of a particular sequence of words.

The NSF Problems

Far more relevant is an analysis of the NSF and its descendants and allies considering what they have done than from the angle of names or even programs. Anyway, the NSF appeared as a political party for exactly the same reason as the other political parties – to ensure for a small group of political leaders the legitimacy of holding positions in the state. Maybe even more than the historic parties or other parties of the opposition, the NSF was from the onset a simple means to save appearances. But in order to understand the genesis and role of the NSF we must go back to the so consequential history of the NCNSF.

At the end of the first period of strife inside the NCNSF set up on 22 December, after a group of dissenters (including Doina Cornea, Ana

Blandiana, Laszlo Tokes, etc.) withdraw from it for the precise purpose of eliminating the remaining group and replacing it with a new political superstructure, and after the settlement of the conflict between those who remained for the benefit of the group led by Ion Iliescu (following the elimination of Dumitru Mazilu and the marginalization of Silviu Brucan), the already described power system got stabilized in Romania, resting on the coalition between the administration and the technocracy. It is very likely that it should have got stabilized in the same form no matter which of the groups mentioned above would have won the confrontation, but what matters is that it felt threatened by them, no matter how unrealistic the threat. Like I said, this power system needs no political parties to operate. Its legitimacy does not rest on political options and on projects to model the future, either supported by the population or not, but on the technical competence it assumes. In this respect, the doctrine shyly sketched by Ion Iliescu as early as January 1990 about a democracy without political parties, was extremely convenient for the power system. And so was the organization of the power instituted after the abolition of the enterprise NCNSF, when the political parties did not play any role and were all of them rallied in some sort of political parliament that, after more or less debate, sanctioned the legislation solutions drafted anonymously and "scientifically" within the power system.

But the pressure put up from the outside and by the political parties inside for the building in Romania of a political system to the pattern of the Western democracies could not be ignored. As a matter of fact, the political parties had already emerged, as organizations backing claimants on the leading political functions of the state. The only ones who did not have such an official team of supporters were precisely the politicians already in power, those who had backed the building of the extant power system. Therefore, in March and April 1990 they started putting together in a hurry a political party. Sure, it was not a genuine political party that should lead Romania in about the same way as the communist party had led it under the previous regime, only promoting different political objectives. It was only about an organization that should allow the people to back the extant power and that should consecrate the power system that had already been articulated in broad lines. And it was not a matter of integrating the political party with the power system either. The power system would not accept the political parties of the governance just as it would not accept the political parties of the opposition for that matter.

The NSF, hastily organized, only a few weeks before elections, had nothing to justify the notion of political parties more than the opposition parties had. It was a simple organization of support for the election campaign and it filled two essential requirements. One was the form of the political system, that entailed political parties. The other parties had to send their representatives to the parliament, and the representatives had to endorse the governments and the legislation. Until the May 1990 elections, the power system, even though constituted, was extremely vulnerable as concerned its legitimacy, which it could only base on the support of public opinion and on the popularity of Ion Iliescu and Petre Roman. It was surely too little. On the other hand, once a normal political system came into being, even if not availing of power, it was the main means of legitimation of its exercise by those who held it.

For the bureaucracy and technocracy, such a system was very convenient. It entailed the existence of a parliament to vote their keeping in power, as well as the technical measures needed for that. Besides, the political party could also be an excellent go-between in the communication with the population. The NSF was built for that precise purpose.

Once the elections were over, once the politicians installed, legitimately this time, in their leading posts, and their representatives sent to the Parliament, the NSF became useless. It proved to be extremely inefficient as an organization meant to conduct pro-government propaganda. The electorate had voted for the NSF because of its leaders' popularity, and now the leaders had loosened their ties with the party, as the President was forbidden any formal political allegiance, and Petre Roman, concerned with his image abroad, had kept all the while at a notable distance from the NSF and he had run for a seat in the Parliament as independent candidate on NSF lists. As these leaders were now holding the major offices in the state, as president and prime minister, the population has turned again to the government structures, increasingly mindless of the NSF. As a political party it was useless once the elections were over. It would become useful again with the next elections. But until then, it would be rather an inconvenient factor of steady pressure. It has developed in a very short while an organization with numberless branches and subsidiaries that dotted the country, and had set up a vast network of communication with the population. During the election campaign, it was used to relay from top to bottom, from the leaders to the electorate, the political and propaganda messages of the campaign. But, after the elections, that flow of messages stopped and, to fill the void, messages started to rise through all those channels, like water in capillaries, from the population to the political leaders. It was not an efficient way to communicate. The overwhelming majority of the messages had no way to get past the NSF parliamentarians and the formal leadership of the party. They had themselves a very limited access to the main holders of the functions and could not influence at all the really important power centers and decisions, all while being subject to a continuous but chaotic political pressure from the population and local organizations, to which they could not respond.

In such a situation, an organization like the NSF is either turning into a real political party or is changing its functionality, so as to respond, no matter how inadequately, to the grassroots pressure. The NSF did not have anything needed to become a genuine political party. It did not have an ideology. Even its electoral message had been articulated not upon an ideology, but as a simple rejection of the other group's claims to accede to the power and, above all, to share among themselves whatever they thought was due to them, more or less legitimately, in their capacity as presumptive heirs to inter-bellum Romania. Especially that latter message was very popular during the election campaigns, both in May 1990 and in September 1992. The NSF electoral message implied that if something was to be shared – and the privatization was understood precisely in that way by almost everyone -, then the NSF was the party of those who sustained that everybody had to get their share of the pie.

Whereas it did not have an explicit ideology – and it even made an asset of that in the 1990 elections -, the NSF still had an implicit one. It belonged less to the party itself and almost not at all to its leaders, but it explains why the people still voted for the NSF and for Ion Iliescu. That ideology rejected any project of an overlay drastic and spectacular transformation. The population felt that the reality was more complex and that the happiness and welfare would not come that easy. Instead, it forecasted a radical improvement of things, based less on very ingenious technical solutions, and more on a sound common sense firmly and, above all, honestly applied to all domains where things had been bad before for obvious reasons. Obviously, the false assumption was precisely the presumptive rationality and good faith, tantamount to the absence of own interests of the elites or of the groups that fought to take their place. Therefore, these beliefs of the population, attributed to the NSF because the population simply had to attribute them to someone and because Ion Iliescu had made it both confident and hopeful, have never generated an ideology, at least not in the case of the NSF.

Just as totally inexistent as an ideology were the NSF leaders. After the 1990 elections, the ruling party remained completely without a leadership. Before elections, Ion Iliescu was formally the NSF president, but he did not attach much importance to it. It is interesting and instructive to remember that in the 1990-1991 period none of the president's intimates wanted to get involved in leading and organizing the NSF. After several variants were aborted because of the lack of interest of those on charge, the actual leadership of the new ruling party went to a group of young revolutionaries who had no real political influence and whose main role was to take care of the logistics of the election campaign. The government formed after the May 1990 elections was not associated in any way with the NSF, as required by the extant power system, neither were in the months that followed the newly installed local governments. The new ruling party remained virtually without a leadership until March 1991, when the government of technicians headed by Roman was adopted as the party's leadership.

But even more inexistent than the leadership and the ideology, was the NSF's activity and so was the activity of any other party. Theoretically, it was a ruling party, but in actual fact, apart from not participating in the governance, it did not even have information as to what was happening inside it. Both the administrative bureaucracy and the technocracy were very reticent with the NSF, for all the support given to its leaders during the elections and for all the fine collaboration after that. It did not seem to be a party with a great political future, considering the vicious attacks on it from the inside, its very bad image outside and its organizational and propaganda inefficiency. Then, it was not even necessary as a element of the power system, and the bureaucracy, having just gotten rid of the dominance of an army of party activists, had no intention to offer itself as subject to another dominance. Therefore, the NSF was very soon designated as having nothing else to do than taking care of the polemic with the opposition parties and of the "political" matters, meaning the problem of the "monarchy", of the relations between minorities, etc., except, of course, for the situations when such problems were real and waited for "technical" solutions. Set up as an organization of electoral fight against Ion Iliescu's political adversaries, and unable to become a political organization, the NSF would simply fall into decomposition once the political war ceased to be the country's major concern. The very fact that it was a ruling party added to this.

First, that deprived it of the unity which the historic parties derived from their being in the opposition. Whereas they were able to easily mobilize their champions and supporters to criticizing the governance, for the NSF it was almost impossible to convincingly mobilize the population's support, the more so as it had plenty of compromises and austerity measures to be blamed for. Besides, the loose ties with the government and the administration did not allow the NSF activists to act in full awareness. And it was a big party, far too big and far too closely tied to the big mass of industrial workers and wage-earners not to be rapidly caught in the contradiction between their interests and the rulers' interests. All along the 1990 – 1991 period, when the NSF had a variable but mass base, its main function was to fill the yawning gap between the power system which the NSF controlled formally and for whose actions it was deemed responsible anyway, and the population that was increasingly affected by the real policy conducted by the power system. The purpose for the main economic measures in that period was to suck in resources from the population and channel them to the industrial system that was traversing a profound crisis but that the industrial technocracy had to keep in operation if it wanted to keep its dominant position in the economy.

Trapped in that way between Scylla and Charibdis, the NSF activits – the active members of the party – were caught themselves in a centrifugal motion. The part of them that was closer to the population started departing from the political group proper. Without drawing nearer the opposition, which did not offer an alternate choice, they remained at the fringes of the NSF, but pressed vaguely for a change the illusion of which was offered later on by the DNSF dissension. The part that was closer to the administration, mainly the government functionaries and, after the local elections, the new representatives of the local authorities, made the political base of the new parties: NSF and DNSF.

The year 1991 marked the sharpening of the conflict inside the industrial technocracy, between the financial technocracy and the enterprise technocracy. The main battle between the two groups – on which we will enlarge below, was fought for the control of the administrative bureaucracy and its use as an instrument to exercise the power. Under the circumstances, both the government and its political legitimacy became important, so the politicians were rapidly enticed into a conflict which was not theirs after all. As the politicians of the opposition did not represent more than uncertain allies, the main camps developed right inside the ruling party. Every one of them rallied around one of the two political leaders that enjoyed popularity – Ion Iliescu and Petre Roman –, using them rather as a trademark and political label than as leaders.

The Iliescu-Roman Conflict

What is strange about the conflict between Ion Iliescu and Petre Roman, that has marked Romania's political history all along the period after the 1990 elections is that, personally, the two leaders did not share the views and positions of the groups whose leaders they became and that, at least as far as they were concerned, the conflict was meaningless. Then, what is the source of the conflict between Ion Iliescu and Petre Roman? Mostly personal disagreements. For a long time, they could be appeased or forgotten when they had to do with politics, because their interests coincided to a great extent. But, obeying by the general rule in the new Romanian political system, each of them was surrounded by some sort of own court, whose members were fighting a silent but tough underground war. And their main weapon was to turn against the rivals the rage or at least adversity of the political leader in whose camp they had found shelter. Roman and Iliescu came at odds for the ridiculous reason that neither was unable to master his own entourage, at least as regarded the conflict with the other one's entourage.

Once the conflict started in that way, the first response with the population and with the NSF rank and file was to ask, maybe even force, the two leaders to resume cooperation. But subsequently, there was a process of polarization, as two big and opposing groups emerged inside the NSF. Later on, out of the need to build a political identity for themselves and to be legitimized with the population, the two groups adopted first differing ideologies, then even differing policies. Two factors favored the process.

First, the multitude of trivial conflicts that sapped from inside at the local organizations of the NSF. Whereas at a central level a government that was autonomous from the NSF had been formed relatively easily, the local authorities were still closely tied to the NSF, given that they had been the promoters and organizers of its county and city branches. But not even the local governments availed of functions and privileges enough to satisfy after the electoral victory all the "outstanding" members of the NSF. The result was that numerous small quarrels, adversities and battles existed on a basis in the local organizations, and they were reverberated up to the center through parliamentarians, they too, taking sides in the local camps. All those conflicts were far from having any political content. Their objectives were very personal, from preferential treatment in granting licences or land distribution to the ambitions of organization leaders to become mayors or prefects. But their legitimation was another story, so, as soon as the opportunity emerged of endorsing a political label to pin to the personal objectives a legitimate requirement, it was enthusiastically endorsed. That process of politicizing the conflict and of polarization of the two leaders' supporters started right after the conflict between them became public knowledge and, obviously, it fuelled also the conflict and hopes of every one of them that they could win a landslide victory, by eliminating the rival while retaining the control of the party as a whole, that would have ensured his success in elections.

The conflict was politicized almost against the two leaders' will. In its first stages, they did not attack each other but key figures in their respective entourage. Petre Roman's attack was directed mainly against the president and speaker of the two Chambers – Alexandru Barladeanu and Dan Martian –, whereas Ion Iliescu was tempted to blame especially Adrian Severin, who was at the time minister assistant to the prime minister and coordinator of the economic reform. The NSF polarization simply transferred the court intrigue to the level of political game, and the two were actually forced to join the combat as the leaders of two differing political currents.

This situation, that became explosive after the fall of the Roman government caused by the miners' riot in Bucharest in September, obviously delighted the opposition and many of the foreign actors who played a role in the Romanian political life that must not be neglected. The great hope that was born there was that, as the NSF was falling apart, a political victory of the opposition became possible. It was obvious that as long as Ion Iliescu and Petre Roman remained in the same camp, no notable shift of the electorate was possible. A political analysis made by French experts and released in the autumn of 1990 emphasized this same thing as well as the fact any consequential political change had to be preceded by the separation of the two. Or, in mid-1991, that was already a fact and it was beginning to acquire also the political color necessary to make any return impossible.

"A Future for Romania" Group

The other factor that favored the splitting of the NSF into two opposite political parties was the existence of powerful pressure at the level of governance. The Roman Government that was formed after the 1990 elections, was a government of the industrial technocracy generally. Both the financial technocracy and the enterprise one were powerfully represented and, for a while, the two groups cooperated well. The brutal offensive of the financial technocracy, launched in the autumn of 1990, caught the enterprise technocracy unawares. Unable to fight, it did only grudge, but that generated a genuine anti-government ideology with the population and the local organizations. In the spring of 1991 a government reshuffle sanctioned the financial technocracy's taking over the control of the government. In the same period though, the parliamentary group dominated by the county representatives, and far more sensitive to the fate of the industrial enterprises in their constituencies, started opposing the government more and more, having as opinion leader Alexandru Barladeanu, who became the ideologist of the enterprise technocracy, preaching the maintenance of the state's intervention in the economy. The NSF ought to have fallen apart at that time, but in actual fact it braced itself to become, if not a genuine political party, at least an organization.

That unnatural evolution was the result of the action of a small group of specialists in politics, international relations, sociology and economics, known later by the name of A Future for Romania Group. Although at the beginning of 1991 the group did not have a name yet, it already had a history. The initial nucleus had existed even before December 1989 and it included young specialists in international relations and security matters who, by the very nature of their work, were aware of the processes of change that had started in Europe after Gorbachev's advent. What worried them was that Romania kept remaining outside chances and its international position was deteriorating, with incalculable, therefore frightening consequences. Conversant with both history and real interests behind the rhetoric about international relations and, especially, with the decision-making mechanisms in the Western cabinets and especially in the international bureaucracies, they watched powerlessly the degradation of both the domestic and international situation. At that time they were positively nationalists and they opposed communism as a system, especially because of the consequences on an international plane entailed by its maintenance in Romania. Immediately after the revolution, a part of that group was co-opted as an expert team under the NCNSF (later on PNUC) Foreign Policy Commission and the group got organized on that opportunity. They elected their chief in the person of Vasile Secares, a military sociologist, specialist in security affairs and formerly lecturer (reader) with the Stefan Gheorghiu Academy of the RCP. He remained the never challenged leader of the group, which was twice unusual. First, because the battle for leading positions was the most disseminated feature of all organizations, then because precisely that group was formed of strong personalities and any one of them could be a leader.

At the end of January, the team, losing patience with the contradictory evolution and the confusion of the NCNSF, addressed an intimation to Ion Iliescu. As a result, he made them his principal advisers. In the beginning, they had a purely intellectual role, confining themselves to drawing up analyses and volunteering advice. In the spring of 1990, they articulated the political program of the NSF and prepared its founding Conference. But, after the 1990 elections, they got engrossed in politics – a part of the group was included in the government, and another part organized Ion Iliescu's team of advisers. In the autumn of 1990, the group was worried again, that time about the government. Apart from the absence of any strategy of transition, there was not even a center capable of articulating it and of watching its application. Obviously, a genuine political force was what was needed, and the group's idea was to turn the NSF precisely into such a force. For that, the NSF had to be reorganized, its connection with the governance had to be ensured, and it had to be equipped with a strategy.

Since November 1990 until February 1991, the group took care of that, drafting a new Statute of the NSF, a new organizational structure and a new political program, entitled "A Future for Romania" which later on became its own name. The central idea of the new reorganiza-

tion was to turn the government, at head with the incumbent prime minister, into the leadership of the new political party, and to give it a
new orientation, although the group did not think Petre Roman to
be very fit for the role and the relations with him were difficult. But
he was prime minister and the purpose was to give the government
a policy and the party an executive. The reorganization was successful, but it caused profound discontent especially with the two
leaders' personal entourages who saw themselves pushed aside in
that way. The reflex was that both Petre Roman and Ion Iliescu became suspicious about the group. Petre Roman because a well organized party equipped with a strategy entailed rigidity, and Ion
Iliescu because, with a formal and organized leadership, the party
was less permissive to his own influence.

The two groupings that were tending to split, for a while encountered the resistance opposed by the group and by the party's new structures. But, in the autumn of 1991, Petre Roman started a direct offensive against the AFFRG, which it suspected to be Ion Iliescu's instrument in the NSF leadership, and managed to co-opt a part of it – the part
already included in the government – and eliminated the other part from
the NSF leadership. Although attacked by Petre Roman, the group refused to join the other camp and, at the NSF National Conference in
March 1992 it came up with its own variant of both program and political leadership. It was a good experimental proof of the seduction which
a sound intellectual construction could represent for people pressed by
the need to choose and confused about the assets, objectives and criteria of selection. The group that participated in the Conference only had
seven men in a hall of a few hundred delegates selected by Petre Roman and other hundreds of invited guests. They were unpopular because Roman was hostile to them and Ion Iliescu did not support them.
Besides, they also had the bad image as former Stefan Gheorghiu professors. They ought to have remained quite unnoticed, but in actual fact
they proved to a stronger opposition to Petre than the group that had
called itself Ion Iliescu's, getting 20 per cent of the delegates' ballots,
instead of less than one per cent that would have been normal. That
spectacular success at the Conference that sanctioned the NSF's splitting was also the last one. After the defeat suffered at the Conference,
Ion Iliescu's camp – including especially parliamentarians – broke away
from the NSF, setting up a new party, the DNSF, and the AFFRG, that

refused to join any of the camps, temporarily exited the political stage in which it functioned independently only for three months.

The Dissolution of NSF and the Ascent of DNSF

Beyond the inter-personal conflict between Ion Iliescu and Petre Roman and their entourages, and beyond the popularization of a big part of the parliamentarians and local leaders for strictly personal reasons, what ensured the social base of the dissolution was the image of the failure of the Front and its government with the fulfilment of the implicit or explicit promises made before the electorate in April-May 1990. That image was gradually taken in by the population first, then by the Front members and, in a last stage, by the Front leaders. The damaging effect for the Front was that the two camps blamed each other for the failure. First, the opposition blamed the Front, then the Front blamed itself and in the end its main leaders blamed one another.

The Front's government first of all failed the population's aspirations and expectations. The population expected the Front, that seemed less inclined toward economic experiments and magic solutions, to administrate a little better the sick economy of socialism and to maintain at least the living standard got in the spring of 1990 as a direct reward for having made the revolution. Such an expectation went very well with the ideology promoted by the enterprise technocracy and, precisely on that basis, its spokespersons – mainly the parliamentarians come from the provinces – were now accusing the Roman Government of incompetence and, later on, of ill will.

But the NSF government was considered to be a failure also by the financial technocracy and the private sector, the main social categories to which the reform had been addressed so far. The economic reform was the only asset of the government, that considered the economic and social crisis to be transitional, as simple inevitable costs of the reform. And the reform was not directed toward ensuring the economic growth and, maybe, toward keeping the industrial system in operation, but toward introducing the market economy which was expected to automatically ensure a new wave of economic and social development. By the introduction of the market economy, both the government and the financial technocracy meant above all three things. First, the abolition of the system of administrative and centralized command of the economy and of the civil society. Then, the abolition of the state ownership and the introduction of the private ownership as well as of the unlimited right to acquire property. Finally, the introduction of capital as a condition of production and of the profit rate of the capital as criterion of appraising the usefulness of the respective production.

In actual fact, the reform implemented by 1991–1992 by the Roman Government and, later on by the Stolojan Government, attained none of these objectives. Which, from the financial technocracy's viewpoint, meant the failure of the reform. The causes were complex of course, but at the simple level of political polemics, a primitive yet credible explanation was offered. The economic reform failed because of the group of "conservatives" in the NSF, considered first to have the president's support and subsequently even represented by him. And the solution that suggested itself was their elimination from the NSF.

Each of the NSF's two camps accepted the political position that was rather imposed on them. However, in the political polemic, neither group gave pride of place to the economic reform. They considered it to be too delicate, complex and unsure to be able to bring about the popular support they wanted. So, they employed surrogates of slogans that seemed more easily to sustain and allowed for ambiguity to continue. As a matter of fact, this ambiguity is an essential characteristic of the Romanian political life. No political party takes a clear and steady stand on any real problem concerning the economic and social reform. The main reason is not a hypocrisy, exaggerated with the Romanian politicians as compared with the politicians of other countries or other times. They simply do not take such stands because they do not know them. Irrespective of the party, any of them is already included in a power system in which they have by no means the role to lead an economic reform. If an economic reform is to be implemented or not and how is it to proceed, these are decisions taken in the power system in which the politicians do not participate. On the other hand, the bureaucracy and industrial technocracy that make these decisions do not pursue any articulate project of transformation. Or else, they would turn themselves into a political party, and the power system would change. They make decisions on the reform, but they do so relying every time on off-hand criteria, improvising technical solutions that should simply allow for maintaining the extant system. Therefore, the two opposite camps in the NSF and, later on, the two parties, have never ever got involved in the maze of real problems posed by the economic reform, developing instead a package of problems of their own from which they derived a new political identity.

Each of them chose a major problem and a secondary one. The major problem substituted the program and the secondary one was used to criticize the adversary. The grotesque character of the confrontation consisted of the fact that the two major themes were far from mutually exclusive and in the end they had but a minor role in the battle. They did not represent differing options as to the settlement of a single problem, but merely differing aspects of the reality, both being equally acceptable to the electorate and the opposite grouping alike. The Roman team endorsed the "democracy" as an element to define itself, whereas the Iliescu team chose the "social security". To oppose democracy to social security or the other way round was politically inadvertent. The two are complementary. On the other hand, neither camp advanced too much in elaborating on the way how they would attain the thus defined objective, apart from stating that they were firmly resolved to accomplish it and just as resolved to eliminate their adversity. Every team tried to convince the electorate and their own supporters that, once the adversary eliminated, that objective would somehow get accomplished by itself. The NSF thought that Ion Iliescu and his associates's being still in the political life was the only obstacle left in the way to democracy. In that respect, the Roman grouping was following in the footsteps of the opposition that had far longer upheld such a stand. In turn, the DNSF tries to convince the population that once the Roman grouping eliminated, the social security would somehow become a fact of its own accord.

In actual fact, the secondary themes played a far more important role than the main ones in the political polemics, and later on in the election campaign. And the secondary themes had nothing in common with the political identity, the government objectives, or with the reform and transition. As a matter of fact they had nothing to do with politics either. They were simple themes of attack against the adversaries, every one of them having a markedly personal character. In that respect, the NSF-Roman chose the theme of its adversaries' communist past, whereas the DNSF chose the theme of corruption of the dignitaries in the Roman Government, especially of Petre Roman himself. None of the themes was elaborated on more than up to the level at which "serious" politicians would bring to mass media the simple gossip cir-

culated in the Government or Parliament lobbies. But they did not in-
tend more than to smear the adversary so much as to make it impossible
for him to be voted. In the end, from all that generalized slandering, the
president benefited the most. Both his own beliefs and his political position as the head of the state, prevented him from participating in such
a skirmish. The DNSF engaged in it without him and his image was less
impaired. The effect on the population was contradictory. In the end, it
did not matter so much, in spite of the fact that elections were held. The
true battle was fought not for winning over the electorate, but for winning the administration. And that is how the DNSF's ascent started.

The shifting of the NSF's weight center from the population to the
administration started even before its polarization in two opposing camps,
with the winning of the elections and the promotion of its own candidates to the control of the central and especially local administration.
The unwritten contract that was applied on the occasion consisted, for
one of the parties, of backing the NSF activists and supporters in occupying the leading functions of the administration and, for the other party,
of using the influence and authoritativeness conferred by the function
for backing the party – in organization and elections. Even such a contract, although widely employed in the political life everywhere in the
world, was rather dubious, but more important was the fact that the
frontier between the necessities of the party and those of the local leaders was quite vague. Consequently, the main result was some sort of
barter in which functions were traded for privileges and administrative
advantages. When the splitting of the NSF started, the local leaderships
were already divided as to how and for whose benefit the privileges and
advantages should be shared, which, like we have seen, favored the
polarization of the two camps. In broad lines, those who were dissatisfied rallied in the pro-Iliescu camp and that made of corruption one of
its basic accusations, whereas the people already in office remained
stuck to the government – on which their maintenance in office depended, hence, to Petre Roman's camp. That tendency of making groups
was general and the numerous exceptions only confirmed the rule.

The conflict between the two leaders, which the population did not
understand and approve of, resulted in a dramatic dwindling of the popular support to the NSF and made it ever more dependent on the party
bureaucracy included in the administration. The DNSF's first target when
it broke off from the NSF, was the administration, as it had to quickly

organize a national network of local branches. More than that, since the elections were around the corner and since the DNSF had only a few experts in politics, election campaign, propaganda, etc., while having plenty of ambitious members – all the dissatisfied who were seeing the DNSF electoral victory as a possibility to occupy the administrative functions denied to them by the NSF, the DNSF concentrated almost exclusively on conquering the administration. It was an objective far more easy to attain than conquering the population.

In the division of tasks that followed in the electoral campaign that objective went to Ion Iliescu personally. Getting the open or underground support of the administration proved not to be difficult when the DNSF – a mere group of politicians without a policy of their own by then – endorsed not only the slogans but also the political objectives of the enterprise technocracy. The administration was on the enterprise technocracy's side. At a local level, consequent to the close ties between the two groupings and especially to the localities' dependence on the destiny of the big industrial enterprises around which they had developed. At a central level, except for a parallel bureaucracy, built by the financial technocracy in order to promote the kind of reform that suited it, the administration was still allied with the enterprise technocracy and oriented toward keeping in function the industrial system. Nor had it any choice. In its effort to find a culprit for the failure of the reform, the Roman wing of the NSF had focussed its attacks precisely on the administration. They blamed the "stagnant bureaucracy" in ministries and administrative institutions, alleged to have sabotaged the reform legislation articulated and introduced by the reformist government. Directly threatened in the event of the victory of the NSF-Roman, the administrative bureaucracy had no choice but to sustain the DNSF. Which it did, thus ensuring its electoral victory.

Two factors can be credited with an essential contribution to the DNSF's electoral victory. On the one hand, the influence of the administration and enterprise technocracy on the electorate. And even more important than that was Ion Iliescu's electoral capital. Even after two years of economic crisis and degradation of the social life, after the conflict with Petre Roman and in spite of the opposition's vicious attacks, Ion Iliescu dominated in 1992 the Romanian political life with his popularity. Although his credibility had somewhat eroded, consequent to the failure of the reform policies he had every time supported unreservedly, he still enjoyed popular support unparalleled by any of his potential opponents.

The DNSF's ascent was favored also by the NSF's confusion. Once the battle against Ion Iliescu was over, as his camp withdrew from the NSF and started building a political party of its own, Petre Roman's party, free of adversaries, was not only stagnating but it found itself having as main concern another series of inner strives. Their specific reasons were of course the leaders' personal disagreements. Although they were not enough to cause new splits in the party, they were eating its members' time and energy. The main cause, though, was the absence of a policy. Once the battle won. in the name of the reform and of a market economy, the party relapsed into its previous state of idleness, because the role of implementing the policy did not belong to the party but to the part of administration that was controlled by the financial technocracy. The Stolojan government was congenial to it, but it was far from dominated by the NSF. And, although the population admired and respected Theodor Stolojan even when he proposed and applied austerity measures, his popularity was never reflected upon the political parties that sustained the government in the Parliament. In spite of the victory won, in spite of the attacks on Ion Iliescu that sometimes were even more vicious that the opposition's own attacks, the NSF remained as ambiguous as ever. As for the labels, it was wavering between liberalism and social-democracy. With the doctrine, the emphasis on democracy placed by the new leadership mirrored the inner conflict in the party and the political themes of the international seminars, rather than a central preoccupation of the population.

True, to come up at the end of 1992 with an ideology focusing on the necessity of political democracy meant a return to the problems specific of 1990. So, as the NSF local organization were decomposing, abandoned by the wage-earning city population that was disappointed by the conflict, and by the peasantry that was following Ion Iliescu, the party of Petre Roman too, was increasingly turning its face to the administration. The more so, as the private sector refused to join, complete with all effectives, in a party which was still too radical, on the one hand, and not credible enough, on the other hand. The NSF had still a big number of councillors and mayors in local governments and an important group of functionaries in the central one. In the autumn of 1992, when the elections were held, the only party that had really been popular in the post-revolution period, had already turned into two camps of the central and local administration that were competing for functions and privileges. Behind them, the two groups of the industrial technocracy – financial and enterprise -, both backing the same power system, continued their fight for its control, by giving political support to their own representatives in the administration against the opposite administrative camp.

As expected, on the eve of elections, the Romanian political life was dominated not so much by the election campaigns, as rather by the political intrigue inside the parties and among them. The formal winner of the elections was in the end the DNSF, but the main beneficiaries were the small parties that made together with the PSDR the new government coalition.

2. The Allies

At the time when the NSF still tried to keep a balance between the two wings of the industrial technocracy, and the governance, in order to improve its external image and the international relations, yielded to compromise after compromise for the benefit of the opposition, a series of small radical political parties were growing at the NSF's fringes. Their specific was to rally the categories of outcasts of the public and political life created by the reversal of the criteria by which the service records were judged. The opposition political parties had haughtily rejected the former political and intellectual elite of the communist regime, recuperating from among them only those who were useful through the viciousness of their attacks against the previous regime and through their credibility. The NSF had been more "flexible", accepting also the support of some "exes", but keeping them at the fringes of both the political party and the administration. Moreover, soon after the revolution, the NSF had to purge some institutions thought by the West to have been the mainstays of the old regime, such as the ministry of the interior and the security, a part of the army as well as the activists of the defunct communist party.

The Socialist Labor Party

Two important categories of people who had been active and influential before were now marginalized in public life. In order to overcome their handicap generated by the revolution, those people decided to develop their own political organizations. And that is how the Socialist Labor Party and the Greater Romania Party came into being.

The SLP was formed as a political party of former activists of the communist party, many of them loosely associated with Ceausescu or even opposed to him in one form or another along their career and having suffered the unfortunate consequence of seeing their ascent barred or of being demoted in the party hierarchy, or even of being ousted from public functions. The NCNSF had recuperated many of the popular figures of the mid-'60s ideological and political detente. Alexandru Barladeanu or Corneliu Manescu were the most representative examples but not the only ones. However, there was a far larger group of former politicians or party activists left outside the political game, who, as they were not accepted by any of the already existing parties, decided to make a party of their own. The SLP was formed like all the other political parties from that angle. Its mission was to create for a small group of former communist party activists the legal form of access to functions in the state and in the public administration. Just like the other political parties, the SLP did not have a policy of its own, did not develop a doctrine and an outlook on the transition. In the beginning, it considered itself a descendant of the former communist party, for propaganda reasons – in order to recover the big number of RCP activists that the revolution had pushed to the periphery of the society -, and also for pragmatic reasons associated with the first intention to claim at least some shreds of the former communist party's wealth. But, it had to accept the revolution and not only Ceausescu's fall but also the fall of socialism. In its new program, it made no more mention of the whole people's ownership of the production means and it no longer considered capitalism to be the enemy. But it proved to be the most severe critic of the economic reform pursued by the post-revolution governments.

The attempt to make political capital on account of the discontents generated by the post-revolution governance was neither the invention not the monopoly of the SLP. Absolutely all political parties, starting with the historic ones an ending with the DNSF employed that theme in their political propaganda. But, the SLP concentrated its activity in the big working-class centers, that were endangered by the crisis of some of the huge iron-and-steel or machine-building combines. It developed in those zones precisely the ideology of the enterprise technocracy, insisting on the state's support to such enterprises, on a good management by local technicians as a way out of the crisis and, obviously, obtained its support on a local plane. Likewise, it gave a high profile to the local activists that had had a good image also before the revolution and whose local patriotism was known by the population and appreciated at least by some. Adding to that the important number of ballots that could be given to it by the former communist party activists and campaigners, the SLP managed to become a parliamentary party after the 1992 elections. But it remained a regional party, influential only in several big workers' centers and recently urbanized areas in Oltenia and southern Moldova.

For the NSF, the emergence of the SLP meant at first quite a relief. A party placed, obviously because of its name and leaders, to the left of the NSF, allowed it to reject a big party of the opposition's accusation, credible abroad, than it was only the party of the former communist nomenklatura. Subsequently, when the conflict started between the NSF and DNSF, the latter found a natural ally in the SLP which vehemently attacked the Roman government, promoted an ideology that was not very different from its own and, besides, it afforded to assert stands which many of the DNSF new political leaders agreed but could not state themselves for reasons associated especially with the international image. Such were for instance the reluctance about the foreign capital and the maintenance of the state subsidies for industry, as well as the price control and the control of the hard currency. Generally, the SLP opposed far more efficiently all attempts to dismantle the mechanisms that allowed the pumping of resources from other domains of the economy to industry, and the DNSF representatives of the enterprise technocracy were only too pleased to back such positions. Just as pleased they were also with the fact that such initiatives did not have to come from their direction.

But the fundamental problem of the SLP, and still is, if it wanted to leave behind its position as a peripheral party of the disoriented and discontented ones, it had also to propose something to mend the "errors" so severely criticized with the other. And in this respect the SLP was just as lost as the other parties. After the 1992 elections, it had obtained the maximum of benefits from such a situation – it had become a party to the government coalition and some of its politicians, second-line ones, had already been promoted to important administrative functions, like state secretary with the Ministry of Culture, etc. However, it abstained from pressing too hard for a share in the government (and the DNSF abstained from accepting, for the same reasons of external image) and had endorsed the principle of permanently voting in support of the DNSF government, all while criticizing its rule on the same permanent basis. It could thus double-deal, benefitting from the small privileges and advantages it could get from an indebted administration, while refusing to share with it the responsibilities of the acts of governing. Moreover, its principal public voice, Adrian Paunescu, former court poet of Ceausescu and his wife, dominated the whole parliamentary group of the government coalition, by the courage, vehemence and theatrical talent of his speeches.

The SLP had reached the climax of its trajectory by mid-1993, when the coalition between it and the ruling party became safe and its breaking by a possible coalition between the PSDR and the opposition, impossible. Any subsequent growth could have been achieved only through its transformation into a genuine political party, equipped with a program, with an outlook on transition and with political objectives addressed to the population and the economy and not to the destiny of its political leaders. Thanks to a congenial conjuncture, the SLP was exactly the party with the most numerous chances to cross the threshold between a group of ambitious and wire-pulling politicians and a political party. The SLP was the only political party that could define a social basis for itself. It did not have one but it could find it in the working class and might have oriented its policy toward representing its interests. But that would have meant to give up the interests of its own political leaders, interests that pushed them to accepting any compromise with the administrative bureaucracy. In the end, the SLP followed more shyly and less successfully, the general policy that all PSDR allies would follow. It considered of the gradual penetration of the central and local administration, both by obtaining administrative offices for their own political clients, and by alluring to party membership the state functionaries who considered – and rightly so – that the association with one of the coalition parties was a guarantee. And so, just like all the other parties, the SLP followed the "normal" evolution of gradually identifying itself with a group inside the administration.

The Greater Romania Party and the Romanian National Unity Party

Before becoming a party, Greater Romania was a magazine, which means that it ought to have an ideology. Its name was borrowed from history. It meant the dream, come true after World War One, of reuniting around the kingdom of Romania (consisting originally of the Romanian Principalities, Moldavia and Walachia, proclaimed independent of the Ottoman Empire in 1878) of all Romanian lands that historical vicissitudes kept bringing in and out of Romanian jurisdiction, as neighboring empires won or lost deals or wars: northern Bucovina and Transylvania, reclaimed from Austria-Hungary, Basarabia, reclaimed from Russia. Some of those lands – northern Bucovina and Basarabia – are even now part of neighboring states's territories. But the Romania Mare (in Romanian: Greater Romania) magazine was less meant to promote a package of ides than to sustain a polemic which the NSF political leaders seemed willing but unable to sustain themselves. Not by the means of the magazine. In broad lines, the Romania Mare magazine, which was Corneliu Vadim Tudor's personal initiative, was and keeps being made of two distinct parts. One comprises only and solely attacks against the opposition, against the historic parties first of all. The attacks arrest the attention by their vehemence and special construction, as Romania Mare does not argue with its enemies, it ridicules them.

In politics, ridicule is a more powerful weapon than rational argument. Romania Mare turned a deaf ear to rational arguments or to the real content of political polemics. It divided the world into two: ours and theirs, where "ours" were good and expected to win, and "theirs" were evil and inevitably doomed to lose. Once established who were "ours" and who "theirs", it was a useless effort for Romania Mare to prove which is which. It went without saying and the magazine was addressed only to those who were already convinced of it. What the magazine did was ridicule "theirs", by using all classical procedures of the satirical literature. It did not matter what was actually saying or doing Doina Cornea, for instance, one of the magazine's favorite targets. What mattered was her silly cap and high-pitched voice. What mattered were the nick-names of them created precisely by the magazine, and the twisted words, the violent language and the grotesque of the imaginary scenes where sex or sports or even cuisine were associated with politics.

Obviously, such a literature was successful with a big part of the population (just as another satirical tabloid, Academia Catavencu was successful with another part). Just the same, it appealed to numerous politicians of the governance, who suffered because of the disbalance created between the popular support they could get in elections and the power ceremonies in which they acted a leading part, on the one hand, and the negative image created by the mass media, mainly siding with the opposition, on the other hand. So, the magazine was read with the same satisfaction with which America's stressed drivers threw tomatoes at cop figures in places specially arranged on speedways. The people would let off the steam, by reading insults against their political adversaries which they could not dare or would not have the opportunity to fancy and speak out aloud.

The other part of the magazine was quite different. It was politics there, simple, imbued with nationalism and that in a first stage had only one target – Hungary and the alleged international plot it staged against Romania. The political statements and actions of the Hungarian government and of the HDUR offered numerous opportunities to sustain it. Subsequently, Romania Mare became the promoter of nationalism matched by xenophobia because the initial premise was extended in a theorem that sounded like this: Hungary and the Hungarian lobbies abroad have managed to mobilize the international community against the Romanians.

The simple ideology of Greater Romania, employed in a less vehement, but even less elaborated form also by the RNUP and the nationalist "tribunes" of the DNSF might be summed up like this: Romania is an extremely beautiful and rich country and always, along its history, the countries around it have tried either to occupy or to subjugate it. And this is what is being tried now, so any negative or critical attitude towards Romania is part of a big conspiracy meant to weaken the country inside and make it vulnerable outside. Those who carry on such attacks against the governance to the country are either knowing agents of the anti-Romanian forces, or unknowing, naive ones manipulated by knowing agents. In such difficult periods, there have always been groups of Romanians who, in spite of the adverse balance of forces, heroically opposed the aggressors and, sometimes, they have managed to thwart their schemes. Now, this group is rallied around the Romania Mare magazine and has Corneliu Vadim Tudor as its leader. Precisely because this group is opposing obscure schemes of conquering Romania, it is fiercely attacked by the agents of such schemes. Hence, one more step forward can be taken, meaning that any attack against Vadim or his supporters is an attack against Romania's sovereignty and independence. Of course, the magazine took that step as well, regarding the criticism against him as lese majesty. If one cares to add to this an endless supply of scenarios involving espionage services, occult power centers, international conspiracies, etc., one will get the classical picture of paranoia.

But such an image is deceptive. The authors of Romania Mare are not paranoic, although they employ precisely the methods that make the paranoics convince themselves of the truthfulness of their own hallucinations. Their initial popularity resided precisely in the fact that they expressed the resentments of important categories of the population that saw themselves all of a sudden marginalized and despised because they had lost the war. Corneliu Vadim Tudor himself belonged to them. Once a court poet of the Ceausescu, author of numberless hymns dedicated to the couple, he had not even the fame enjoyed, for instance, by Adrian Paunescu, of having been a great lyrical poet. Nationalism, which he had to attribute to Ceausescu as well, was his only excuse and that is why he exacerbated it.

Obviously, he was not the only one. Two important groups, for which the SLP was not a solution, joined the Greater Romania Party. First, a group of military, army, militia or securitate officers who were purged after the revolution, often only because they had held relatively important functions in the respective institutions, or, even more simple, because they stood in the way of spectacular ascents, that were numerous after the revolution, both in the army and in the Interior forces. The other group mainly consisted of intellectuals, especially historians and men of letters, the main partisans of the nationalism promoted by Ceausescu himself in all the twenty years of his "rule". They were joined by a big number of pensioners, either retired officers, or intellectuals for whom patriotism was no idle speech and who were unable to explain the country's pre- and post-revolution degradation, unless they referred to the conspiracy against Romania.

Of course, such a heteroclite combination generated big oscillations in the policy promoted by the magazine. For instance, when it came to identifying the major adversary. Hungary offered itself as a privileged target, but Hungary was too small and too weak to represent by itself a convincing explanation. Behind Hungary, one could identify the West, first of all the Americans, because for a while they openly sustained the political ascent of the opposition, or, in a traditionalist variant, like in the interbellum period, the Jews, considered to have made an occult international connection of power. But, many of the officers and intellectuals rallied around the magazine were not so much anti-Western as they were anti-Soviet, on an ideological line on which Ceausescu has built his political autonomy and his credibility with the West, and they considered that the major danger was coming from the East and not from the West. The result of that line was the apology of marshal Antonescu, for whom the magazine was building an image as an patriot and victim of the Soviets. That ideological hotchpotch ultimately led to an image of Romania surrounded by enemies. It is not surprising that, although identifying a big numbers of enemies, România Mare does not identify any ally and, although most of its theses spring from the interpretation of international conjunctures, it simply does not have a foreign policy idea.

A magazine, even one that promotes relatively successful ideologies, does not justify such a detailed analysis here, but, on the eve of the 1992 elections, România Mare became a political party – Greater Romania Party, and won enough ballots to enter the parliament. In November 1992 it was included in the government coalition, with which it signed a protocol of collaboration in February 1995 and, in spite of the numerous clashes with the rational politicians of the ruling party, and mainly with President Iliescu, it has remained one of its reliable members to this day.

Quite the opposite was the evolution of the RNUP. The GRP was born as the action of a group of people who wanted a room at the top of the society and that, for that purpose, endorsed a sham ideology. Instead, the RNUP was born around an ideology and ended by being a simple group of people who wanted to secure a lukewarm place for themselves in the society. The RNUP emerged as a reaction not so much to the formation of the HDUR, as to the political and ideological pressure put up by it or around it. Because of the historical experience, the population in Transilvania is far more sensitive to a potential Hungarian danger than the population in any other region of the country. And immediately after the 1989 revolution, such a danger did not seem impossible at all. Not only were eccentric voices of marginal groups inside and outside – extremist organizations, groups of Hungarian emigrants in the two Americas, etc. – heard now louder than usual, but even officials of the Budapest government made really worrying statements, such as that about the rejection of the Trianon Peace Treaty, etc. All these things, plus the effects of the policy of self-enclavization of the Hungarian minority, promoted by the HDUR, were perceived far more acutely in Transylvania than in Bucharest, and the Romanians in the region, considering that Bucharest was unable to understand what was happening, chose to create their own political organization. The RNUP, set up in Cluj, a city with rich traditions in the Romanians' fight for national emancipation in the past century and at the beginning of this one.

So, unlike all the other small parties, the RNUP had from the onset a mass social basis and focussed its ideology and political profile on themes that were quite different from those of the other parties. Absolutely all major issues of transition were secondary to the RNUP which viewed everything as subordinated to the essential problem – what will be Transylvania's destiny? Therefore, in spite of similar rhetoric, the difference between the GRP and RNUP was essential, at least in the incipient period. Whereas the GRP promoted an aggressive ideology of Romanianism, with very strong implications as to the hierarchy of the groups that had access to power, since after all what it was after was the acceptance of its own group among those entitled to claim the power, the RNUP promoted an ideology of resistance to the offensive of Hungarianism. That program-like self-limitation meant at the same time the RNUP's most important asset and the biggest handicap.

The asset was the RNUP's possibility to address all Romanians in Transylvania, irrespective of their stand or views on all the other matters of the transition. As long as the danger seemed imminent, between 1990 and 1991, the RNUP had no difficulty with getting important support in the sensitive zone, meaning Trasylvania. On the other hand, precisely because it ignored all the other problems, far more acutely perceived in the other regions of the country, its impact there was incomparably weaker. The anti-Hungarianism was meaningless in Moldova or Oltenia, whereas the problems of privatization, the monarchy or the attitude toward the foreign capital were far more important. Therefore, in the zones, the GRP simple nationalist ideology, that entailed options as regarded the problems of transition, was more pervasive, but it had a negligible impact in Transylvania.

Just as heterogenous as the HDUR from a political point of view, the RNUP started being sapped by inner problems as soon as the "Hungarian danger" was heeded less by public opinion. One of the sources was precisely the RNUP's fundamental ambiguity in all major issues of the transition. A liberal wing and a technocratic one seemed to slowly develop inside the RNUP, but that process of clarification was dwarfed by a more rapid structuring among groups of leaders who were competing for the privileges entailed by the position as a politician at a national level. An inner strife started in the RNUP which, on the eve of the 1992 elections, ended with the victory of the most radical wing, led by Gheorghe Funar, first because it was it that carried the simplest and most clear message. In his campaign for presidency, Gheorghe Funar realized that the RNUP's anti-Hungarian message was not enough to win him ballots also in the other regions of the country. Therefore, he tried to add a liberal message, a declaratory reformism which he should be able to oppose to the more complex but more moderate message of President Ion Iliescu. The fact that such an attempt totally failed, with Gheorghe Funar getting for presidency a lesser support than the RNUP got for the Parliament, convinced soon the hardliners that the if they wanted to get ballots and popular support, the only and safest way was to confine themselves to anti-Hungarianism and the rhetoric of the endangered nation.

The 1992 elections propelled the RNUP not only to the Parliament, but also to the government coalition where it was an uncertain, uncomfortable and compromising ally for the technicians of the administration. But it became the more indispensable as the political intrigue was growing more complex and the keeping of the alliance with the RNUP became for the leadership of the ruling party a condition not only of keeping itself in power. A new stage was beginning in the Romanian political life, in which the parties' role was increasingly being taken over by the trans-political pressure groups in the Parliament. The stage of the original parties was followed by a new stage, of "parliamentary democracy".

3. The Political Parties' Administrative Basis

The stage of the "original parties" ends in the period right after the 1992 elections. Its main feature is that political parties are not included in the power system, although they keep playing an important role in the system of legitimation of the power. Such a paradoxical situation is possible only because of the lack of importance of the political parties' activity. What matters is their simple existence, the fact that they are more than one, have differing names, participate in election campaigns and elections proper and allow for the holding of the Parliament seats according to a system of rules recognized as legitimate by the international community. Consequently, the system of political parties is very important for the attainment of the objective of the first transition, the one meant for international integration. Second, it is important for securing the legitimacy of the real power system, built behind this pseudo-political "cover" of the parties.

As demonstrated earlier, such a situation was not result of some plot or shrewd manoeuvering of the real holders of the power – the industrial technocracy and administrative bureaucracy. The main factor that allowed this to happen was, above all, the current political parties' chronical inability of assuming real political objectives that should allow them to master and model the transition. The parties were simply unable to go past their initial condition as simple groups of claimants on public honours and functions. The fact that the society did very well without a political leadership – based on the power system created after the revolution – facilitated the maintenance of the parties at this embryonic stage.

In time, they have developed the mechanisms needed for exercising the role assigned to them and which they have accepted without wondering at least whether they ought to be or to do more. They have developed a specific set of problems, on which the big debates inside parties and the polemics among them proceed. The monarchy, the relations with the Hungarians and, for a change, with the Jews and Gypsies, the external image, Basarabia, etc., these are the major political issues of the Romanian politicians. Of course, they do not ignore the real issues of the economy or social life, for instance, but they transfigure these issues up to a form that should allow for their "political" approach, meaning free of any relevant content for reality.

The privatization is a good example in this respect. In principle, it ought to be one of the directions of the economic reform, which would mean first a clear political option, followed by a technical process, rather sophisticated because of the countless connections between privatization and the other components of the economic policy. But, in the Romanian policy the privatization has been used as a label in the polemic with the political adversary. The basic idea is that, just as in connection with the economic reform there are some that are more reformist than others, in connection with the privatization there are some more dedicated to privatization than others. The simplest ideology that has developed against the background of the polemic focussed on the false question "Who is the greatest adept of privatization in Romania?" Has towered the Romanian political life for four years. For a while, the domain was monopolized by the Opposition parties. They built their electoral campaign and lived politically for two years after the elections, especially by accusing the government coalition and the cabinet of the absence of a real will to implement the privatization. Moreover, even the parties in the government coalition employed the theme in order to retain some own identity in relation to the PSDR and to compensate the negative image that went with their stand on other problem such as the national one. The RNUP tried for a while to distinguish itself from the PSDR precisely being more concerned with the privatization.

But, at the beginning of 1994, bored of being permanently accused that it opposed the privatization, the ruling party launched the slogan of mass privatization, meaning the concomitant privatization of an important number of enterprises, announcing a government program of privatization of three thousand enterprises inside one year, a program which obviously did not go past the stage of fine intentions. Meanwhile, the political contest on "who wants more and faster privatization?" continued, new and new privatization programs were launched both by political parties and by more or less independent politicians who wanted to build for themselves an image as reform-oriented. And so it happened that since the passing of the privatization law in 1992 until the end of 1994 the working out of programs, models and methods of privatization, as well as the polemic on them replaced the privatization as a process by a torrent of paper matched by an ever heavier torrent of words. The only common point reached after that polemic was the general agreement on the necessity of a different privatization than the one that began with the passing of that law and on everything having to be started all over again. The result of that belief materialized in the Law of Speeding up the Privatization, proposed by the Vacaroiu government in the summer of 1994. Its history, which rather consists of mere anecdotes, is extremely significant as regards the absence of a real content of Romanian politics. In the first half of 1994 all parties felt comfortable in the absence of a real process of privatization. The PSDR and its allies were just putting together, in the parties' political apparatus, the mechanism of political-administrative control of the economy, consequently they had no intention whatsoever to waste their work by transferring the enterprises' control to entrepreneurs and investors, either Romanian or foreign. Therefore, where the privatization was concerned, the government coalition was favoring especially the MEBO system which allowed also for the demagogy about the "popular capitalism", and also preserved the control in the hands of the extant management, which, in turn, was politically controlled. The Opposition too, was happy that the PSDR was not venturing in privatization, as in that way it had a matter to grudge about and to point out the political difference between itself and the government coalition. And it also could show itself to advantage to the public opinion both at home and abroad. That harmony of interests was smashed in the summer of 1994, when President Ion Iliescu, responding to international pressures, most emphatically asked the government to do something about expediting the privatization.

The government's response was the Law of Speeding up the Privatization, which became in fact the main instrument by which the privatization was almost totally blocked for a whole year. Except for its title, the law does not at all refer to speeding up the privatization. It rather entails the taking of the whole process all over from the beginning again, with the distribution, on account of the 30% earmarked free to the population, of coupons meant to replace the property certificates issued by the Roman government. Improvised in less than a week, during the parliamentary recess, when the PSDR, as a party, was inert, it was a governmental, not political, initiative and it therefore encountered the immediate resistance put up precisely by the government majority. It took one year of debates, discussions and convincing work with the government politicians to have them ultimately pass a law that, in its essence, does not change a bit of the old law. But the amount of speeches, articles, interviews, statements and polemics that followed on that matter is huge. One can say that a "live political activity" proceeded in connection with the law, a true godsend both for the parties of the parliamentary majority and for those of the Opposition. Obviously, that "political" approach to the privatization is irrelevant for the economy and for the real problem of its transformation. But for the parties it is the necessary surrogate for maintaining the appearance that they still address the reality.

The fact that there was an ever bigger gap between the political parties and the reality appeared as obvious already in 1991, in the analysis of the activity of the Constituant Assembly and of the political parties' attitude toward the fundamental problems posed by the articulation of a Constitution. The local elections in 1992 made that reality and its perception even more clear. At about the time when the NSF started to fall apart because on an equally false package of problems, and the Democratic Convention was coming into being outside any political option, as a group of claimants for whom the options about transition were secondary in relation to the supreme objective of holding the functions of representation in the state, the "A Future for Romania" Group tried to announce the end of the political parties in the form in which they had come into being soon after the revolution and the necessity of their transformation. Although put in a scientific form hard to understand by public opinion and politicians alike, the message was too strongly sustained by reality not to be credible, but its success was drastically limited by the drawing near of the parliamentary and presidential elections of 1992. The ebullience for the clarification of the options inside the parties was actually "frozen" by the prospect of the elections and replaced by the more pragmatic struggle among groupings for imposing their own candidates on prominent places in the electoral lists.

So, if they did not deal with politics, what were the political parties and politicians dealing with? First, with the inner relations of the parties. There is an extremely low limit that ensures the unity of a political party built on the criteria and objectives of the parties now in existence, and it is set by the small number of members a political leader's entourage can bear. Once this number is outgrown, the competition among leaders begins in any party, a competition among entourages. The major parties of the country, be they in power or in the opposition, were big enough to have three or four groups each, engaged in a permanent, more or less overt, strife inside them.

The strife remained underground as long as by public image or personality a leader managed to dominate the party and to keep his rivals in an inferior position. It is the case, for instance, of the CDNPP, where Corneliu Coposu managed to keep his dominant position in relation to Ion Ratiu and other, less outstanding leaders, of Petre Roman, who continued to dominate the Democratic Party, although competitor groups emerged, or of the SLP in which Ilie Verdet won the battle versus the group who challenged him, forcing it out of the party. In situation when several leaders came to have close positions, the strife would become open and splits occured. It is the case of the NSF, already mentioned, or of the numerous splits of the Liberals. When the dissenters did not have power enough to cause the party to split, they resorted to migration, as did the dissenters of the Civic Alliance Party, Democratic Agrarian Party of Romanian or Greater Romania Party. That situation generated a real politician hunt, especially among parliamentarians, with the parties trying to obtain by new enrolments of deputies and senators what they did not manage to win in elections, meaning a bigger number of ballots in the Parliament.

In periods between elections, the internal problems become more important than those of the relations among parties, which is an important condition favoring the "parliamentary democracy" that is tending to get entrenched now. But, the strife among parties keep being the second major occupation of the politicians. The function of the strife among parties is to define the political problems and keep them topical. Since, because of the gap between parties and reality, the political problems do not have a source in reality, they have to be created. The mission of the fight among parties is precisely to create them concomitant with the impression that the parties are doing something. The mechanism consists of an endless train of news conferences, statements, releases and speeches. They are not so much addressed to the public as to the adversaries, who respond by the same means. An absolutely essential role in this process devolves to the mass media that, if they ceased to reproduce the political statements that generate political acts, would let the Romanian political life die probably in a few weeks. But, as they have to come up with political coverages, the newspapers, radio and TV stations take over all these "messages", extend them with an impressive amount of inferred significance and probable scenarios and thus keep alive a political activity is mostly pointless and useless.

Obviously, after five years, all this useless fuss has lost much of its popularity. Whereas in the beginning the population was unreservedly – and indiscriminately – getting involved in the battle among the political parties, it started withdrawing from politics as the divorce between politics ant the reality was getting more obvious. That, of course, faced the political parties with important problems, the most serious of all being not so much the absence of an attendance, since they do talk among themselves, but of party membership and of the mass of supporters. Under the circumstances, the parties were running the risk of simply thawing away, with nothing left but the group of leaders and their close entourage.

To counter that process, they turned to the bureaucracy, the most efficient way of keeping an organization alive. The classical solution is to build a party's own bureaucracy after the hyperstatist model of the communist party. Such a bureaucracy was however extremely expensive and the more difficult to built as one went lower on its hierarchic levels and closer to the population that has just quit politics. Therefore the need to be more than just an isolated group of leaders, the political parties turned to the already existing bureaucracy, meaning to the administration. It is not a new orientation. In the inter-bellum period, the "historic" parties relied on the interconnections with the administration. After 1948, the communist party had established a hierarchic connection between its own political bureaucracy and the one of the administration, which allowed for the relatively separate maintenance of the two. But, after the revolution, such a relation was no longer possible. The solution endorsed by parties was to gradually reunite their own bureaucracies with the administrative bureaucracy. They made a double move for that purpose. A first component consisted of appointing to administrative functions their own political clientele, the party members or even leaders who in a normal organization, would have held exclusively party functions.

Obviously, such a method comes in hand more for the parties of government coalitions but, in Romania the political intrigue made possible the access in this way to the administration also of representatives of the Opposition. That is how come into being, after the Vacaroiu Government's investiture, the Reform Council, first made up mainly of representatives or supporters of the Opposition. By some sort of tacit compromise, the principle of some success of the Opposition to the administration was accepted by everybody and it is it that has led to such a strange mechanism of appointment of public functionaries according to political allegiance, as is consecrated by law in the case of the Television, Radio Broadcasting or Property Funds.

The other method consisted of alluring public functionaries to political parties. This method is equally used by all parties, with various degrees of success. An important advantage goes to the parties in the government coalition that can sanction by administrative means the refusal of political integration. Both methods are in principle criticized by all political parties and equally practised by all, and the battle fought is fierce enough to give rise to another series of endless polemics in the political arena. And the last and only legitimate method is to win the local elections and take over in this way the control over the local administration, the role of which in the power system is extremely important.

The process of integration of the political parties with the administration has gained momentum after the 1992 elections, when the political system started adjusting itself to the new stage of the "parliamentary democracy". The integration was facilitated precisely by the parties "originality". After all, it was precisely the objective which the parties were after – to have the functions of representation or that entailed privileges in the state administration occupied by their own political leaders. Two years after the 1992 elections, the political parties tended to reduce themselves more and more to a position of mere subgroups within the administration fighting among themselves for the redistribution of the highest administrative functions. Very soon, the government reshuffle and the possible government change came to mean nothing more than the possibility of occupying, with the own clientele, the peak administrative functions.

Such an evolution of the parties means at the same time a restriction and an extension. A restriction, since they are thus tangibly restricting their ability of becoming the standard-bearers of important social categories or groups and of doing real policy. It also means an extension, since the parties cease being simple annexes of their political leaders. On the contrary, the leaders start now being regarded as political spokespersons of the administrative group which they have "swallowed up".

The political intrigue, and the political battles start reflecting more and more the confrontations inside the administration. The scandals around the Ministry of Culture or, even more spectacular, the scandals of the selling out of the Romanian merchant fleet and those concerning some economic activities of the army, a part of the political strife on the banks' executives or on the national corporations, are rather the reflex in the political sphere of the confrontation among various groups inside the administration than polemics of a direct political nature. The final result is worrying though. The parties' integration in the administration, a process in which it is the administration that assimilates the parties than the other way round, annuls almost all politics and also the chances of a revigoration of politics through a spectacular "transfiguration" of the parties.

VI. INDUSTRIAL TECHNOCRACY'S WAY TO POWER

The industrial technocracy has been the main beneficiary of the December revolution, but it had to go a long and thorny way for this. First, it had to prepare the revolution, creating an alternate ideology to replace the ideology of society's leadership by the political vanguard of the working class. It had to win the administration over and it did it by simply penetrating the administration and by taking over a part of its key positions. The revolution brought its liberation from the domination of the communist party's political bureaucracy, but with that the problems of the industrial technocracy were not over. It had barely ridden itself of a political control and was threatened with another one, in the name of the revolution this time. The dismantlement of the NSF enterprise Councils was the moment when, at long last, the industrial technocracy broke free of any political control. Moreover, it was capable to formulate and promote itself political decisions of the most important ones. But the power system was formed and got stabilized only later, when the technocracy devised the ways of cooperation with the administrative system. It took quite a while to have everybody convinced that such a cooperation was absolutely indispensable.

In the summer of 1990, the industrial technocracy had already overcome its biggest post-revolution problem: the challenging of its power right in the industrial enterprise. In a first stage, the challenge have come from the revolutionaries who had organized themselves politically. Subsequently, it came from the trade unions. The trade unions, that got reorganized after the revolution, started immediately the attack on the enterprises' and institutions' technical and administrative management. By some kind of leader's instinct, the union leaders understood very soon that they and their organizations would not survive and people would identify soon an adversary, and even one that could be defeated. To begin with, they equated the adversary with the enterprises' managers. What contributed to that was the general tendency after the revolution to change as many executives as possible and the general resentment toward the authority exercised under the old regime and the ambitions of other candidates for executive functions. In the first months after the revolution, by manoeuvering larger or smaller groups of workers, always noisy and aggressive, the union leaders managed to change sometimes several series of managers and also to get spectacular pay rises, extras of all kind, work time cuts, etc. Almost a year passed before the relations between managers and trade unions reached an equilibrium and the trade unions changed their fire, targeting it, instead of the enterprise managers, against the central administration, better said against the government. The change was also favored by the opposition political parties' efforts toward turning to their advantage the pressure and propaganda potential of the union movement, as well as the trade unions' gradual organization at a national level. The leaderships of the trade union federations and confederations had to take over the fight at their level in order to justify their usefulness, and they did not have managers to fight against. So, they fought directly against the government, and their claims rapidly took the form of elements of economic or social policy and, sometimes, even a direct political form.

Although the power system was still under construction at that stage, the technocracy was already able to influence to a great extent the political decisions through the "technological requirements" of the production. As a matter of fact, it was in that period of improvised leadership and use of the power that were articulated the two main instruments by which the technocracy models the administrative and political decisions. One is the threat the economic results of its activity can pose at the macroeconomic stability. Romania had to go through a grave economic crisis for such a mechanism to be eventually established. The other was the threat of the danger entailed by the social consequences of economic and political decisions that seem advisable at certain moment. The first great victory scored by technocracy was the "price liberalization" in the autumn of 1990. The price liberalization was a reform-oriented name given to a process otherwise quite well known to Romanians by the name of "price rise". After more than half a year of pay rises, work time cuts, decline in labor productivity and bad management, the only way in which the industrial enterprises could still continue their activity was to increase the prices. Theoretically, the price liberalization was considered to be a step ahead toward setting in motion the autonomous mechanisms of the market. The prices, they said, would be established on the relations between demand and supply. That manual equation was however quite unrealistic, at least for the Romanian economy, because most of the producer enterprises had a market socialist economy. The second big victory was the development of that new mechanism of unlimited subsidising, through bank credits. That mechanism was, from the technocracy's viewpoint, superior to the budget subsidy mechanism – although it too, was retained for some industries and for agriculture for a long time, and part of it still exists, although not officially – because it eliminated the administration's control over the destination of the subsidies. Finally, the third big success of the technocracy in inducing the decisions on economic policy was the financial blockage. The financial blockage proved that when the technocracy decides not to obey by the economic rules established by the administration, the latter has no other choice than to change the rules. One of the rules is that a buyer has to pay for the commodity, product or service, which he buys. The administration, with all its legislative and institutional mechanism, is the warrantor of the observance of this rule. When the enterprises simply refused to pay, through a mass violation of the rule that seemed elementary, the administration had no choice and accepted that new rule of the game: when the enterprises do not pay, the administration pays, more exactly, the administration makes the nation pay. When the enterprises no longer wanted or were able to pay, their debts were written off and they were given more money to pay the salaries – in order to keep the social stability – and to go on with the production until the next financial blockage. In the five years that have elapsed since the revolution there were three financial blockages and all of them were settled by the same recipe.

Those victories and many other, smaller, ones have proved that the industrial technocracy can dominate the decision, through the agency of the administration and of the government, without having to take over directly the management of the economy and of the country. But it took a while until the lesson was learned and, especially, until the new mechanisms of communication between technocracy and administration were established.

For, the technocracy's major handicap in administrating the power is its lack of unity. Communism had managed to ensure a unity of the technocracy, but it had done so through a common subordination of the technocracy, political bureaucracy and administration (the economic ministries) as well as by having the economy bear the negative effects of political decisions. The revolution and the reforms that followed eliminated those dependencies, but they crumbled the technocracy. For a while, those circuits tended to remake themselves as the technocracy tried to build a new unity at an administrative level, using the ministerial bureaucracy for that. Therefore, when the Law of Commercial Companies tried to undo the bureaucratic-type ties between ministries and central departments on the one hand, and the industrial enterprises, on the other hand, it was not only the "conservative bureaucracy" in ministries that opposed, but also the enterprises' managers. It seemed as if surrealistic anecdotes attributed to cultural stereotypies were revived: the enterprises executives want to be subordinated from an administrative point of view because they are not able or do not know how to solve the problems by themselves. And they really could not, as long as the industry as a whole could not survive without a centralized redistribution to its advantage of the national resources.

Another process took place concomitantly, that would have a decisive influence on the power system: a change in the relations between the industrial elites. In the period of industrial development of the '70s, an elite of the industrial technocracy came into being, which later on represented the nucleus of opposition to Ceausescu and his economic policies and the main promoter of the alternate ideology that de-legitimated the communist power system That elite consisted of the technocrats that were closest to the peak technologies. It was dominated by engineers and it was concentrated in the research and design institutes as well as in the technologically more advanced isles – the computer counters or newer enterprises like Oltcit, or enterprises associated with what meant high-tech for the Romanian industry, like the aviation industry, nuclear technologies, et. The post-revolution period brought about the destruction of the elite. The economic crisis that grew sharper since 1990 affected first of all the scientific research and design, which were virtually destroyed, and the high-tech enterprises, that lost their products' outlets. The economic crisis and the absence of any government policy oriented toward the technologically advanced industrial zones virtually led to the vanishing of that elite, consequent to its lack of economic competitiveness in the battle for power. The Romanian technological research and development, powerful in the pre-revolution period precisely because it was separated from production, through its financing forced by administrative means, became the victim precisely of that separation. Its last victory – the financing for a minimal keeping in operation, through a unitary contribution of one per cent of the whole industrial activity, then redistributed from the national budget – meant its dooming to the situation of simple annexe, deprived of power and real industrial function of an industry that secured its survival through en excessive consumption of either raw materials or energy, manpower, but anyway, not sensitive to the technological progress. The setting up in 1992 of a Ministry of Science and Technology, far from being able to redeem it to its pre-revolution privileged situation by tying it to the administration, turned it for good into a peripheral activity, like that of culture or environmental protection.

On the other hand, the crisis caused the emergence of another industrial elite, defined contingent upon the economic and financial might of the enterprises or the gravity of the social problems with which they can threaten the society or the political system, as is the case of the Jiu Valley mines or the Resita industrial zone. Obviously, central to them are industrial giants. Their managers make up the new industrial elite of Romania and they have taken over the role as leaders of the technocracy. Their way to power was not a smooth one. It took two years and the winning of more than one economic political battle.

1. Pushing the Humanist Elite Aside

For that, it had to eliminate several competitors, some potential, others already installed in power. Soon after the revolution, the main elite that approached the power was the intellectual elite of the Romanian cultural and artistic world. Of all elites, the humanist one had the greatest access to international mass media and public opinion, as many were known not only at home but also abroad. The population knew many by name and figure, and from among them some of the most popularized dissidents or protesters against Ceausescu had distinguished themselves. During the revolution they played an important role in mobilizing the mass and then, by TV appearances, in orienting the mass. Besides, they availed of the advantage of a precedent, the success of the Civic Forum of Czechoslovakia, that brought to power precisely that intelligentsia and that seemed to set a general model for the course of the anti-communist revolutions.

In spite of all those assets, relatively easy to use in the political battle, the cultural intelligentsia was not a serious adversary for the industrial technocracy. It should be stated from the beginning that the humanist elite had no understanding of the economic problems and it was ready from the onset to ignore and even sacrifice the Romanian industrial system complete with its technocracy. It was the bearer of an absolutely naive ideology about the meanings of the Romanian revolution and about how to turn it to advantage, even as regarded the orientation of the country's further evolution. By the very nature of their profession and activity, the members of that elite understood pre-revolution Romania's crisis especially as a human and moral crisis and felt more than other social categories the alienation that had been generated by the communist regime. After the revolution, they remained stuck with the same problems and, almost without realizing it, within their confines. They were the main promoters of all changes addressed to human rights and individual freedoms, but they completely ignored the fact that the real power was to be found where the resources were concentrated, meaning in the economy generally and in industry particularly.

For the technocracy and for its political representatives, concerned mainly with the economic problems and the further administration of the country, such problems were unimportant, but the changes proposed could do no harm. They could even help. On the one hand, they were taken very seriously by the West, as a signal of change, and, on the other hand, they maintained an absolutely necessary tension and pace of changes. And, as long as the humanist elite was caring especially about such problems, it remained harmless, in spite of its resolute joining, as early as the first days after the revolution, in the battle for taking over the control of the political power and the elimination of the grouping led by Ion Iliescu who was after all representing precisely the political interests of the technocracy.

But the same humanist elite was also the promoter of another direction of change. It considered that the revolution meant first of all a moral transformation and it dealt with it rather as with a new religion than with an opportunity to reorganize the society, the economy and the international relations. As a matter of fact, at least some of its representatives rapidly came at some sort of extremely unproductive political mysticism. The naive ideology which they promoted, influenced also by the turn-of-the-century speculative philosophies, made them think that, after half a century of dictatorship and communism Romania was morally ill and only a Jacobinic purification, based on self-flagellation matched by a witch hunt could deliver the society of communism. Communism itself was considered rather as an intellectual malady than a way of organization of the society and of the power. Therefore their essential thesis was that the change had to be first of all spiritual and moral in nature. Many of them had enjoyed favors and privileges during the communist regime and in certain periods they even had had important functions in the communist hierarchy. And the more inclined they were now to be tough and intolerant, as a way of dispelling any doubt about their own healing of the communist disease.

The Humanist Intelligentsia's Criticism of the Transition

Starting from that base, the humanist intelligentsia was the first that tried to articulate a criticism of communism, on the one hand, and of the transition on the other hand. It was also the only one that associated them with a direction formulated for the further development of the revolution. But the base it started from was precarious. Mostly, it was built by taking over the mythology specific of the cold war about the two societies that opposed each other – communist and capitalist. Therefore, both the explanations they produced and the solutions they proposed were either naive or extremely simplifying. Moreover, they ignored all economic and social realities and the fundamental requirements of the population that was obviously oriented toward construction and not toward destructive madness, no matter how purifying. The results matched the ideology.

Communism was simply equated with the "evil" and the evil was pictured with its classical features: jails, torture, apprehension and execution without a trial, arbitrary court decisions, terrorization of the population, a.s.o. Because they saw communism as a incarnation of the evil, they could in no way accept that it ever had a popular support. So, they explained its success and maintenance for half a century mainly on account of the characteristics of a regime of occupation capable of keeping the population obedient by force, and of suppressing a continuous clandestine resistance movement which succeeded in the end, in 1989, and the most recent representatives of which were precisely the humanist intellectuals. In broad lines, the story was not different from the one which the communists had produced about the former regime and the underground communist movement, in order to explain and legitimate their own success. And some of the active personalities of the new intellectualist movement had participated in building both stories.

Trying to find a convincing illustration of that image, the representatives of humanist intelligentsia had to conjure up events and characters from the '50s. What they did not realize was a criticism of the incipient communism of the '50s was inconsequential for the '90s. That period was over and it was not the December 1989 revolution that had ended it, but the industrial communism of the '60s and '70s. The objectives of the humanist intelligentsia was to trigger a trial of communism, starting from disclosures about the past period and leading it into the post-revolution period. Their whole strategy of access to the power relied on the possibility of using such a process in the fight against the new, postrevolution leaders. There was no more efficient way of ignoring the realities of the '90s than that.

And that doomed their offensive to total failure. In the beginning, the trial of communism was presented by its promoters and perceived by public opinion like some sort of witch hunt proclaimed against the former members of the communist party. Launched immediately after the victory of the revolution, in a public rally on the 1989 Christmas Eve, the idea was immediately and unanimously rejected and its immediate political objective – the elimination from the NCNSF of Ion Iliescu and the other former leaders of the communist party – failed. In a country that had had three million party members, the proposal to eliminate the communists from public life had no way of enjoying popularity. And in a revolution that depended totally on the army's congeniality, it was a grave political error, since 99 per cent of the army officers and cent per cent of the senior officers had been party members. In that month of December 1989, the leaders with political ambitions of the humanist intelligentsia were exulting because they had been able to rally without big difficulty several tens of thousands of people in the Palace Square in the Capital. But they completely ignored the effect which the slogans and objectives presented at that rally had on real factors of the power – the army, the administration, the economic managers. Actually, they ignored their very existence and capacity of reaction.

The failure extended even to the immediate form of those objectives, which was to eliminate in principle from the public life all those who had leading functions in the communist party, the famous point eight of the Timisoara Proclamation. That was another failure. Not that the population would have been very found of the former leaders of the communist party. But it was obvious again that the measure was targeted against Ion Iliescu who was the most popular figure in the country at the time. On the other hand, the procedure of making decisions about people in consideration of their "records", meaning of labels of a general character that did not take account of the individual himself in any way, was too similar to the procedures employed by the cadres' departments of the former communist party to be approved of. And those intellectuals could be – and were – criticized precisely for that thing, for the fact that they proposed an anti-communism just as impersonal, authoritarian and inflexible as the communism which they were condemning for precisely the same characteristics.

In the end, the trial of communism died lamentably. The idea of a string of trials staged to former communist dignitaries in the '50s was ridiculous and impossible to achieve. And the idea of staging a moral trial of communism, in the absence of Nuremberg-type trials, became obsolete, because nobody understood very well what such a moral trial meant, how could it be done and what would have been its concrete results

Just as simplistic and inefficient was the humanist intelligentsia's attempted criticism of transition. Since it ignored the economic and social realities, but, of course, it did not ignore the existence of the economic crisis and of the popular discounted, it tried to explain the failure of the transition according to the model by which the industrial technocracy built an ideology to explain the failure of communism. In brief, the economic crisis and the failures of the transition were to be blamed, to their mind, only on the post-revolution political leaders, naturally with Ion Iliescu on top of the list. They were no longer accused of incompetence, but straightly of ill will. They had betrayed the revolution and were now leading the country toward a disaster only in order to keep their leading functions which they had taken by conspiracy on the first days of the revolution. The solution was to have those leaders replaced by the true anti-communists, hence, by themselves. And to achieve that any means would be allowed, inclusive of "another revolution", by which they meant some sort of street insurrection that should take over the power by force. The humanist intelligentsia courted the idea from 1989 until 1992 when the passing of the new Constitution in the Parliament stabilized for good the post-revolution power system. The humanist intellectuals tried to win over all the intellectuals, through organizations like the Civic Alliance. They tried to convince the unions to join them. And they even turned for support to the underworld from which they recruited some sort of task forces that were responsible for the violent actions during demonstrations against the government or against the President.

Thus, paradoxically at first sight, it was precisely the humanist intelligentsia that developed a first form of post-revolution extremism and gave it a political and even doctrinary guise. Among other things, this made it more and more unpopular. But, for all its extremism, in the scarcity of options of any kind that characterized the post-revolution period, the political contour realized by the humanist intelligentsia was an important reference point. The political opposition endorsed all its theses and made them their own theses and built upon them not only the electoral campaigns but the whole political activity. As was expected, that is precisely why it lost, but anyway it did not have a choice, because it was incapable of building its own ideology and there was no other one to take over.

The Defeat

That specific of the ideology built by the humanist intelligentsia had also other consequences. First, it allowed the technocracy to adopt an offensive strategy against the humanist intelligentsia, identifying it as a grouping and its personalities with its own exaggerations. Second, it made possible for the humanist intelligentsia to be presented as an inflexible grouping which, at the time when compromise became the watchword in the Romanian political system, essentially contributed to its elimination from the political mechanism.

The technocracy's attack on the humanist intelligentsia was the tougher as the danger that it should really seize the power was real, especially all along the year 1990. On the other hand, it was easy to defeat it, for all the political, financial and logistic support it got from abroad. Its weaknesses were even bigger that its assets. The humanist intelligentsia was not only ignorant of the economic and social realities but it had absolutely no ties with the administration and technocracy alike, including the influential military technocracy. It has never managed to extend its connections to the workers or farmers, or at least to the new layer of entrepreneurs that was coming into being at the periphery of the state economy. Partly aware of these weaknesses, it tried a rapprochement to some trade unions, capitalizing on their leaders' political ambitions, but to no avail. The trade unions themselves were too much tied to the managers of the industrial enterprises and the governmental administration with which they were negotiating, so they could not ignore those, as the humanist intelligentsia professed in theory and practice.

That elite's second big weakness was that it could not hold other power than the political one, and for getting that power it could rely only on the electorate's ballots. Or, that is precisely that made it more vulnerable, on the one hand because of its political message and, on the other hand, because of its elitist character that made it attribute to the common people not only an inferior statute but also less attention. The specific of its theses managed to attract primarily the group that considered that, for one reason or another, a witch hunt would be to their advantage, and those were not very numerous. By bringing together also the partisans of the numerous opposition parties, the Civic Alliance managed in November 1990 to mobilize, together with all the other opposition parties, over one hundred thousand people in Bucharest in an anti-government rally, but its audience outside the Capital was minimal, and after that success it fell into continuous decline. It ended by melting into the various parties of the opposition, including the Civic Alliance Party, or by giving up the political activity altogether.

The industrial technocracy did not attack and eliminate the humanist intelligentsia – as an elite with at least ruling ambitions – only because the latter intended to come and rule the country, meaning to occupy the political summit of the power system. Such a perspective did not matter for the technocracy for, as long as it retained the control over the main national resources, concentrated in industry, the true power belonged to it.

But, the humanist intelligentsia was firmly resolved to do away with everything communism had meant, and that determination did not refer only to the communism of the '50s. It extended also to what communism had managed to develop in the last two decades: industry. In a bid to build the image of a society as different as possible from the communist one, the humanist intelligentsia had turned, in order to define the orientation it expected to give to the transition, toward inter-bellum

Romania, which it tried to give an idyllic description. "Back to capital-ism" said one of the elite's leaders, when he was asked whereto he pro-posed that post-revolution Romania go, emphasizing by that both the opposition to socialism and the period which he considered as being the reference point. In actual fact, although it is sure that inter-bellum Ro-mania did not mean communism, it is doubtful that it meant capitalism and by no means did it mean the end-of-the century industrial capital-ism which the industrial technocracy wanted. On the contrary, that meant a direct and fierce attack against it.

First, consequent to the thesis of restitution of the nationalized as-sets. The restitution was rather exasperating than frightening the indus-trial technocracy, because it meant the relapse to a primitive form of ownership, very little or not at all suitable to Romania's industrial struc-ture. Second, as a result of the theses regarding the country's transfor-mation into a society economically relying on farming and tourism. Having no economic knowledge, the humanist intelligentsia was an-chored in some sort of "bucolism", dreaming of the remaking of the traditional values and of the Romanian village and of turning the Ro-manian nature to advantage through tourism, in order to generate the hard currency needed for imports. Industry was the sacrificial lamb in all that vision, and the intelligentsia never tired of criticizing the giants of the heavy industry, built by Ceausescu, for which it did not find other justification than his stupidity and megalomania. And, in order to show it clearly that it was firmly decided at least to try such an option, the humanist intelligentsia also found a political expression of that sui generis recipe of transition, in the form of the restoration of the monarchy.

It is just possible that the industrial technocracy should not have heeded too much the Civic Alliance's economic slogans and that it should have let go the propaganda campaign in favor of the idyllic inter-bellum period, but the monarchic option was obviously detrimental to it. There was no better and more vivid example about what meant specifically the remaking of the structures characteristic of the inter-bellum period than the dissolution of the technocracy in agriculture – as a power struc-ture – pursuant to the land reform and the dismantlement of the Coop-erative Producer Farms. Sure, the problem had been partly settled in the end, through the keeping in operation of the State Agricultural Enter-prises, the transfer of the personnel to the administration and the heavy pumping of financial resources to that zone in form of soft agricultural loans and programs of agricultural reconstruction. But, that important sector of the economic power had been severely disorganized by a political measure and the technocracy could not accept another experiment of the kind. What mattered was also the humanist elite's cosmopolitanism and its outspoken preference for the West which, although making it likeable in the Western mass media, made it less likeable for the industrial technocracy. In economic language the absence of nationalism is tantamount to giving up any protectionism, and the Romanian industry, even more disadvantaged in the domestic market by the competition with the Western industry than it was in the external market, badly needs the shield of a protectionist legislation in order to survive.

2. The Working Class' Battle for Power

By the beginning of 1991, the humanist elite was already eliminated as a potential danger. Another elite, that of the revolutionaries, did not even come to exist. The "revolutionaries" and the "heroes of the revolution", those who were at the head of the crowds of demonstrators in December 1989, considered themselves for a while entitled to participate in the administration of the power. They were accepted as long as their presence could add to the legitimacy of the incumbent power or, on the contrary, to the challenge of that legitimacy by some candidate or another for the political summit. Whenever they intervened in the public life in an active and organized manner to claim new privileges and rewards, those were always unreservedly granted. Along the five years since the revolution the claims grew as much and the very number of claimants increased to such an extent as to make the population suspicious about them, adding to their image as the most active and brave participants in the revolution also the image of those who had the most to gain from it. Although they were numerous, credible, influential and organized, they have never made up a post-revolution elite of the power. They confined themselves to becoming a bunch of privileged. They have never had any post-revolution objective, any clear ideology or stand. If they really were the leaders of the demonstrations on 21 and 22 December, then they offer the best illustration of the fact that the revolution did not have objectives for the period after Ceausescu's fall. For the industrial technocracy, they have never represented a real problem in the competition for the control of the power, although in the period right after the victory of the revolution, some of them sustained the idea of a total purge of the old rulers, from political leaders to economic and industrial executives.

The Trade Unions' Offensive

Finally, the last potential candidate for the control of the power, which the technocracy had to withstand, was the group of union leaders. Of all the constituted or embryonic elites, the union leaders were the most dangerous for the industrial technocracy. As shown before, the technocracy managed rather easily, when it had to face elites, either constituted like the humanist one, or embryonic, like the revolutionaries', which tried to impose their control through the political level. The problem was settled through the very creation of the power system, in which the political level at the summit had but a minor function in making decisions, through the annihilation of the government's political function, through the political attack on the other contenders and through privileges and favors dispensed to the opponents that could be thus neutralized. Such privileges and favors could be addressed either to groups, as was the case of the status of the "revolution heroes", or to individuals, ranging from embassy functions or parliament seats to lucrative posts in administration boards.

None of those methods was enough to counter the union leaders. First, because their attack was not coming from the political levels but, which was far more serious, right from inside the enterprises and institutions led by the technocracy. And the attack endangered directly the resources' control at their very source – the enterprise. Besides, the unions leaders were no writers or literary critics, naive and easy to scare away. They were energetic people, selected after fierce battles fought for holding the leading positions, adept with handling the mass of workers, who would not draw back when a fight was in sight, irrespective of the means.

The trade unions that came into being after the revolution were to a great extent the heirs, if not in all cases, of the people and structures, at any rate of the short tradition and values of the NSF ad-hoc councils. Most of them were formed in the period in which neither the enterprise managers nor the central administration, including the political power, had any legitimacy other than the workers' support. Its withdrawal would mean the automatic loss of any authority. The union leaders took advantage of that power in order to dismiss and appoint managers and other executives of the enterprises, and the fact that the higher bureaucratic bodies, like the ministries, confirmed those dismissals or appointments, war mere formality. The first half of 1990 was the golden era of trade union power, in which, inside the enterprise, the union leaders availed of authoritativeness both with the union members, or at least an important part of them, and with the factory's administrative management. It was also a period of big claims. First, because the workers themselves felt entitled to reparations for all sufferings they had gone through in Ceausescu's last years. Then, because the only method by which the union leaders could secure for themselves the workers' support, thus keeping the unions' power and their own authoritativeness, was to snatch something either from the enterprise's administration or from the government.

It was also a period of definition of the unions' area of preoccupations. In a first stage, taking over the NSF councils, the unions tended to take care of the whole range of enterprises' problems, from personnel policies concerning salaries, holidays, pensioning, labor conditions and the appointment of the enterprises' managers, to production problems having to do with investments, structure of expenditures, markets, prices, etc., plus, of course, the global problems of the economy and of the country itself. The basic argument of the trade unions was that any of those problems was consequential for the union members. Tending to monitor and supervise the whole activity of the industrial management, plus the problems of governmental macro-economic policy, the unions started to constitute themselves, in the early half of 1990, into some sort of new soviets of the workers, putting up serious pressure on the power system that was coming into being at a central and local level.

For the industrial technocracy, that new candidate for power was extremely dangerous for two reasons. First, because its power was challenged right in the enterprise, where the unions opposed a new system to the administrative decision system. The budding union bureaucracy was tending to first occupy the place vacated by the political bureaucracy, yet with an obviously superior legitimacy, since it relied on an improvised worker democracy. And, against that budding union bureaucracy, the industrial technocracy did not have even the argument of greater technical competence. The union leaders were, most of them, former members of that technocracy themselves. They were mainly engineers or economists of the enterprise, people familiar with its technical and economic problem, that could easily resort to the expertise of other specialists of the enterprise. The only thing that could be opposed to them were the bureaucratic rules of the industrial decision, a rather weak argument in front of the united force of the enterprises' personnel, for, the trade unions rallied just as well the workers and the technical and administrative staff.

The other major danger spelt by the trade unions was their tendency to strengthen the functions and authoritativeness of the governmental bureaucracy, to which they turned not so much because they needed an umpire, but rather because it had the role to formally reinforce the decision proposed by the trade unions. So, the technocracy was faced with the prospect of seeing the power shifting precisely from its position partly toward the trade unions and partly toward the higher bureaucratic echelons, meaning toward the central administration.

The industrial technocracy eventually won the battle but, like I said, it was the first serious confrontation it had to cope with. What ensured its victory was a double offensive, conducted both at the level of enterprises and in the relation with the governmental administration. The main idea was to turn the disadvantage of being trapped between the two levels – trade unions and government bureaucracy – into the advantage of being the only factor of the three to have direct ties with both of them. By using over and over again the workers' pressure to change the managers, the union leaders ended by inducing the appointment of managers with whom they had cooperative relations from the onset and who were now interested in protecting the unions in their relations with the government administration. In turn, the enterprises' managers ended by proposing to the union leaders an alliance in order to sustain jointly the enterprises' interests before the government bureaucracy. The unions' strategy changed, the labor conflict shifted from the workers-managers form to the enterprise, or group of enterprises-government one.

Such a shift was facilitated by the relations between the administration and the enterprises' management, inherited from the old regime and still in operation. The old system had concentrated the resources under the government administration's control and had articulated a vast web of regulations that ensured that control. The enterprises' managers could easily shrug away any claim by the trade unions and point a finger to this or that regulation that had to be changed first in order to grant the claim. In that way, the trade unions were gradually pushed to putting pressure on the government and on the administrative bureaucracy instead of challenging the power of the enterprises' managers.

Moreover, the alliance between the union leadership and the enterprise management materialized in the promotion by the union leaders of some of the management's claims as trade union claims. When the management was unable to obtain itself additional resources for the enterprises' benefit, which in principle meant additional subsidies, no matter in what form, the problem would be mooted by the trade unions in their negotiations with the government. In reciprocation, the management would back the union claims for pay rises or bigger extras, etc., either by offering the necessary technical arguments or by simply sponsoring financially the strikes and demonstrations. And so, paradoxically, the trade unions and enterprises' managers have come to organize together strikes or union offensives the target of which were the government or relevant ministries. Sometimes, when the main target was of a legislative nature, or a ministry like the Ministry of Finance or the Ministry of Labor, they could count even on the support of the office workers in the respective ministry, when managers lobbied old acquaintances in ministries.

All the while, the enterprises' managers extensively used the advantage of direct, personal and traditional ties with the technocracy in ministries in order to counter the attack of the union leaders. As a matter of fact, to the extent to which that attack really meant a pressure for the redistribution of the power between the technocracy and the workers, there was no defection either inside the technocracy or in the alliance between the technocracy and the administration to counter it. In that respect, the administration has always been on the side of the technocracy, with which it had already started a symbiosis under the previous regime, and never against it. The technocracy got a serious support in that respect from politics. First from the government. The little policy the government has made all along the post-revolution period was in direct connection with the trade unions and, obviously, against its access to power. The post-revolution governments have always yielded to the unions' economic or pay claims. After longer or shorter negotiations, having or not to resort to strikes, the trade unions have always got their pay rises or financial extras. To the extent to which their claims only reproduced claims of the enterprises' management, sometimes even of the industrial branches, the government too, yielded whenever it had what to yield. But it has never yielded to what it called "political claims" of the trade unions, meaning the trade union leaders' attempts to share in the real power. And it did not yield to the unions' attempts to increase their control of the enterprises.

The key to the whole battle was the appointment of managers. It was on it that focussed the trade unions too, as early as the first days after the revolution and, periodically, the waves of the battles mounted up to higher echelons, such as the relevant ministers or the senior functionaries of ministries. It was there, after the short-lived dominance of the trade unions in the first months after the revolution, that was eventually settled the battle to the advantage of the technocracy, with the unconditional support of the administration and of the politicians. There were cases when enterprise managers, whom the government or the ministries wanted to change, who remained in office only because the trade unions had asked for their dismissal and the rulers wanted to avoid the appearance of the unions' victory. As a rule, the administration fiercely defended not the managers themselves, but the principle by which the trade unions did not have access to that kind of decision. Just like the decisions referring to the enterprise's activity. And when it could not manage alone, it applied to political support. The politicians themselves did not hesitate to take advantage of all their influence with the public opinion, turning it against the union leaders, in order to protect the technocracy. No wonder, because, in actual fact, the big match of the power played around the revolution was between the elites and the working class and it was lost by the latter.

The Working Class and the Power

Actually, the working class – the industrial workers and especially its elite, the skilled and highly skilled workers – lost the power as early as the former regime. It did never have a real and significant control of it but, in certain periods of industrialization, it did play a really influential role which it lost entirely only by the end of the regime. The political bureaucracy of the communist party, that claimed to hold the leadership in the name of the working class, had to take account of its elite. It did it by creating a system of privileges almost as vast as its own system of privileges. By contrast, the administrative bureaucracy and the industrial technocracy used to get their privileges based on a system of illegalities and abuses tacitly accepted by the political bureaucracy, first because anyway it could not annul it efficiently and the, because it was a very efficient means of control by blackmail of the technocracy. However, the working class did not sustain communism for the sake of such privileges and advantages. It sustained it because the policy of industrialization, urbanization and development of the '60s and '70s was obliviously to its advantage. Even the extremely high rates of accumulation of that period, that sometimes reached 30-33 per cent of the national income and that were leading to endless regimes of austerity, were fully compensated by the working class' growth in numbers and social importance. We should add to this the vast social programs, such as the housing construction, free of charge education and medical care, job and pension safety, etc., as well as the living standard rise that occured in the period of economic growth.

No need to wonder how was it possible that a handful of people, no matter how skilfull, even with the support of the political influence of the Soviet Union – tangibly diminished after the withdrawal of the Soviet troops from the country – and even benefitting from an efficient political police, should be able to keep a whole people under control, without real problems. We would make the error of judging the realities of communism according to a mythology created after the fall of communism. The working class did support communism, as it was its main beneficiary. The industrial workers were not interested in sustaining an authoritarian regime, in the restriction of human rights or the maintenance of a political bureaucracy that was parasitic to a great extent. But, it accepted all these as an inevitable cost of industrialization, of the economic growth and equalitarian distribution of its benefits, just as they accept now the unemployment, declining living standards and non-equalitarian distribution of the incomes as an inevitable cost of economic transformation. And just as, in the same period, they were accepted also by the industrial technocracy and cultural elites, well integrated with the system both of them.

For a good part of the '80s, the working class was still supporting socialism in Romania, in spite of the fast economic and social deterioration. Socialism could not have survived another ten years relying only on the capacity of the regime of reproducing itself politically, if its basis, the class of industrial workers, had denied its support and its legitimacy. But it lasted for yet another period. First, because there was no alternative in sight, and then because there was hope that the deterioration was caused by the efforts to pay off the foreign debt, so things were going to radically mend after that. When that prospect too, died, when Ceausescu's announcement that the foreign debt was paid off was not followed by a further economic growth matched by detente of consumption and improvement of the living standard, the working class started understanding that the regime it was sustaining was not capable of another economic revigoration, and the economic crisis and the deterioration of the everyday life were the price paid to keep the system in operation and not to liquidate the foreign debt.

At that moment though, the industrial workers were no longer in power, and their influence on the power was zero. The communist party's political bureaucracy had long ceased acting as an interface between the country's political leadership and the working class. Its role had been reduced to extorting pressures on the workers, which it did by using not so much its political authoritativeness that had dwindled away, but by using the authoritativeness of the enterprises' administration and organizational structures. Surveys on the sharing of the decision and authoritativeness in industry, made even before the revolution – never published and never heeded by authorities – pointed to that double process that was characteristic of the break between the communist party and the working class. Initially, the political bureaucracy had assumed the role to politically control the industrial technocracy in the name of the workers who were subordinated to it from a technical and administrative viewpoint. In the next stage, that of the "golden era", meaning of intensive industrialization, the political leadership developed an autonomy in its relations with the grass roots. The communist party's political leaders, who no longer depended in any way on workers in order to maintain their posts or to get promoted, but only on the success in the intrigue inside the political bureaucracy, barred the workers' access to power, but kept using them as a means of pressure against the mounting industrial technocracy. The communist party had already departed from its class basis not only in actual fact but also ideologically. This time Ceausescu no longer claimed to be the representative of the working class but of the whole people, a pretense all dictators share. That obviously more vague claim tended to shift the weight center of legitimation from the industrial organizations to the administrative organizations and from the political party to the state. The confusion still obtained, because Ceausescu never gave up what was called "the communist party's leading role", his main defence against any offensive by a possible contending elite. But he was increasingly acting first as the head of the state and not as the head of the party. That did not happen in the Soviet Union, for instance, where the communist party's general secretary was unquestionably leading the country, although he did not need a state for that. At that stage, the political power had become autonomous in relation to any social basis, and the authority of the political bureaucracy on the workers was exercised through the administration and technocracy. The party secretary used to pass down the decision to the enterprise's manager of the department chief and they would execute it, by using their technical and administrative authority. No more political authority over the workers.

The third stage of the process started when the political bureaucracy had to use its power against the working class in order to get from it more work hours in more difficult conditions and for smaller pays, a drastic cut down of individual and social consumption, and to suppress any attempted protest or rebellion, as were those of the Jiu Valley miners or Brasov workers in 1987. The fourth and last stage was the revolution, in which the workers rose against that power and against the policy it promoted. It was precisely the workers' uprising that led to the victory of the revolution. It was the workers who, on the morning of 22 December, stirred the Bucharest population and ensured the victory of the demonstrations against Ceausescu that had started the day before and had been suppressed by the militia and the army on the night of 21 to 22 December. And, what is important is that they started from factories, as workers and not as "simple citizens".

For a short while the victory of the revolution meant the working class' return to power. But it could be a short-lived reality which was anyway running against the current. None of the elites that were poised to compete for the power was willing to accept the working class' sharing in it. The cultural elite would not take it, because it had no connection whatsoever with the working class and would rather ignore its existence. Its projected future of the country, vague when it was not about the role it would play itself, relied on an idyllic image of the Romanian peasant, farming the land and hosting foreign tourists in order to raise the hard currency necessary for imports, while paying little attention to industry and its people. For the industrial technocracy though, the workers had a well defined place in the technical organization of the production and that was the place as executants, unconditionally obeying by the industrial discipline. It could not think of any reason why it should yield the political power or at least part of it, to the industrial executants.

The December revolution was termed as an anti-communist revolution. Eventually, things did take that course, toward the dismantlement of all structures and realities that could be considered as specific to communism. But it is doubtful that in December 1989 and even for many weeks after that the workers really wanted to give up communism. If the name is used to define the political and economic regime of Ceausescu's last years, then the revolution was definitely an anti-communist one, and the workers too, were anti-communist. But if you mean by communism an economic and social system in which the working class shares in the power because it is a working class and not because the workers too, are citizens like all other citizens, then you cannot take the anti-communist character of the revolution for granted. The workers did not rise against a society where the working class is in power. On the contrary, they rebelled against a regime which, although declaring that it ruled in the name of the working class, had left no trace of power for it, having started instead to govern against it. And the workers equated that regime rather with Ceausescu than with communism itself.

What the working class was after in December 1989 and in the next months was rather a comeback to the principles of the ideal communism, that utopic world depicted in the popularization literature. Much if not the majority of the population regarded the revolution as a way of eliminating Ceausescu, viewed as the source of all evils, as a way of improving the extant socialism rather than of building capitalism. When, in his first speech after the victory of the revolution, Ion Iliescu accused Ceausescu of having betrayed the ideals of communism, he was right and he was not speaking up just a personal opinion, but one rather disseminated and shared mainly by workers. He was right because just like any applied communism, the reality of the one patronaged by Ceausescu had no connection with the utopia about the classless society in which everyone works as much as he can and gets as much as he needs. Just as it had nothing to do with a society politically ruled by and for the benefit of the working class. The opposition insisted on those statements made by Ion Iliescu, in its own election campaigns in order to convince the population that he was in fact a badly dissimulated nostalgic of the former regime. But it only managed to convince the people that he was still tied to the ideals of the native communism of his first supporters and it is not at all sure that was to his disadvantage in the electorate's view.

As a matter of fact, soon after the revolution, the working class did seize the power for a short while, after which it was discretely pushed aside, sometimes with its own helping hand.

The trade unions were the workers' last effort to share in the power, one way or another. In enterprises, the trade unions continuously tried to control the managers' technical and economic decisions. And at a national level, the union confederations tried to impose or change economic and social policies. None of the attempts succeeded. Although, at least in the beginning, the pressure put up by the working class through the trade unions was big enough to make the holders of the power bow. It became obvious on those moments that, while availing of the power, the working class had no ides what to do of it. It used the power to get pay rises and work time cuts, to give itself extras and material advantages as well as greater social security. All proved to be short-lived and in the end it had to pay for them through a deterioration of the living standard even more dramatic than if it had not asked for and obtained them at all. But it did not try in any way to stabilize its position in power. It is doubtful that it would have managed, but anyway it did not make any systematic attempt to that effect, such as, for instance, an attempt to get politically organized.

The industrial technocracy was ready to use the trade unions in order to press harder on the administration for a redistribution of some resources to the enterprises' advantage, but it was not willing to let the unions control the use of the resources. The political parties too, were attracted by the idea of using the unions as a mass of political manoeuver, both in elections and in more sophisticated schemes, such as overthrowing the government through a combination of no-confidence motion and general strike. And, of course, they too, had no intention whatsoever to yield a part of the thus obtained power to trade unions.

The Annihilation of the Union Leaders

Generally, the solution proposed by the holders of the power at all echelons was to co-opt in power not the trade unions but the union leaders, which, of course, is something else. Co-opting the trade unions would have meant turning the workers into co-participants in adminis-trating the power. It could have been done, at the enterprise's level, for instance, by including a representative of the unions in the administra-tion board, a proposal that was debated in 1990-1991 and was rejected even by the union leaders. Co-opting the union leaders alone does not mean any enlargement of the circle of the participants in the power, it only means turning the workers, through their leaders, into a very use-ful mass for manoeuvering, political as a rule. And it has also another consequence. A divorce gradually occurs, between union leaders and union rank and file, as regards both the interests and the objectives.

It is only human that the union leaders should have political ambi-tions. Many a times they are even more justified than those of many politicians. Like I said, in order to accede to their position as leaders and keep that position, they had to go through a complex and intricate process of selection and through fights and intrigues at least as sophis-ticated as those inside a political party. The building of the union con-federations, that bring together unions of all branches and from all over the country, took a tremendous organizational effort, and now the union leaders have an experience with the organization and leadership of big masses of people and intricate bureaucracies that is obviously superior to the politicians'. In brief, they are more knowledgeable and experi-enced as leaders than most of the politicians and bureaucrats.

But, the closer they got to politics, the more they tried to introduce more or less transparent political objectives in the union movement, the less authoritativeness they had with their own organizations. A first sig-nal was the aborted attempt to create a political party of the trade un-ions, some sort of political wing of the union movement. The "Conven-tion of Social Solidarity", put together in a hurry and clumsily on the eve of elections, with the more or less overt participation of the three big union confederations: the CNSLR (National Council of Free Trade Unions of Romania), Fratia (Brotherhood) and Alfa, got a ridiculously small number of ballots in September 1992. The failure of the general strike in the spring of 1993 was the best proof that the workers did not go for a policy conducted through the agency of trade unions. It showed that the workers were ready to go on strike in enterprises for pay rises, maybe even to go on a branch strike extended across the country, but not on a general strike to change the government.

Such an attitude of the union members, meaning mainly of the work-ing class, seems surprisingly. In other European countries, there are clear and direct connections between the political parties and the trade unions. There are parties that came into being as political movements of trade unions, just as there are political parties that organized important union movements, and the connection between them has continued. On the other hand, none of the political parties that have been consequential after 1989 has stood out as a party representing the workers' interests in the fight for power. The workers' lack of interest in their leaders' political adventure is not caused by the working class' lack of interest in the power as such. It is simply caused by the fact that the policy which the union leaders have tried to associate with the unions is irrelevant for the working class.

Each of the big national confederation has a membership bigger than any of the political parties or alliances. There are big confederations, like the CNSRL or Alfa that have more members than all political parties taken together. They avail of the necessary potential to play a key role in the national politics. It is just that they do not have any policy. They don't even have a basis on which a policy could be eventually built. That would mean to define the interests of the workers and to propose a role for the working class in the society which is being built or which is resulting from the transition. In this respect, the union leaders are totally powerless. Many of them have taken courses in the West on the trade union movement and have had the opportunity to learn precisely how the unions operate there, including their relation with the political parties. Likewise, none of the foreign organizations and bodies that deal with the transition in Romania, influencing it in one direction or another, have ignored the unions, extending to them expertise and logistic support. But, the union leaders themselves have been less concerned with the philosophy of the union movement and of the working class, and more with the organizational structures and mechanisms of leadership and negotiation, etc. On the other hand, what befits the union movement in a developed Western country does not necessarily befit the union movement in Romania in the course of transition, although it is neither obvious nor easy to realize.

The result is that the Romanian trade unions have not gone past the stage at which their fight concentrates on pay rises. The union leaders' tactics, whether they started an enterprise or nation-wide conflict, has been to demand pay rises as the core of a long list of claims political in character or associated with the fight of the bureaucratic factions in the enterprise, such as the change of managers. When a strike was needed in order to impose claims of the second class, they could be sure that the workers would go for the strike in order to get their pay rise. The technocracy's invariable answer, be it at the enterprise's level or at a national level, through the agency of the government, was to grant all pay rises, which would thus eliminate the workers from the game, and none of the political claims, which would thus ensure the defeat of the union leaders.

The pay rise was no big victory either. After the revolution, the industrial technocracy too, saw itself forced to reduce the consumption of the population generally and of the working class particularly, in order to ensure the necessary resources to keep in operation the nucleus of the Romanian industry. Under the circumstances, the pay rises are obviously not a part of the economic policy objective. The pay consequent to strikes have been easily annihilated through inflation. Along the five years since the revolution, the trade unions have organized one victorious strike after another, but, in spite of them and in spite of the pay rises got through them, the real salary at the end of 1993 was only 60 per cent of the level of October 1990.

Trapped between the economic mechanisms of inflation, that annul its economic victories, and the policies that do not matter for it, the union movement evinces a tendency of gradual decomposition and loss of credibility after the climactic year 1991. Adding to this is also another, more subtle but not less dangerous phenomenon, namely the union bureaucracy's getting autonomous in relation to the union rank and file.

Actually, the unions evince a tendency to repeat, at a far higher pace, the history of the communist party's alienation from the working class. By making its organization more intricate, they have developed a union bureaucracy made up of union leaders at all echelons and employed personnel, organized in numberless committees, councils, etc., that have developed its own rules of promotion of the leaders. In the current stage of organization of the union federations and confederations, the union democracy is no more than an idle word. The union leaders no longer depend, for their position or promotion, on the union members' support, but on the power relations among the various factions of the union bureaucracy. The elections, conferences and congresses, when they are held, although the union leaders are never in a hurry to organize them, have become purely formal. The means of manipulation of the ballots by organizers are generally not different from those employed by the defunct communist party in organizing its own "party democracy".

Second, just like the former political bureaucracy, the new union bureaucracy too, is tending to resort to the authoritativeness of the structures of the enterprise's technical organization in order to maintain or strengthen their own authoritativeness with the union members. Like I already showed, most of the enterprises have reached a collaboration "on top" between the administrative and union leaderships, so, at present, the two categories of leaders are mutually supportive. As this collaboration is based first of all on the inter-personal relations between the manager and the union leader, it does not change in any way the distribution of the power, in the enterprise, in the economy or in politics.

In this context, it is the more easier to simply engulf the TU confederations' leaders in the political intrigues as they are farther from the enterprises' life and closer to these intrigues. The result is double. The union leadership gives up the articulation of a policy specific to workers and their representation at the level of the political system. It simply adopts slogans of the political parties which it tries to attach to the working class or at least to the union organizations it controls. Besides, it adopts them at random. At what level, the union leaders, deprived of political criteria and appraisals imposed by their own organizations, but willing or having to interfere with the political life, endorse the political slogans or objectives of those politicians who are personally closer or who, in the ad-hoc market, offer more personal advantages to the respective leader. The result is complete confusion at the level of the union movement and generalized confusion in the political life. It is very difficult to know some or other union leader's political combination, because the market is steadily open, and a trade union leader would always change sides in keeping with conjunctures and offers. Consequently, the trade unions' "political" trajectories shall go through the most spectacular changes, the more so as the politicians join in this game just as free of scruples as the union leaders.

The Trade Unions and Politics: the Miners' Riot in June

The most spectacular instance of abrupt change in a trade union stand was that of the Miners' Free Trade Union Federation of the Jiu Valley, the author of the famous "mineriads" – the miners' riots. Thrice between 1990 and 1991, miners' riots had a significant influence on the

Romanian political life. But every riot meant a different intervention in politics, in favor of a different camp, and the intervention was obtained by different means. Miners first came to Bucharest in February 1990. They came to support directly the NCNSF generally and the President Iliescu particularly. It was in reply to the opposition's attempt to overthrow the NCNSF through some sort of "insurrection" according to the principle that at that time the power belonged to him who could seize it. Throughout the year 1990, the opposition courted the idea of insurrection embodied in the slogan: "the only solution – another revolution", but it obviously never assumed the responsibility for the street riots which, if it did not organize, was at least ready to capitalize on.

Such an "insurrection" was close to success on 18 February 1990. Armed with clubs, the insurgents, whose nucleus consisted of the organizations of "revolutionaries" backed by the Capital's underworld, attacked the headquarters of the government and of the NCNSF, forcing their way inside the building. As usual in such demonstrations, the police did not interfere, and the rulers panicked. The Television, in the spirit of the tradition of revolution on TV, was live broadcasting the confrontation, and, consequently, a big part of the Capital population and of the workers tried to go and help the NCNSF, organizing a counter-demonstration in support of Ion Iliescu and his associates. But, having no organization and no leaders, they were mildly pushed toward a side of the square, and, protected by the crowd of passive spectators and peaceful supporters, the insurgents forced their way into the building. Eventually, the army came in and restored the initial situation without difficulties and without victims, put under arrest a few aggressors and numerous naive onlookers who had entered the building out of curiosity.

But there was a moment when the insurrection seemed victorious and that moment made the miners come from the Jiu Valley to Bucharest to help the NCNSF. It was not a union initiative, although the union leaders later on hurried to assume it. The miners came together with at least some of the technocrats, with their engineers and shift chiefs and although it was then that were used for the first time show elements that would later on stir fuss – miner's uniforms, lanterns – they were remarkably disciplined. The ride from the Jiu Valley to Bucharest takes one day. By the time the miners arrived in the Victoria Square, the conflict had already been settled by the army, and the situation was under control. Their arrival, although not changing things, had the same significance as the Bucharest workers' coming out of factories on 22 December. The working class in whose name the miners were speaking was willing to support the newly installed power. Little mattered that the base of that faith was still the ideology of the regime that had just vanished. No power could be legitimate on those days without the workers' support and it was precisely why the miners had come to Bucharest. Not so much to fight against the insurgents as to legitimate those already in power.

The miners' arrival in June 1990 was different and it proved an important evolution that was however not understood then. The attempted insurrection was repeated on 13 June, almost immediately after the NSF's victory in elections was certain. That time, it was far better prepared. It began when the police tried to evacuate from the University Square the demonstrators who had occupied it for more than a month. After the initial enthusiasm and especially after the opposition lost the elections, the University Square was idle. The demonstration had seriously lost quality, and the students, intellectuals and generally the political opposition had been replaced by half-tramps, half-bohemians who remained there on their own and had built, without being troubled by police, some sort of hippy camp that was running a thriving and illegal trade. On the morning of 13 June, police cracked down on the demonstrators in the Square, arresting a part of them, beating others and dispersing the remainder. A few hours later, powerfully reinforced with far better organized insurrection bands armed with petrol bottles, the demonstrators resumed the offensive, scared the police away and, accompanied by a big number of spectators, started attacking institutions like the Television and the Ministry of the Interior.

Rulers panicked, not so much because of the demonstrators, who were no force by themselves, but because of having suddenly seen themselves isolated. It seemed as though the situation of Ceausescu, left all of a sudden with no support in front of the peaceful demonstrators back in December, would repeat itself. Virtually, the police had vanished from Bucharest, except for those besieged in the headquarters of the Ministry of the Interior, who were rather in need of help themselves than able to help somebody else. Moreover, the police had no superiors to take orders from, as both the minister of the Interior and the Police chief could not be found anywhere. The army too, seemed to hesitate. Until late in the evening, the military units that were supposed to guard the attacked buildings, stood by, taking no action. The government building was not attacked as the demonstrators passed by indifferently, on their way to the Television building. That proof of the insurgents' having a leadership, of their discipline and ability scared the rulers even more. They turned to the population for support, but the Bucharest would watch the events on TV rather than go out in the streets to help the fresh winners of the elections.

The fact is that the situation was not for one moment really grave. But that was seen better from the city than from the Victoria Palace. The numbers of the demonstrators was never bigger than several hundreds, the city was quiet and nobody felt like making an insurrection or rioting the streets. The people had voted, the political battle was considered as won and everybody expected the government, more lawful now than ever, even if it was still the old government, to reinstate the order, for that is what the governments were for. Even the political leaders of the opposition would not get involved in such an adventure. Finally, in the evening the army got moving and after a short intervention at night, that turned into a street battle with fire arms, it reinstated the order.

But, in the afternoon of 13 June, the miners left for the Capital once more. That time, though it was no working class coming to help the power installed by it after the revolution. Now, the technocracy, scared that, after having won the elections, it might lose the power, was simply handling the miners through the trade unions. They were not called to Bucharest on President Ion Iliescu's order or with his knowledge, although the cry for help launched by him to the population on TV was used to justify their coming. It is not known to this day precisely who had the initiative to call them. Most likely, some zealous leaders of the new ruling party. But it is sure that the technocracy widely cooperated. It organized the transport. It allowed and even facilitated the miners' departure for the Capital. And, in Bucharest, it supported their action at least morally. Its representatives did not for a moment show off as leaders or organizers of the miners' riot and did not assume for any moment the responsibility for it. But they did organize and support it.

The technocrats were so scared and the frustrations accumulated so many that their nerves no longer resisted. The miners were not only allowed but even directed in police operations that were meant less to find the participants in the 13 June attacks and more to settle the accounts. The miners beat the students and whoever happened to be in the University Square, broke in and devastated party headquarters and even the homes of some opposition leaders and raided the capital's market places for gypsies. The June "mineriad" was heavily featured and commented on by mass media and used to completely disgrace the government in the eyes of the international public opinion. As was only normal, President Iliescu was overcharged. Not only was the calling of the miners attributed to him – which, in fact, was not true – but he even had to publicly thank them. Thanks to the television, the images showing miners beating people in the University Square and Ion Iliescu thanking them, travelled around the world. On that occasion, Romanian politics got a label which could not be definitely detached to this day, although meanwhile the interests, consequently also the stands of the Western governments regarding Romania, have changed.

The major significance of the June miners' riot, which took long to be understood, was however different. With the May 1990 elections the working class existed from the history of the revolution. Its last political gesture had been to vote a regime directed first of all against its interests and especially against its sharing in the power.

It was the beginning of a new stage. The industrial technocracy had managed to stabilize its own power by establishing a political power that should represent it and promote its interests. It proved now that it could also manipulate the working class. And that the trade unions were the most efficient means for that. The lesson would be used again. The miners who rallied in front of the Victoria Palace to defend it from the opposition's attacks would return. But, that time, in order to conquer it and to overthrow the government, the same government which, in June 1990, they thought they had rescued. A complicated evolution led to that reversal.

The Union Leaders and Politics: the Miners' Riot in September

By September 1991 those processes functioned, changing many of the previous year's realities. In February 1990, the Jiu Valley workers had made a political demonstration. In June, the same year, the trade unions were used as a task force in the political fight. In September 1991, those who came to Bucharest were not even the trade unions, they were simply "the men of Miron Cosma", the Jiu Valley union leader.

Most of the miners had remained in the Jiu Valley and had no intention to get involved in Cosma's adventure. The history of the September "mineriad" is more simple, but far more consequential and meaningful than that of June 1990. Everything started against the background of a labor conflict in the Jiu Valley. The labor conflicts in the Jiu Valley were endemic. Periodically, the miners, through their union leaders, would draw up long lists of claims which they would present to the government. Periodically, the government would draw up just as long lists as promises. They would always be kept only partially and after long procrastination. Some promises were never kept and they would invariably show up in the next lists of claims and promises.

In September 1991 the starting point of the miners' riot was again a list of claims, as well as the miners' usual request that the prime minister should go to the Jiu Valley to meet them. It was a matter of prestige to them, a way of asserting their importance and of countering the campaign conducted by the press and by the political opposition against the miners with reference to June 1990 "mineriad". As usual, the prime minister refused to go there, but he sent a delegation on the spot to negotiate with the unions. As usual, after marking time as much as could, the delegation ended by yielding and granting the claims. The list of claims was accepted and the miners even called off the strike. The same day, they demanded again the prime minister should go to the Jiu Valley, and at night they left for Bucharest, that time for the purpose of overthrowing the government. Like I said, not all of them left. Not even all union leaders. The trip was taken by Miron Cosma and those who unconditionally followed him. Most of them did not even know very clearly why they left. They only knew that what the government was doing was not good and that they were going to set things in order.

Important evolutions had taken place in the Jiu Valley meanwhile. Although the government had willy-nilly granted a part of the miners' claims, life in the region was not easy at all. After the 1990 miners' riot, a genuine mass media campaign was turned against the miners. They were featured as barbarians, ignorant savages come from the bowels of the earth to suppress the democracy with their clubs. Nobody wanted to mingle with them. They were stigmatized and Miron Cosma was naturally given the biggest slice of that treatment. Under mass-media pressure and against the background of inter-personal conflicts even the other mine trade unions had turned their back on them and had formed a competitor federation.

Maybe even more important than the mass media campaign was the widescale sabotaging of the region. Coal is the only thing that is being produced in the Jiu Valley. Everything else needed for a living, from food to durables is being brought from other zones. As a result of the opposition's political pressure and of the negative image thus created, genuine sabotaging started of the region's supply with staples, especially food, that had to be brought from neighboring counties and that were sent elsewhere. The life in the Jiu Valley was getting harder and harder and the prices higher and higher. Miners had money but they had nothing to buy for it.

And, on top of it all, the government too, was increasingly turning its back on them. As early as June 1990, Petre Roman, incumbent and future prime minister, had seen to it that he should not be identified with them. As long as the miners were in Bucharest, he made no gesture that might associate him to them. He did not show up near them, he did not make speeches, he did not thank them and he did not talk to them. Right after their departure, he gave a news conference to foreign correspondents in Bucharest to show he was not solid with the miners' advent. He disapproved of the miners' behavior. He contradicted President Iliescu's theory that what happened on 13 June was an attempted insurrection and presented the events as a simple street brawl between police and the underworld. Very careful with their image abroad and more conversant with the cultural stereotypes of the Western mass media, Petre Roman and his associates left the whole responsibility of the "mineriad" to the President and the NSF to which they did not belong at that time. After that, the government's attitude toward the miners was strongly influenced by the wish not to be seen as rewarding them for their June intervention. That ambiguity of the government and of the next most popular leader of the power, Petre Roman, counted tremendously in casting the blame on the miners and in making at least their leaders feel betrayed by the power.

The more so as after 1990 the opposition radically changed its attitude toward miners. Actually, it changed its whole political strategy that had rested before on the unfortunate ideology of anti-communism. Now, the political opposition insisted on the government's incompetence and corruption, trying to take advantage of the discontent the economic crisis and declining living standard were bound to generate. The miners were not forgotten in that process. An historic reconciliation was staged. Bucharest students visited the Jiu Valley and the miners were only too happy to prove that they were normal people and not savages and to show off the inhuman working conditions in mines. Leaders of the political opposition too, took trips to where neither Ion Iliescu nor Petre Roman had wanted to go as they had feared a further worsening of their external image. Miron Cosma himself was contacted by the opposition and forgiven for his mistake of June, of course, if he would change his political views.

But little mattered Miron Cosma's political views. As usual, the real conflict was not the conflict between rulers and the political opposition. The latter had been annihilated with the elimination of the cultural elite from the game. The battle, even more serious than the one fought against the working class, was now being waged inside the industrial technocracy, among its main groups. The idea of using the miners against Petre Roman and against what he represented from a political viewpoint might have come also from the opposition, which had tried also before to win the trade unions over. At any rate, it was not the opposition that incited the miners, for the mere reason that it could not have done it. But, of course, it tried to take advantage of their rebellion. So, the situation was rather complex. For reasons which nobody understood, the miners where now coming to Bucharest against the power that they had supported back in June. The political opposition did not control them, of course, but it was ready to use them and for that purpose it mobilized its own task forces. The technocracy has already divided into two groups in full competition, one around Petre Roman, the other around President Ion Iliescu. That was the big match the stake of which was the power, the real power this time, and the course Romania would take.

It was not clear at all what the miners wanted and who manipulated them. Most probably, nobody had total control over their movement. It was obvious that they were coming against the government headed by Petre Roman, and the technocracy which was already opposing them was shrewd enough to take advantage of the confusion. And the confusion was total, given that the conflict was going on right inside the leading elite and nobody knew for sure who was supporting whom and precisely what was the real purpose, behind an apparently innocent advice or decision. It was suggested that, while the miners were on their way to Bucharest, Petre Roman should go to Petrosani and talk to the miners that had remained there and that were definitely less bellicose. Such a move would have left Miron Cosma without an objective (formally, he was coming to Bucharest because the prime minister had refused to go to the Jiu Valley) and would have eliminated him from the game, because the negotiation with the premier would have been conducted while Cosma was in the train, somewhere between Bucharest and Petrosani. But Petre Roman suspected there was a trap behind that unusual idea and in the end he refused to travel to Petrosani. Some advanced even more daring proposals. More determined cabinet members proposed that the miners' train be stopped by the army, either by using the tanks or even by blowing up the rail. But the army had no intention to let itself involved in such a mess, so the proposals were dropped.

Once arrived in Bucharest, the miners got as reinforcements the gangs of brawlers of the Capital's underworld, who joined them without an invitation, and made serious efforts to stir clashes with the police and with the guards of the Government headquarters. The miners' new riot proved in the end to be as useless as had been the previous one. Without having an importance of its own, it proved to be important through the intrigue that proceeded on its account. And through the significance, unnoticed at that time, of the fact that the trade unions ceased to play any real role in the power system, whereas their leaders could be further used, if they were able to rally enough people to invoke a popular support to a political objective.

As shown above, three groupings tried to take advantage of the miners' riot. The technocrats grouped around Petre Roman knew that the victory over the miners' riot would consolidate their position so much as to render possible a subsequent victory over the adverse group of technocrats. The adversaries, the group of technocrats rallied around the NSF internal opposition to the government, were ready to use the miners' riot in order to overthrow the government and the prime minister. And the political opposition hoped to use the miners in order to eliminate both groups and seize the power itself.

What the opposition ignored but the people in power did not, was that, no matter who would win the fight, he had first to take the miners out of the Capital. For that, the only solution that seemed feasible was again the army's intervention, but there were fears that the army, if it had been attacked by the miners, would have had to resort to weapons. No politician was willing to assume that responsibility and, to extricate himself from that mess, Petre Roman thought it fit to reshuffle the government. The communique released was rather confusing, but the idea was that the premier tendered his resignation and he would form the new government. The next morning, the Senate's Executive Office acknowledged the government's resignation, and paid no more attention to what else the communique was announcing. Nobody was sure that such a form was correct but, under the circumstances, it did not matter too much. After launching the official news about the government's resignation, the Senate went home, so Petre Roman tried to apply to the Assembly of Deputies. He did not get any support from it either. Besides, he had to leave in a hurry because the miners had decided to besiege the Parliament House. The miners' entry in the Parliament House was spectacular, but it had no other effect, apart from having scared the deputies. With the government freshly dismissed, the miners did not even have someone to negotiate their claims with. At that moment, the political opposition, ridden of the NSF government with the miners' helping hand, tried to use them in order to overthrow the President as well. An open conflict between Ion Iliescu and the miners could only be to its benefit. Miron Cosma, the "barbarian", the "savage come from the bowels of the earth", etc., was the guest of honour of the National Peasant Party's Congress, greeted with ovations, as if he had been a champion of democracy, and speeches were delivered to honor him. Among other things, he was also urged to attack the Presidency as well.

The miners did attack the headquarters of Romania's Presidency, but its guard used the recently acquired tear gas and rubber bullets and scared them away. In order to ensure an as honourable retreat as could and to convince them to leave, a meeting was arranged between the President and Miron Cosma and a protocol was signed. After that, the miners returned to Petrosani, the Stolojan Government was formed, and the opposition had to give embarrassing explanations about its alliance with the miners.

The September miners' riot marked the trade unions' exit from the political game and the union leaders' entering the game. After the 1992 elections, there started some sort of general auction for the acquisition of union leaders by political parties. Obviously, no political party needed the leaders alone, but at least complete with the union name. Nobody could cherish many illusions about the number of ballots such a combination could contribute during the elections. The failure of the unions' party during the general elections and the failure of the candidates openly supported by the trade unions during the local elections had been total. What was still of use was the extra legitimacy that a union leader could contribute. Also, an important organizational gain could be counted on, since the unions' organization was by far better than that of the political parties, no matter which.

After the 1992 elections, the union leaders seemed to be more attracted to the opposition, the more so as the only strategy they knew was to be permanently at odds with the government. The only thing that seemed to prevent them from completely siding with the opposition was the fact that the union members felt less inclined to join the political parties generally and the opposition ones particularly. On the other hand, the ruling party, through the government, was offering more palpable and immediate advantages. As a first step, a number of second-line union leaders were taken in by the administration, becoming state secretaries or directors-general in ministries while also retaining their functions as union leaders. That was a still unheard of combination. But Romania had gotten used to original solutions. Later on, the main union confederation in the country, CNSLR-Fratia, split into two, with the leaders of one of the groupings choosing the integration with the government coalition, and the other ones the alliance with the opposition. The trade union movement was thus definitely emasculated and the working class exited for a long while from Romania's political history.

VII. THE INDUSTRIAL TECHNOCRACY'S FRATRICIDAL WAR

1. The Combatants

Whereas 1990 was the year of winning the battles for power fought against the cultural elite and the working class, the next year, 1991, would record the beginning of the war inside the technocracy itself. The technocracy had acted by then united enough in the fight against the potential adversaries. The cultural elite had been eliminated as a real danger when the danger of an insurrection or of another revolution had been left behind. Its climax had been in December 1990, when the cultural elite counted to turn the anniversary of one year since the victory of the revolution into another mobilization of the mass against the rulers. The scenario was applied, big demonstrations were organized and the climactic event was the truck drivers' strike. They demonstrated in the Bucharest streets with their heavy machines and then they blocked the speedways leading to Bucharest cutting the city's supplies.

For all those efforts, the population had no intention to overthrow the then most popular figures, Ion Iliescu and Petre Roman. Both emerged more powerful from the confrontation and the cultural elite abandoned for good the fight for power. As far as the unions were concerned, they had not been completely annihilated yet, but their glory was fading. Fratia was already engrossed in politics, and although its leadership had enough control of the union members' actions, it had proved unable to mobilize the population in support of union actions with political motivation. The huge CNSLR was still in full process of restructuring, and its leaders were preoccupied with the internal strives rather than with the political scene. Other unions were still not playing any role, and later on, when they were able to play one, they only acted as political annexes of some group or another. In enterprises, the battle for power had already been settled in favor of the technocracy, with the result consecrated by the new legislation on the management of the commercial companies and on trade unions.

The technocracy was already victorious. The power system had been consolidated and stabilized. It seemed that it had nothing else to do but govern, thus taking over at long last, the control of the transition. But, it was precisely the victory that disclosed and even increased the tensions inside the technocracy. The battle fought for the elimination of possible elites, was followed now by an internal war to decide which of the technocratic groups would manage to conquer the power to the detriment of the other ones. For, the interests of the various components had already become too diverging for a compromise to satisfy any of them. Besides, nobody tried to articulate a compromise.

One could say that the confrontation was to a great extent caused precisely by the fact that nobody was aware that what was happening was some sort of civil war, that the groupings that were fighting were only the components of one and the same social layer. The political rhetoric added much to the artificial radicalization of the stands, at least at the surface. And since, eventually, most of it proceeded about a very personalized conflict – between Ion Iliescu and Petre Roman, it might be concluded that everything was caused by an unfortunate circumstance, and here we have a case in which the personal characteristics of some leaders had a major influence on the history of the transition. Actually, the political battle between the two leaders and their supporters, so spectacular and extensively covered by mass media, was only the top of the iceberg. The real battle was fought in the depths of the economic life and it erupted at the political surface only when, in order to win, each of the conflicting parties needed to control that top of the power system with which they both agreed in principle.

The Enterprise Technocracy

One should not be surprised that the industrial technocracy is not a unitary social and economic category. An important source of this lack of unity was the lack of unity of the process of industrialization carried out under the previous regime. In turn, that lack of unity was caused by big oscillations in the economic policy.

Romania began its industrialization according to Lenin's recipe of developing the heavy industry. A first wave of industrialization consisted of the building of those huge metallurgical, iron-and-steel and machine-building works. Mainly, they were bearers of ante-bellum technologies, meaning that their basic unit was the workers' team, the nucleus of which consisted of several skilled workers, assisted by a relatively big number of half-skilled or unskilled workers. In those processes, the role of the machine was to enhance the skilled workers' abilities and substitute an even bigger number of unskilled workers. The whole process was technically assisted by a small number of highly-skilled technicians – engineers –, whose interventions in the productive process were random. The purely economic operations, concerning the accountancy of the productive activity, the supply and sales were considered as mere annexes and that is precisely what they were, given that the decisions concerning the enterprise were strictly stipulated in plans and administrated at a national level instead of the enterprise's level.

Such a structure was not only typical of a certain technological level and of certain industries. It was specific to the communist system as a form of social organization and account for the ideal structure, both by its social composition and by the network of power in the enterprise, for a political regime in which the working class – meaning the skilled workers – was considered to be the most important in society and the source of legitimation of any wealth and power. With the '70s, those structures started being modernized. Automation and engineers were being introduced at a relatively wide scale. However, things were not pushed as far as to endanger the basic structure. Some of the technological processes did undergo wide-scale automation. But whole enterprises were not automated and, although the skilled workers' role was somewhat diminished, they remained the main component of the production. Even when the robotization of the production started, it was only partial and the robots, bought rather in order to be in fashion than out of the wish to change the characteristics of the production, were simple curiosities in enterprises.

The next stage never ever started seriously. Important pressure for that existed inside. A part of the technocracy, tied to advanced technologies, pressed for the development of the most dynamic industrial branches, from electronics to synthesis chemistry, as well as for the wide-scale dissemination of their applications – computers and modern telecommunications. Even harder were the foreign pressures, as the Romanian products traditionally exported to the Western market became less and less competitive. The West was changing its technological and economic structures, and the price scissors tended to favor the products bearing the new technologies or the traditional products but at standards of quality and remunerativeness which only the new technologies could ensure. For communism, the opposition to the economic restructuring entailed by the new form of economy was a political option, since it also entailed a restructuring of the power sharing. Here, communism was contradicting its own ideology, since it claimed to be the most congenial environment for the scientific and technological de-velopment and profoundly interested in promoting it. In Romania, the problem was solved by isolating the potential isles of advanced tech-nology and disconnecting them from the essential economic flow. The computers were piled up in computer centers and were used on calcu-lating the salaries, at the most. Experts too, were packed up in research and design centers meant to serve enterprises that were not at all inter-ested in technological innovation. On the one hand, they did not have the money for that, as all investments were planned in a centralized manner, and, on the other hand, the priority problems of the enterprise technocracy were not to be settled through technological updating. So, the group of experts tied to advanced technologies became an intellec-tual elite, concentrated in the big cities, most of them in Bucharest, with an extraordinary reduced real functionality, isolated from the real economy and its power centers, but with a very high school prestige. It was diverted from its real mission: instead of becoming the spearhead of the industrial technocracy, its new wave, it was turned into a cultural elite deprived of any power.

Like I said, it was easy for the industrial technocracy to eliminate that elite from the competition for power after the revolution. It did not have any real economic basis, it did not control any resource, it was entirely dependent on the funds earmarked by enterprises for projects or updating works, which were never regarded as vital, but rather as luxury or as a fashion which were the first to be given up after the revolution.

Why was the industrial technocracy opposing the modern technolo-gies and the changes that went with them? Of course, it is understand-able that this layer of enterprise executives – managers, chief engineers, chief accountants, heads of section and of department, etc. -, scattered all over the country, having tremendous authoritativeness in their own enterprises and in the communities where they functioned, specialized in the administration of chiefly mechanical productive processes and in heading big masses of medium-trained workers, all of them could by no means have friendly feelings for the small group of technology aristo-crats in the Capital who, in turn, did not understand what a factory is and that its destiny depended far more on the fine relation with the ministry functionary who allocated indispensable imports or raw mate-rials, than on any technological improvement. The opposition between the enterprise technocracy, far more small-town and pragmatic, and the cultural elite of the new technologies, far more Bucharester, cosmopolitan and theorizing, is understandable if it is viewed as a relation between two social groups. But why, on eliminating that elite, the enterprise technocracy did not become the bearer of the new technologies itself? Why did the enterprise technocracy, that had supported the movement initiated by the elite against communism and against Ceausescu, not take over the "natural" standard of technological development in the name of which the revolution had been made after all?

The understanding of this apparent paradox is essential for the understanding not only of the battle for power that was fought inside the technocracy but, even of the content of the spontaneous transition that took place in Romania in the last five years. And the answer consists of understanding the objective of the industrial production, the bearer of which is the enterprise technocracy and which it imposes on industry and on the whole society as long as it is in power.

An enterprise consists of two main components. One is the productive process, a complex technological process, which includes all resources, from raw materials and equipment to people. Its control means first of all the settlement of technological problems and of matters of production and labor organization. The enterprise technocracy is experienced and competent as regards the management and control of this productive process. It knows both its general principles and its peculiarities and specific. It is experienced with the settlement of all important issues tied to supply, labor organization, with controlling the thousands of workers all along the process, with taking action in conditions of crisis, etc. The problems posed by the process are mainly technological, and the enterprise technocracy is for that reason dominated by engineers.

But these is one more component of the enterprise, tied to production not as a productive activity but as a business. It is the enterprise's accountancy, financial and commercial activity. This activity is indifferent to the technological process. It does not care about people but only about their pays, it does not care about raw materials and equipment, but only about their costs and their participation in the product's price. It does not even care about the product as such, but only about its ability to sell and about what could be done to sell more and at better prices. That component too, has its own specialists. It is not controlled by engineers but by economists, by the category of economists that might be equated with the businessmen, the entrepreneurs of the Liberal literature.

The enterprise technocracy, dominated by the engineers tied to the technological process of production, has as its objective the keeping in operation and, if possible, the development of the technological process. Which is only normal. But what matters for them above all is to secure the prevalence of the enterprise as a technological process over the enterprise as a business. This objective is essential, that in its absence they lose their dominant position. Their special situation, as the people in control of both the enterprise and its resources, results precisely from the existence of such a prevalence. It is inherited from the socialist economic system. Socialist economy too, has as main objective the maintenance of the technological process but, within this process, it was interested in maintaining the workers and their key position in the process, since the workers made the base of the communist party's legitimation. The overthrow of the communist political regime led to the dramatic deterioration of the workers' position in enterprises, as they were now reduced to the normal situation of technological dependence on the technical managers of the technological process. But, what obtained from the old regime is the subordination of the enterprise's business facet to its technical component. The role of the enterprise's "businessmen" is to meet the requirements of the technological process – to raise funds for the production, to bring in due time the needed raw and auxiliary materials and people and to sell what the enterprise produces. The enterprise technocracy's responsibility is double – to keep the technological process in operation and to keep its own authority over the economists.

For that, the enterprise technocracy badly needs to cooperate with the government bureaucracy, it too, oriented toward maintaining first of all the technological processes, either for nationalist reasons, or as it worries about the problems which their mass shrinking would generate. The problems may be social, caused by mass firing of workers, or economic, caused by the impact which the shrinking of an enterprise's production might have on other enterprises, dependent on its production in the technological chain, or even security problems, if it is about a strategic production, like the arms or energy production. The administrative bureaucracy will settle many of the enterprise's financial and economic problems, by reorienting, to keep the technological process going, resources of the society, through soft credits, public investments, state orders, through the tax and rate system, etc. But, above all, it will promote as priority criterium of decision the prevalence of the technological processes over the business – in form of priority of the use value of their products in relation to the economic conditions of production. As long as it can count on the administrative bureaucracy's support for that purpose, the enterprise technocracy can keep the technicians of the economy in the enterprise under control and in a subordinated position.

Such an objective of the enterprise is however quite the opposite of the one that has led to the emergence and dissemination of the "new technologies". Their fundamental role is precisely to subordinate even more the technological processes of the previous period to the business criteria of efficiency and remunerativeness. Half of them were meant directly for facilitating transfers of money and equities and unlimited access to information about market, policies, conjunctures, etc., on which the business rests. The other half was meant to change the extant technological processes, so as to have them comply with the criteria by which the business proceeded – greater labor productivity, smaller stocks, cheaper products, newer products, etc. The enterprise technocracy could not become the promoter of the new technologies unless it recognized first the priority of these criteria and values over its own criteria. And unless it accepted that the control of the enterprise should pass from its hands to the hands of the enterprise economists turned overnight into genuine businessmen, at least potentially.

Therefore, the enterprise technocracy did not become the supporter and promoter of the new technologies and shrugged at the subsequent collapse of the cultural elite. As a matter of fact, it had more important things to do. It had to react to the major challenge, come from the financial technocracy, against the power system to which it was central.

The enterprise technocracy was the dominant component of the industrial technocracy and, in a first stage, it did not seem to have to withstand any serious competitor. Not even before the revolution had its dominant role in the industrial technocracy been disputed. To the extent to which there were also other components of the industrial technocracy, they were integrated in subsidiary layers or categories. So, the technical intelligentsia tied to the new technologies had been assimilated as a simple cultural elite; other components has been assimilated with the administrative bureaucracy.

The communist regime too, had attributed unquestionable priority to the enterprise technocracy, because it attributed priority to the workers. As a matter of fact, one of the permanent and general preoccupations of the communist regimes had been to built the enterprise not only as a productive unit, but also as the main nucleus of social life. A big number of activities, from the educative ones to sports and recreation and, especially the major housing issue, had been appended to enterprises, considered not so much as work spaces as rather as "work collectivities". Such a preoccupation has been common to all communist regimes, and in some variants, like the North-Korean one, it took extreme forms. The concentration of the social problems around the enterprises entailed several advantages. Some were of a material and financial nature. Others were associated with the possibility of controlling better the population generally and the workers particularly, for in enterprises, the workers were organized as work force into a rigorous hierarchy whose chiefs' authority rested on the authority they had in the productive process. Anyway, the result was an obvious increase of importance of the technical chiefs of production, of the engineers, since they were also the workers' chiefs.

Right after the revolution, it seemed that the only ones that might challenge the supremacy of the industrial technocracy with some changes of success would be the foreign investors, therefore the entreprise technocracy sustained the ideologies of autochtonous competence and extraordinary big riches of Romania, as well as slogans like "we don't sell our country", to compensate the political enthusiasm generated by the foreign investors' apparent interest in the Romanian economy. Moreover, concerned with finding a solution to keep the control of the economy, while not opposing unreservedly to the collaboration with the foreign countries, which it needed for capital injections required for technological updating, the entreprise technocracy promoted and supported intensely the setting up of joint ventures as a main form of foreign investments in Romania. The joint ventures in which the Romanian party used to reserve for itself the control of the majority stock was extremely popular in 1990-1991 with the Romanians but less so with the foreign investors. The main significance of such a combination was ultimately to obtain more subsidies on account of the foreign capital. Maybe if such joint ventures had been set up some ten years earlier they would have been far more efficient, hence more sought after. But this way they stirred only little interest with the big investors and when the image of a serious political instability and of uncertainties of financial and monetary policies added to this, the foreign capital ceased threatening the autochthonous technocracy.

But the competitor would show up from the inside and, in the conditions specific to the first years after the revolution, it knew spectacular thriving. It was the component of the industrial technocracy which we might call "financial technocracy".

The Financial Technocracy or the Market Economy without Industrial Capitalism

The communist regime had concentrated and centralized at the level of the administrative bureaucracy most of the functions of the entrepises as entities that were doing "business". First, all functions tied to the market, from the purchase of raw materials and the sale of products to the establishment of the production strategy (what is being produced, in what amounts and at what time, etc.), of the prices, pays and even of the labor structure. Second, it had concentrated and centralized all economic relations with the outside world, hence with the environment in which the business obviously prevailed over the technology. The whole Romanian foreign trade was controlled by 58 specialized foreign trade institutions integrated rather with the administration than with the economy. Finally, it had centralized and concentrated everything that had to do with the entrepises' capital, from its appraisal and the establishment of the profit rate to decisions on investments, on increasing the capital, on entrepises' cooperation or merger, etc. But, above all, it had centralized and concentrated the capital outside the productive entreprises. For the central political bureaucracy to be able to keep its control of the economy, it was very important that the entrepises should not avail of sizeable capitals. An enterprise's financial autonomy under the communist regime was zero and that is precisely why its "business" zone was virtually inexistent. Theoretically, the capital belonged to the state, which meant that the decisions made on its use were first of all political. But in actual fact the capital was concentrated in banks and handled by office workers, technicians of the domain. After the revolution, they made the nucleus of the financial technocracy and also the engine of its ascent.

One of the important reforms after the revolution, although very discretely implemented, was that these former administrative units in charge of administration of the entrepises' capital or "business" turned autonomous. The first to become autonomous were the banks. That happened against the background of the ideology of competence that dominated the revolution and in the same "impulsive" manner that dominated all measures taken immediately after the revolution. The basic idea was that the administration of the national capital should be entrusted with specialists, who were the most competent to decide its use and destination. So, the banks became all of a sudden the masters of their funds, autonomous where the decisions were concerned and subordinated to the government only to the extent to which it retained levers of intervention in appointing their executives. The banks' turning autonomous had two important consequences. The first affected the entreprises that availed only of small funds of their own, barely enough for the entreprises' current operations, that did not allow for any enterprise policy. If they needed money, the enterprises had to ask for credits and it was up to the banks to decide how much, when and in what terms the credits would be granted. In that way, the enterprises were practically and efficiently subordinated to the banks. It may not have been the worst of solutions for that matter, if the banks, in their capacity as administrators of the capital, had been promoters of some industrial policy and had considered themselves responsible for the destiny of the enterprises which they financed. For instance, if the Bank for Development had pursued a certain policy of development, if the Agricultural Bank had promoted a farm and the Romanian Bank for Foreign Trade had promoted an export policy, etc. But it did not happen that way, because of another consequence that was felt by the banks this time.

The banks' autonomy was not confined only to removing their activity from the direct control of the government and of the political authority. And the process was not so fast either. On the one hand, it was because the former office workers, now the new "bankers", were used to the collaboration with the relevant ministries, and, on the other hand, because the government could put pressure on the executives of the banks that, although formally not subordinated, were still appointed by the government, either directly or through the agency of the Board of Directors. In a first stage of formation and ascent of the financial technocracy, the banks' autonomy did not consist first of all of their executives' autonomy, but it was almost complete as regarded the objectives of the banking activity. And there occured an important change. Until the revolution, the banks' main function had been to provide the enterprises with the funds necessary for their activity. In that respect, the relation between enterprises and banks was quite the reverse, with the banks being some sort of financial subsidiary or piggy bank of the enterprises. They did exercise a certain control on the way how the enterprises employed the entrusted funds, but that control was only the technical form of the political control over the enterprises through finance, which added to the other form of political control, through cadres' policies. Turning autonomous, the banks defined themselves as units the main purpose of which was to make profits. The market economy started in Romania with the banking system, but in a manner than afterwards proved to be contra-productive, since it separated the capital from its main source – industry – and prevented the dissemination of the market economy precisely in the industrial domain.

New relations thus developed between the major money holders – the banks – and the major producers – the enterprises. The banks found themselves to be the only capital owners in an economy the essential feature of which was the hunger for capital, and to have no other objective than to get rich. It was not at all clear to them what they could do with the profits that would build up in huge amounts. In the end, the solution endorsed by most of the banking institutions was to consume a part of the profits in order to distinguish themselves socially and to assert themselves as an elite, and the other part in order to get even more profits. They started giving themselves huge salaries as compared with the average pay per enterprise, starting right with the bank executives and thus drawing a clear separation line between them and the administrative bureaucracy, on the one hand, and the enterprise technocracy, on the other hand. Under the former regime, the salaries in Romania complied with a rigorous hierarchy according to the administrative function. The post-communist governments maintained that system out of inertness and in the absence of any policy regarding the work force. The salary schemes still start from the salary of Romania's President – the biggest pay in the administration and continue down to the pettiest office worker. Among other things, the system gave rise to funny disputes since, for the administration to be able to raise its own salaries they had first to raise the President's salary and Ion Iliescu objected as a matter of principle to the rise of his own salary. But the banks soon discovered to be in line with the administration's schemes and that they had the possibility to make there absolutely autonomous decisions. True the majority in the Boards of Directors consisted of representatives of the administration, of various ministries that is, but their allowances would be calculated contingent upon the salaries of the banks' executives, of their presidents as a rule, so there was no chance that they should object to any rise.

They bought buildings, furniture and equipment, apartments for their employees, plush cars for directors, holiday houses, sports grounds, etc. They gave soft credits on special pay-off terms to their own staff and, generally, they did all they could to distinguish themselves as an exclusivist and clearly delimited elite. Sure, all this could be done without an adequate ideological and propaganda preparation. The more so, as the general economic crisis which affected the population's living standard made the banks' excessive profits unpopular. The "bankers" explained that by the banks' need for prestige, by the relevant international standards and by their wish to curb the drain of the personnel from banks to other domains that offered big incomes, especially the private sector. They started instead alluring specialists from all domains and they were soon able to combine financial elitism with the intellectual one.

And one must not forget that all banks had their head offices in Bucharest. The banks' leadership was – and still is – concentrated in the Capital, and it runs the financial operations across the country through subsidiaries. For a change, the customers were to be found especially in the provinces.

As for the main customers, the state industrial enterprises, the banks simply treated them as cows good to milk. The enterprises had to apply for credits, as it was the only way in which they could get the funds necessary for their mere functioning. They also applied for credits for some development projects, most of them being investments started before the revolution, So, the banks' profits were secured by the taxation of the financial operations they were running and by the interests they were cashing. They did not care at all about the enterprises' destiny or at least about what the enterprises did with the borrowed money. One of the most important achievements of the banking technocracy was to free the banks of any tie and responsibilities to the enterprises for which they were providing financial services. And, above all, to prevent the enterprises from shaking off their absolute dependence.

There were numerous and very big enterprises that still availed of funds and that would have been ready to join and set up their own banks, some sort of mutual financial aid houses from which they should get the necessary funds. It could have been done in two ways. The first meant that groups of enterprises should put together the funds needed to start a bank and then use it both for current financial operations and for loans, in obviously convenient terms and conditions. The other was to build banks for industrial branches. That would have allowed for a better correlation among the enterprises belonging to the same branch as well as for the use of government funds or of loans meant for branch policies. But, because of the pressure exerted by the banking technocracy, both solutions were forbidden by law. The credits a bank could give to its founding members were limited to at least 20 per cent of all credits given, which made the banks unable or unwilling to help their own founding members. The setting up of branch banks, too, was forbidden, and that prevented the enterprises in a certain industry from getting associated. The arguments invoked were technical in nature in most cases, but there were also ideological arguments. One argument was that the possibility of competition should be maintained and the formation of monopolies or cartels should be prevented. All classical arguments of economic liberalism were invoked in order to secure the banks' absolute monopoly over the capital and to prevent the enterprises from breaking that monopoly. One of the methods resorted to for that purpose was to block means, that had become classical, of obtaining capital for the commercial companies that had valuable development projects, on a medium or long term but did not have the needed money to implement them.

The first and most important method of all was to concentrate the credit operations on short-term credits, from several months to one year. The banks simply eliminated the medium or long-term loans from their policies. There were numerous technical arguments, referring to inflation, to the impossibility of making long-term forecasts, to the political instability or the enterprises' insolvency. All those arguments, very serious and sound, had as fundamental criterium the bank's potential profit. The bank's orientation to profit was considered as "natural". Sure, the banks are no charity institutions, but in this economy which is entirely oriented to anything else but profit, the emergence of a sector oriented only and solely to profit has generated serious distortions. Then, in a genuine market economy, an enterprise can raise money also in other ways than by turning to banks: by floating shares or bonds for instance. An analysis of the way how the companies raise the funds they need for projects in the most developed countries (Japan, the United States, Germany and Britain), shows that they rely first of all on their own funds (from half up to three quarters of the total funds) and only after that on funds attracted from the outside. And within the latter, the loans are by no means the most frequently used form. Lots of factors come in here, pertaining to the specific of every economy but, for the Romanian enterprises, that did anyway not have funds of their own, there was no way of getting capital other than the bank loans. But for one remarkable exception: they could set up joint ventures and use, in that way, foreign capital in order to extricate tehmselves from troubles and to avoid their subordination to the Romanian banks. That possibility, like I said, was limited. And even more limited was the foreign credit. Besides, its getting required as a rule the cooperation with the financial technocracy. A foreign bank or other financial institution was ready to give Romanian enterprises loans only against guarantees given either by Romanian banks or, even better, by the government itself.

The financial technocracy could not have obtained the least of prevalence over the enterprise technocracy in the absence of the government bureaucracy's cooperativeness. It was possible because, just like the enterprise technocracy had its own camp constituted inside the government bureaucracy in the relevant ministries, the budding financial technocracy relied on another administrative grouping, the basis of which was the Finance Ministry. The cooperation between the Finance Ministry and bankers was natural. They shared the same domain of activity. They originated not only in the same professional body, but also in the same group – both had been mere administrative functionaries under the previous regime. But after the revolution, the relations among the various groupings inside the government administration tended towards a reshuffle to the disadvantage of the enterprise technocracy. In the summer of 1990, the second Roman Government, formed after the May 1990 elections, dismantled all industrial ministries, turning them into departments of a huge ministry of industries. The industrial technocracy retained for a while strong positions in the Ministry of Economy, but gradually they were lost to the Finance. The Ministry of economy and Finance, set up by their merger in 1991, meant mainly a victory of the "financiers".

Turning autonomous – with an autonomy reinforced by the absence of long-term objectives, apart from the trivial one of maintaining an as high profitability as possible -, strongly supported in the government administration, operating in a little spectacular zone and at bay from the attention of both the population and politicians, who usually do not understand much of the banks' language and long columns of figures, and using to its benefit the mounting ideology of the "market economy", the financial-banking technocracy got the support also of another valuable ally – the big international financial institutions. The big international financial institutions (the International Monetary Fund, the World Bank and the European Bank for Reconstruction and Development) had the difficult mission to turn the Western support to Eastern Europe into one of the levers of these countries' passage to a market economy. The moment was important to those institutions, since it meant their comeback to the linelights of the international policy after a period in which they had kept a low profile. Then, the passage from the former socialist countries' centralized and planned economies to market economies was the opportunity of an unprecedented experiment, and the specialists of those institutions would not want to miss it. But, although the politicians of all formerly communist states were, at least in words, unreserved supporters of the market economy, the economic transition has proved to be difficult in all these countries. In some of them, like Romania, it seemed even more difficult than in other ones, because of the smaller financial aid meant to the country, of the bad image with the international public opinion and of the Western government quarters' disbelief in the Romanian rulers' political will to coordinate such a transition. So, the task of those institutions in Romania was not easy at all. Their specialists realized that the legislative and administrative measures alone were not enough. For the institutions of the market economy to function there had to be economic and social operators to promote them. In search for autochthonous partners and associates, they found in the banks if not the ideal actor at least one that was speaking the same language.

From the Western experts' viewpoint, the Romanian banks were suffering from sins and deficiencies, some of them chronical. They still were too closely tied to the administration, as they were institutions with state capital. They were too small, their capitals rather small too, their equipment scarce, their staff not skilled enough and they were being badly managed. Consequently, the whole Romanian banking system, was far from being a modern one. Besides, it was rather resistant to changes. However, it seemed to be sincerely interested in the market economy, which was true. Besides, it was unquestionably the master of the Romanian capital. All those assets of the banks generated the idea that, since the governments did not too willing or too able to promote a firm economic reform, that role could go to the banks. The idea of centering the economic reform around the banks and of using their control of the industrial capital in order to stimulate the restructuring of the Romanian economy developed after the manual models of the market economy, too simple to function, failed in Romania either because they were not adequate enough, or because they were not applied. The renunciation of those models which drew inspiration especially from the economic relations specific to the American business, made the experts look for inspiration to other types of market economy. The transformation of the banks into institutions meant to model the economy seemed to draw inspiration from the German capitalism, less speculative, less liberal and more oriented to long-term projects than the American one. The idea seemed to be worth trying, consequently, the foreign institutions and experts increased their pressure for a bank reform – with but minor results -, and tried to protect the banks against the attacks on them and on the new financial technocracy. Those attacks were presented to them as coming from "conservatives" or from "nostalgics of the old, centralized regime", whereas the banking technocracy called itself reform-minded and the international institutions were ready to believe. For such a project to be at least tried, the banking system had to become not only very powerful economically – in step with the decline in the enterprises' own financial force –, but also to benefit from significant political support. That last condition seemed to be filled with the formation of the Stolojan Government.

That was the golden period of the financial technocracy. The banks were thriving. In the first two years after the revolution they had made handsome profits and now more and more people were turning to them. Many private banks had already appeared and even more were about to be set up. Their prestige had visibly grown and the bankers could no longer be ignored, not only as economic actors but also in politics. A part of them were already starting to take a discrete interest in political evolutions and to support just as discretely some political party or another with funds necessary for political activity and especially for election campaigns. The privatization even of the state banks was in sight, and that threatened to outrun the mass privatization announced by the government. The Capital S.A. financial company was set up in 1991, in which even EBRD participated, meant for the privatization of the Romanian Bank for Foreign Trade (BRCE). The news gave the creeps to the whole industrial technocracy, because it was through the BRCE that virtually all Romanian foreign trade was handled. It worried even the government bureaucracy – the part of it which was not tied to the banking technocracy – for, it meant a dramatic restriction of its control of the foreign trade and hard currency exchange. But, after that climactic moment, came the decline, and the financial technocracy started losing ground to the industrial technocracy. It was more than a circumstantial defeat, it meant that the financial technocracy lost the war for the control of the power. Some of the reasons for that defeat were tied to the evolution of the political battles between the representatives of the technocracy's two groupings. But other ones regarded precisely the weaknesses of the banking system and of the financial technocracy.

Behind the gilded facade of the banks' prosperity and their great prospects of their executives, there however lied a contradictory reality. The banks did make big profits but those profits were somehow coming automatically. The enterprises, especially the big ones, had to run their financial operations through banks and, obviously, they were charged for that. The banks were giving loans at low interest rates, often even lower than the inflation rate, but in turn they would borrow money from the National Bank, that took an even lower interest rate. So, the banks actually prospered without working too hard for that. And that was felt even in the banking activity. It was slow, complicated, inaccurate. Since the loans used to be granted in an arbitrary manner, without precise criteria, they favored the graft and all kind of interventions, from personal to political ones. Although being the major money holders in the country, the Romanian banks did not concentrate big capitals, unless one considered the standards of Romania, where nobody controlled big capitals. By international standards, their capitals were small. Consequently, they were only loosely connected to the European and international financial system. Moreover, their capitals were small also considering the financial necessities of major investments made by the big enterprises. They were unable to finance big projects in petro-chemistry, power engineering, construction or urbanism, etc. Their capitals in lei, the national currency, were small, and those in convertible currency were even smaller, so, apart from the BRCE no other Romanian bank could guarantee a loan in the international capital market. Only the government could. They had neither the force, nor the organization or the skill to become a financial nucleus of restructuring of the Romanian economy. Besides, they did not have the least intention to become one. Because of the way how they were built, because oh the way how they functioned and of the environment in which they existed, the Romanian banks were interested in promoting the market economy but they were not interested in promoting capitalism, to say nothing of a developed capitalism.

There is no paradox in this statement. The market economy emerged much ahead of capitalism and it prospered for a long historical period without needing capitalism or industry. At the end of World War Two after a period of intense industrial development, needed in the war effort, Romania had a market economy but it was far from being a capitalist country and the least so was it an industrial country. Communism (or socialism, irrespective of the name, it means only what happened in Romania after World War Two) tried to develop the industry, avoiding capitalism though, and it managed to built it up to a level at which the concept of industry built upon the principle of only one, huge national factory, with all kind of sections dotting the country's territory but managed from only one center of decision and resources proved incapable of ensuring the further development. The transition that followed the revolution, having no orientation toward a national project, opened several possible roads. The easiest of them was the road leading to the remaking of the market economy outside the industrial system, and the banks and the banking technocracy were among the most important supporters and promoters of that road.

The non-capitalist market economy does not need, in order to exist, that the whole economy obey by the rules of the market and seek the profit. On the contrary, it relies precisely on vast economic sectors that are not market-oriented. All along the period of European history between the Middle Ages and the industrial capitalism (approximately the 14th–17th centuries), that basis was ensured by the agrarian economy of the societies in which the towns were the reserved domain of the market. It is worth mentioning that at that time too, the banks were prosperous, running about the same operations as they run now: mediating payments, giving loans and exchanging the various national currencies. The innovation contributed by the Romanian transition is that the economic basis is industry, which is not market-oriented, but which ensures a prosperous sector of the market economy. The fact that industry keeps remaining outside the market, actually inside the specific market generated by socialism, does not upset the banking system at all. On the contrary, it even ensures a superiority which the banking system is not willing to lose. The restructuring of industry and the launching in a capitalist-type market of the big industrial enterprises, in a form similar to the corporations of advanced capitalism would rather be difficult for the current Romanian banks, because that would call for their own inner restructuring and for the adjustment to an environment in which they would no longer have the absolute monopoly of the capital. Therefore, they prefer a behavior closer to that of pre-capitalist moneylenders and money-changers, that to the modern banks and financial companies. But in the attempt to maintain such an economic system, they are opposed the interests of the enterprise industrial technocracy. The latter wants not only to rid itself of the banks' financial domination, but also to build an autonomous financial basis for itself.

The battle between the industrial and financial technocracy would be fought not so much on an economic or financial ground, as on the administrative and political one. The cause is simple. As both the industry and the banks are, in spite of the autonomy won after the revolution, institutions with state capital, the state could intervene in order to impose one reality or another. Ant the "state", meaning the government bureaucracy, could be forced to do it only by political pressure. Such a battle was obviously an internal one. The two groups were in after all components of the same industrial technocracy that had taken over the power after the revolution. The relations between them were far from being only hostile. In other domains they cooperated. They had acted together or supported each other in fighting common enemies, like the human elite or the workers, or even the big foreign capital. Politically, they had backed the same NSF in a first stage, which now, after the conflict, they would tear into two parties, more fiercely turned against each other than against the traditional adversaries: the historic parties. True, both the DP (NSF – Roman) and the PSDR (NSF – Iliescu) would try to get into alliance with the former enemies against the former partners. In that battle, the financial technocracy would turn for support to an almost "natural" ally economically and socially but, because an unfortunate conjuncture, remote politically – the big merchants, emerged after the revolution as "private entrepreneurs".

The "Merchants"

Right after the revolution the legal possibility was opened for the functioning of private entrepreneurs. Neither the enterprise technocracy nor the financial one opposed their emergence and development. The idea was not new. Something like that had been tried before, even under communism, in about the late '60s, when the economists of socialism had courted an economic project similar to the Leninist NEP (New Economic Policy) of the '20s. Anyway, what was set aside for the private enterprises was the small business, services and petty commercial activities. But a few factors contributed to a quite different evolution.

For instance, these new economic enterprises were not supposed to start with an initial capital big enough to allow them to reach significant dimensions and turnovers. That forecast proved to be completely unrealistic. First, because some of the new companies did start with enough capital to approach the business, in the new context, with sufficient means. A primitive accumulation of capital had already occured in the last years of socialism, when the underground economy had acquired an important share in the total economy. Then, some of those new businesses started with foreign capital, as partners or representations of medium or even big Western firms. In those latter cases, the financial growth of the new private companies proved sometimes to be overwhelming. Finally, those that proved to be the most successful were not the suppliers of services to the population or the producers, but the brokers, those who mediated either the state's business or the business of the big state-owned enterprises.

As a matter of fact, the private sector in Romania started being successful when it was accepted that at least a part of the country's foreign trade should be handled by private companies. Such a decision virtually led to the self-dismantlement of the state's specialized institutions. Their personnel either privatized the enterprise or deserted it, setting up new foreign trade companies where they did precisely what they had done before, using the same clients as before, when they had been state employees. The source of such a situation was double. On the one hand, the powerful pressure exerted by the new entrepreneurs on the administration and politicians in order to obtain the legalization of such an activity, and on the other hand, a naive outlook on the capital.

The Romanian politicians and rulers after the revolution were subject to strong ideological pressure both from inside and from outside. They were mainly accused of being only a dissimulated variant of the former communist leadership and of wanting to raise obstacles in Romania's road to a market economy, either because they did not believe in it, or because they were unable to give up the old values and conceptions. Wishing to evade those pressures, they got caught in an elementary trap: they made decisions and promoted changes not so much for the sake of the change as especially in order to prove their adhesion to the ideology of those who attacked them, and their firm wish for change. Obviously, they could prove nothing in that way and could by no means stop the criticism. However, the trap worked and it is still working, the easier as neither the politicians nor the rulers avail of clear criteria to appraise the consequences of their own decisions. The wildcat, explosive and "wrong" development of the private sector is the direct result of such decisions.

The naive outlook capital which, as a matter of fact, under the pressure of the industrial technocracy's dominant ideology was shared also by the public opinion and experts alike, and especially the politicians, also made an important contribution. The entreprise technocracy was obviously inclined to equate the capital with the value of the capital assets. It was its economic basis. Their prevalence over other component elements of the capital was tantamount to securing its own prevalence in the industrial enterprise. Consequently, it was inclined to underrate the importance and value of far more ethereal components, more difficult to appraise, such as the trademark, a portfolio of orders or an outlet. Or, simply the competence of employees and their information. When the capital of economic institutions owned by the state had to be appraised, all these "imponderable" factors were skipped. When the entreprise technocracy's conception was applied to the privatization of some foreign trade companies, it appeared that their value was roughly equal to their furniture and office equipment, which was actually immaterial as compared with the value of the contacts, customers, information, etc. It happened about the same with the privatization of publications, publishing houses or other institutions that supplied industrial or financial services. The first result was that, by using minimal investments, the private sector saw itself not only possessed of impressive capitals, but also placed in the most profitable economic positions. Along the financial flows, they were placed at the input-output places of the convertible currency, investment funds and foreign aid.

Another factor that contributed to the success of the private sector immediately after the revolution was the relative affluence of money with both the population and the government. To compensate the excessive austerity imposed in the last years of the communist regime, the post-revolution government started a regime of expenditures if not inordinate, because there were no resources for that, at any rate without clear criteria. The population's pressure for increasing the supply of consumer goods and the comfort added to the enterprises' pressure for imports of raw materials, spare parts and auxiliary materials needed for production, and the administration's pressure for prestige symbols of the function – from furniture to cars – or modern office equipment. The expenditures of both population and government mounted spectacularly in that early period of the privatization and it notably helped in the development of the private sector.

One cannot omit the cultural aspects either. The new culture of money was obviously a novelty for generations of Romanians. Not only the new generations, but also the older ones had been affected by the socialist culture in which money was valued rather negatively, anyway thought to be inferior to labor motivations like the social importance, the satisfaction derived from work and even from hard work. Such a culture did not necessarily lead to austerity – it had to be imposed when it was economically necessary, through the simple but efficient method of cutting the supply – but, more simply, more seriously, to ignoring the money, sometimes even to despising it. Such an attitude was obvious especially with intellectuals, whether technical or humanist in nature, or it is precisely they that turned all of a sudden into the country's rulers, either as political or government leaders or as leaders of the opposition. The consumption craze that got into the Romanians right after the revolution was matched by a spending craze and an aristocratic spite for rigorous accountancy and calculation of profitability and efficiency. Besides, that cultural deficiency was paralleled by the absence of elementary knowledge about the laws and mechanisms of financial circulation.

All those materialized in naive behaviors toward money both of authorities and of the public at large and even of the economic operators.

The success and then failure of the Caritas-type money-spinning schemes are a fine illustration but they are not the only ones and surely not the most consequential. Corruption too, can be included here, as an expression of a conception that made the administration functionaries turn the effort for catching up into a genuine social plague when it seemed to them that they had been outrun in the race for money. One more illustration of unrealistic and sometimes surrealistic behaviors is the housing and rent market, especially in Bucharest and especially with the homes of the "villa" type, which, for almost three years, were maintained at prices comparable with those in the world's big capitals, without of course having similar comfort features.

All those factors facilitated the development of the private sector, but especially its success expressed in profitability. Especially in export-import operations, the success could be so spectacular as to sometimes confuse the Romanian companies' foreign partners. Shy at first, the private entrepreneurs soon became an elite that almost "naturally" drew closer to the financial technocracy. Anyway, they had common interests, since the private entrepreneurs could not run their business without the loans extended by the banking system. And they had the same kind of relations with the enterprise technocracy which they saw not only as the hen that laid golden eggs but also as a sector that had to be kept under control.

The emergence of the private entrepreneurs and the development of the private sector generated many hopes both with politicians and with economic analysts. They were regarded, by an ideology that was still equating the private ownership with the capitalist system, as a nucleus of Romania's future capitalist economy. They were hoped to be dynamic, resourceful, promoters of high standards of quality and efficiency and they were impatiently expected to extend from services and trade to production in order to bring, especially here, the growth of remunerativeness needed in order to set the Romanian economy afloat. In actual fact, far from being and acting like genuine capitalists, the private entrepreneurs did not go past the stage of pre-capitalist merchants. True, they were profit-oriented, they were dynamic and resourceful, but the profits did not come from higher quality or a greater supply of products, they came from their ability to suck in the profits from the state sector which was still mindless of the profit. And the dynamism and resourcefulness that characterized their actions was rather associated with the ability of functioning as a mechanism of redistribution of the national wealth than of contributing to the growth of the national wealth. It is precisely from that started the conflict with the enterprise technocracy. From the moment when they started playing a significant role in the redistribution of the resources, the merchants joined in the most conflicting process of the transition – the distribution of the power. Actually, together with the financial technocracy, they seized the power soon after the 1990 elections.

2. The Victory

Until the 1990 elections and the formation of the first legitimate government after the revolution, the industrial technocracy's main battles had been fought against competitors that were rather noisy than dangerous. They accused the rulers – among whom, far from including the politicians alone, they listed the whole state administration, as well as the executives of the economic enterprises, either industrial or not – of the absence of a true wish for change and of pro-communist nostalgia, given that they were associated with the realities of the old regime. True in all that ideological polemic was the fact that the industrial technocracy definitely opposed radical changes in its own situation. For the "historic ones", as well as the humanist intelligentsia, who completely ignored the economy, the idea of erasing the whole political and economic history of socialism, and of building from the pieces left a "new" society, for instance to the pattern and look of the inter-bellum one, was tempting for political reasons and from the perspective of doing away for good with the former pre-revolution elites. The industrial technocracy obviously was far more realistic and did by no means ignore the economy. The period right after the revolution was, safe for the union pressures, its golden period. It had gotten rid of the control of the political bureaucracy and of the pressures of abnormal objectives exerted on the industry. It had at its disposal resources that were infinitely bigger than before. It cooperated well with the administrative bureaucracy and the new government's economic policy slogan – technological modernization – was tantamount to the reiteration of the enterprise technocracy's prevalence over any other elite. Romania had politically turned its face to the West and, thanks to that opening, the big foreign companies started showing an interest in investment opportunities in Romania, caring but little about the form of mixt society which the industrial technocracy was promoting.

Before the May 1990 elections, the power system was already built and it was clear that the elections would bring no major change. The future seemed the safer as the famous reform project articulated under the guidance of the Romanian Academy, for all its ambiguities, was obviously to its advantage. Besides, the enterprise technocracy, which was for the time being content to remain a provincial and silent basis of the industrial technocracy, did not oppose changes generally and not even the evolutions to a market economy. The price liberalization, for instance, suited the enterprise technocracy just as much as it suited the other components of the industrial technocracy and the private sector too. Not so much because it allowed them to increase the profits, since it was not the profit that was the enterprise technocracy's objective, but because, through the simple mechanism of the price rise, they could solve all problems concerning the production as a business, without bringing about an enhanced importance of the economic enterprise technocracy. Also, the growing autonomy of the enterprises and the reduction, and then elimination of the government-coordinated balances of imported raw materials and products meant for production, were considered to be to their advantage. True, that was pushing them more to the arms of the new "long-distance merchants" – the private entrepreneurs, and was pumping toward the entrepreneurs a big part of the enterprises' funds, but the enterprise technocracy would rather have such a collaboration than allow for the ascent of their own economy through the development of the enterprises' own foreign trade and marketing activities that might gain prevalence over the technical activities.

The enterprise technocracy was willing to cooperate also with the financial technocracy. The enterprises needed money and banks anyway. By using the government coordination, the enterprise technocracy had managed, in spite of the new banking autonomy, to keep to a great extent the banks in a position of finance suppliers, without great reserves, of the industrial activities. The main role devolved there to inflation. The inflation, which was eating up the population's savings, was also reducing the importance, both economic and social, of the money owners to the benefit of the owners of equipment, installations and utilities, hence the prevalence of the enterprise technocracy. Moreover, it was useful in order to impose on the population an austerity which it politically rejected, without however exposing itself to the hostility the communist regime had brought upon itself by imposing austerity by administrative means. And, in conditions of negative interest rates, it forced the banks to subsidize the ever higher costs entailed by the keeping of the enterprises in operation.

That idyllic cooperation among the three great actors of the Romanian economic life and of the power system would end in the autumn of 1990, when the financial technocracy launched its big offensive for taking over the control of the economy. Although conducted to a great extent with economic means, its main battles were fought for the control of the administration generally and of the government particularly, and from there it quickly shifted to the political domain. It was the only genuine political battle in the post-revolution period and it proceeded inside the power.

The Financial Technocracy's Offensive

We have got used, these last five years, to seeing any confrontation about the power presented as a confrontation between pro-reformists and anti-reformists. And the battle inside the power, although never presented as a confrontation between the enterprise technocracy and the financial one, has been excessively matched by a rhetoric of the reformists' fight against the conservatives. What is true in all these avalanche of political speeches and so-called analyses and explanations is that, whereas some wanted to introduce certain changes, the others objected. But, it should be stressed that the changes did not mean the reform so much talked of, and the opposition of the so-called conservatives referred to the changing of the power system and not to the reform proper.

The financial technocracy and, subsequently, the layer of the big private merchants, were not that interested in introducing a market economy in Romania. Some of the characteristics of the market economy, such as the private ownership, the transfer to it of state monopolies, the convertibility of the national currency, the price liberalization and the limitation of the state's control of the economy, were obviously measures that suited them and that they backed. True, all these elements are to be found in the market economies. And it is just as true that all of them taken together do not result in a market economy. If one puts together the wheels, horn and chairs of a car one does not obtain an automotive vehicle. Ant they, the financial technocracy and the merchants, did not want more than that. Anyway, in order to remain what they were, they needed the existence of the huge state industry. To begin with, they needed it right in the form in which it remained state-owned. As long as they could control the state through the agency of the government and of the governmental administration. The final objective was to take over its control and the privatization was unquestionably the safest and most convenient way of doing it.

For the enterprise technocracy, the market economy was not a threat as long as it did not mean the rising of a new economic elite to take over the control of industry. Consequently, they did not oppose so much the reform generally, supporting instead some of its components. But by no means did they support the elements that would have led to the diminution of their economic and social importance. But it pressed for other elements, such as the recapitalization of the enterprises and the freeing from the banks' control. For the enterprise technocracy the privatization could be a disaster just as it could be the moment of the big victory. Everything obviously depended on how would the privatization be implemented and with what consequences. Therefore, without opposing the privatization as such, the enterprise technocracy opposed the method of privatization promoted by the financial technocracy, which meant, beyond the profuseness of slogans about the market economy, the latter's taking over the control of industry. In the end, the enterprise technocracy proved remarkable versatility, managing to turn the main institution in charge of the financial-style privatization – the State Property Fund – into some sort of mutual financial aid house of the industrial enterprises and also into its main financial outpost in the fight against the financial technocracy.

Finally, one more aspect has to be understood. To feature the battle thus waged as a fight between the enterprise technocracy and the financial technocracy is correct but incomplete. This is only the economic aspect of a far more complex confrontation, given that it was fought not between mere economic categories but between real social groups. And they had also less economic characteristics. At least two require consideration. First, it is at the same time a battle between the Capital and the provinces. But for small yet notable exceptions, the big industry is especially the territory of the provinces, where the power structures look quite different from those in Bucharest. A big enterprise is often the center of a city's or even county's economic and political life. And if it is not the main center, then it surely is one of them. Consequently, the social basis of an enterprise manager, for instance, goes far beyond the confines of his own enterprise. For the same reason, the stake of the fight is bigger than the mere control of the respective enterprise. Just the opposite, the financial technocracy, as well as the big private business are concentrated in the Capital. It is here that are based all banks and foreign trade companies. It is mainly in Bucharest that have developed also the big private companies. And it is in Bucharest that are based also the representatives of the foreign capital. Bucharest and the provinces went different ways after the revolution. Whereas the provinces remained dominated by the complex economic and social institution – the industrial enterprise, the Capital soon became especially a financial and commercial center. Sure, there is industry in Bucharest as well, but it does not dominate the city, the more so as it has willy-nilly retained its provincial character.

The other aspect concerns the prevailingly cosmopolitan character of the financial technocracy and of the private sector, as opposed to the prevalently autochtonous character of the enterprise technocracy. The world of banks, finance and foreign trade – the foreign trade is only the most striking characteristic of the private sector, whether it is about big companies or just small shops or tobacco and beverage peddling near the Subway stations – is infinitely more international and more tied, even dependent to a great extent, on the foreign capital, hence on the foreign policy. On the other hand, the foreign capital and the big international financial institutions have found in them a more handy partner of dialogue. Obviously, the financial technocracy too, used that connection in order to consolidate its position with the extra legitimacy the West could provide.

The other way round, the enterprise technocracy was far less open to the outside world. It had fewer contacts and lesser communication and, above all, it did not speak the same language of profit and economic efficiency that characterized both the western business and their technicians and academics. But it had contradictory interests for a change. Some of the macro-economic policy measures promoted by them directly affected the industrial enterprises, and the enterprise technocracy was obliviously very sensitive. Besides, it had serious misgiving about the foreign capital as soon as that capital tried to go past the frontier of joint ventures, turning from the industrial technocracy's partner into a very dangerous competitor, because it was powerful. Therefore, in the battle that followed, the industrial technocracy resorted to nationalism. It was obviously not the promoter of an extreme nationalism, imbued with xenophobia and autarchic tendencies. The excessively nationalist policy or demagogy were just as upsetting to the industrial technocracy as they were to its adversaries, since it needed the West, it needed foreign investments, more modern technologies and foreign outlets. The enterprise technocracy's moderate nationalism would take the form of economic protectionism and, for certain domains, defined as bearing strategic importance, the form of national security.

In the economic field, the battle was syncopated, as the two camps would alternate the cooperation, vital for both of them, with the confrontation, at times when the financial technocracy would accuse industry of financial undiscipline, while industry would issue threatening signals about a total collapse of production and social unrests. As shown above, on an economic plane the enterprise technocracy's main objective was to keep the restructuring at the enterprises' micro-economic level, independent from the policy of macro-economic stabilization, and the fact that it managed was the economic basis of its political and administrative success. The macro-economic policies, including the stabilization ones, only mean the adjustment of the size, speed, itineraries and other characteristics of the financial flows in an economy. They obviously are in the hands of the financial technocracy and, to the extent to which they manage to impose changes in the structure of production behaviors they express the dominance of the financial technocracy on the productive sectors. However, in a normal economy the financial technocracy takes care of the hen that lays golden eggs, the industry that is, doing its best not to kill it, but to stimulate and help it. The condition obviously is that it should adjust to the new financial reality and change its structures and behaviors.

It is precisely what the enterprise technocracy refused to do, endorsing the reverse strategic objective, i.e. of having the financial mechanisms adjust themselves to the situation extant in industry, in about the same manner in which a gas station adjusts itself to the cars it has to supply and not the other way round. True, in the text-books of an economy generally and of market economy particularly the problem is about the same as the egg and hen in question, meaning the two aspects that are so interconnected as they are virtually impossible to separate. It is on this interconnection that are based all forecasts referring to the economy and the economic behaviors which will be stimulated or inhibited by various macro-economic measures, such as the tax system, the interest or inflation rates. Such a system is foreseeable, controllable and it can be influenced. It is upon theses characteristics of the system that rest all developed market economies that would collapse into chaos if things were different. It is only that the things are like this only as long as the extant power system is not challenged by any consequential force. This is the unspoken sociological premise of the whole modern economic theory, with its intricate mathematics from which the change of economic behavior results as rigorously as does Y from f (x). In economic terms, the sociological premise becomes "uniformity of the motivation", "human essence", and other suchlike fairy tales. As the enterprise technocracy had no intention to yield the power only in order to stick to the economic theory, it did what any social group in its situation would have done, namely, it gave priority to the power criteria instead of the economic ones. The immediate consequence was the industrial crisis on the one hand, and the financial blockage on the other hand.

The post-revolution industrial crisis is the resultant of several factors. Some of them are tied to the industrial characteristics inherited from the previous period. Other ones were introduced by the revolution. But, most of them are tied to this battle for the building of the power system, in which the enterprise technocracy had to stand first of all the working class and the financial technocracy. Inflation, the dramatic devaluation of the national currency and their consequences too, are connected to the same battle. They are mainly effects of the pressures which one of the groups exerted on the other. And, of a certain blackmail that sounded like this: "if we are to fall, let's fall together", which either elite used in order to force the administration to intervene in its favor in the critical moments of the skirmish. The only thing which is not represented by the economic crisis is precisely the one which the politicians and specialists have used in order to justify it so far, namely that it is a cost of the reform. It is not a cost of the reform, first because no reform results from this crisis. Second, because the painful effects of the post-revolution period are not the result of measures meant to turn the economy into a better one, but of measures meant to ensure the prevalence of one of the competing groups or another. The economic and social crisis is to an overwhelming extent the effect of the elites' fight for taking over the control of the society, one to the detriment of the other. To say that they are costs of the economic reform is a very convenient way of explaining them and of keeping the population's protest at low levels. It means to say that they are inevitable. Well, they are not!

On the other hand, the financial blockage is the direct result of the enterprise technocracy's refusal to behave according to the prescriptions of the financial technocracy, which, of course, would have meant to accept the latter's domination. The financial technocracy's method, considered as infallible, even by the western experts, was rather simple – any other behaviors than those recommended by it were more expensive and more unprofitable. The enterprise technocracy's big challenge posed to the whole financial-monetary strategy was to ignore the profitableness as a criterion on the one hand, and to push things as far as to make the consequences of the financial mechanism unacceptable. That is precisely what happened. The industrial enterprises refused to get restructured under the pressure of other criteria than the technical ones. They accepted to shrink the production, they accepted to rise the prices, thus narrowing their outlets, and also agreed to break all the rules of financial discipline, buying without paying and selling without cashing. The result was not a singular bankruptcy or several singular bankruptcies, but an almost generalized desisting of payments among enterprises. The only thing the enterprises continued to pay for, in a syncopated manner sometimes, were the salaries. The situation was termed "financial blockage". It happened three times in five years and it ended every time with the victory of the enterprise technocracy: the debts were taken over by the state and transferred to the public debt, and the enterprises were able to go into more indebtedness in order to continue to exist.

The theoreticians of economics have not managed to this day to explain how was it possible to break what seemed to be a package of immutable laws of functioning of an economy and there is no wonder. For, when it came to discussing the change of roles in the power system, the framework of the economy was abandoned. When the economists try to explain an economy, they start from the assumption that an enterprise and the people acting in its behalf are one, and the people endorse the objectives of the organization. Which is precisely what happens in normal situations, and the assumption is good. Under normal conditions, when the power system is stabilized, the enterprise technocracy identifies itself with the enterprise. It is only natural, since without the enterprise, it would no longer exist. But, the five years after the revolution and the attack on the power system are no normal conditions. So, instead of sacrificing its role in the power system in order to save the enterprises, the enterprise technocracy decided to employ the enterprises as a weapon for keeping itself in power. And it succeeded!

The enterprise technocracy was able to prove that a victory of the capital over the production was not possible, but it did not sketch one way of cooperation. For that reason, the victory of the enterprise technocracy has never been complete and the whole process has been resumed all over again, every time.

In the first years after the revolution, the enterprise technocracy was on the defensive. Right after the "golden" period, which lasted into the autumn of 1990, it perceived the danger of losing the control of the government administration. At least a part of the government resulted from the 1990 elections was determined to make policy, a policy directed precisely against the enterprise technocracy and in favor of the financial technocracy. It was demonstrated on that occasion how important the political action could be. True, the control by the legislative and the executive allowed, in a period so open to changes as the transition period, for the reorientation of the changes to almost any direction. The Roman Government oriented them toward supporting the ascent of the financial technocracy, with the result of consolidating the latter's position and, through the privatization law, of ensuring its domination over the economy. But on that same occasion, one could see also the limits of the exclusively political action deprived of a real social basis. The political summit of the financial technocracy was only an unimportant minority, even if extremely active, both in the ruling party and in the administration. Its whole offensive relied on the enterprise technocracy's inability to react, on the authority the government control gave it over the administration and on the wrong assumption that the new private sector would ensure the social support it needed. All the three assumptions proved to be groundless.

Indeed, the enterprise technocracy was not organized, but it had proved before that it could however act in a unitary manner. The efficiency of the resistance to the micro-economic restructuring was a good proof in that respect. On the other hand, it was remarkably influential with public opinion. Soon, both the banks and the public sector started being considered rather a plague on the still vigorous body of the national industry. The main ideological battle was fought about the government's intervention in the economy. The state administration's non-intervention in settling the ear-marking of the resources in the economy was considered a way of yielding it to the capital holders – the alliance among the financial technocracy, the merchants and the foreign capital. On the contrary, keeping the capital holders under control and the redistribution of the capital through government intervention was considered to be the main way of sustaining the industrial technocracy. Actually, what the industrial technocracy wanted was the possibility to use the state capital in order to cope with the financial technocracy's pressures. For that, it needed to be able to use the administration's authority over the state capital, hence the state's intervention in the economy. Not any kind of intervention, just one meant for the reproduction of the enterprises the way they were and, with it, also of the economic and power relations between them and the other participants in the economy – from banks to population.

In the political domain, the enterprise technocracy has proved to be more efficient than any other elite. Whereas the financial technocracy seemed to control at least the fashionable world of the Capital, the enterprise technocracy controlled the provinces and the needy strata of the population, meaning the electorate. Therefore, the enterprise technocracy's main weapon were the parliamentarians of the ruling party and of the parties allied with it. It is precisely from their ranks that started the political offensive against the Roman Government, which ended with the split of the NSF and the victory of the Iliescu-DNSF group against the Roman-NSF (DP) group.

Finally, the financial technocracy was in the end uncapable of bracing itself for a coherent effort. The private sector was too tightly tied to the administration, without the approval and decisions of which no business could be successful, in order to afford a political conflict with it. It chose to adjust itself, replacing the uniformity of the economic rules and mechanisms with the uniqueness of the decision bought by bribe. That allowed them to continue their business and keep their profits even without getting a prevalent place in the power system. So, it proved in the end to be an uncertain and double-dealing ally. About the same was also the position of the foreign capital, capable of accepting any rule, inclusive of the rule of breaking all rules, if by that it could win.

Ultimately, even the international financial institutions disappointed the "bankers" when, by giving priority to international policy criteria, they sacrificed precisely the economic principles and, with them, also their main supporters in Romania. But, especially after 1992, the international policy toward Romania changed. The war in Yugoslavia, that seemed to last for ever, the mounting tensions in the Balkans and the unforeseeable character of the political evolutions in Russia made of Romania's political and social stability and of the cooperation with it an increasingly important factor. So, all of sudden, Romania, that had been accused until then of ill-will in the application of the reforms for a passage to the market economy and of maintaining a political and economic regime still too close to communism, became a success in the domain of the reform and was rapidly integrated with all European political structures. The funds, that had been previously denied started pouring in, and the Western and American officials, that had that far excluded Romania from their East-European tours, started stopping over in Bucharest, to praise the successes scored with the economic reform.

The instability of the alliance with the private sector, but especially the political change of mind of the West toward Bucharest caused not only profound disappointment with the political summit of the financial technocracy in the Roman Government, but also its defeat in the political fight. The Roman Government's overthrow after the miners riot in September still did not mean the victory of the "Iliescu wing" and the revamping of the power structure. It only stopped the financial technocracy's political and administrative offensive. The Stolojan Government was the expression of a compromise. The gist of the compromise was to wait, as regarded the radical measures that had to be taken for the benefit of one camp or another, for the results of the September 1992 elections. They favored the political representatives of the enterprise technocracy – the DNSF was precisely that, but the victory was not a fact yet. True, the political victory meant the elimination of the most aggressive political summit of the adversaries – the NSF Roman. It was considered to be far more dangerous than any other adversary had been before, consequently the battle between the DNSF and the NSF too, was tougher and more fierce than the ones before, vs the historic parties or the humanist intelligentsia. But, it did not mean also the winning of the confrontation. As shown before, the political factor had but a minor role in the power system that was defended by the financial technocracy. By winning the elections with the support of the DNSF and its allies, the enterprise technocracy could not get more than the ability to prevent others from making policy against it, by simply occupying the key political place – the Parliament, with a grouping that in principle was congenial to it but could not do more than blocking its adversaries. A positive support, meaning a real political support from them, the enterprise technocracy could not expect. The real support could come only from the executive and from the government administration. There, the battle went on for a while, silent, underground, but no less fierce, since the financial technocracy still availed of a powerful team at that level.

On joining in the battle for power, the financial technocracy too, did not put all political eggs in only one basket, betting exclusively on the Roman Government's success. Just like for the enterprise technocracy, the government and parties were for it too, a relative matter. The fall of the Roman Government and the resignation of the Stolojan Government after the 1992 elections did not make the financial technocracy pass automatically to the opposition. On the contrary, after having tried with the two previous governments to play the political card, it tried, after September 1992, the technocratic-administrative card, meaning exactly the method of power control which it had attempted – and partially succeeded – under the NSF rule. In the first two years after the revolution, the financial technocracy consolidated its positions in the administration, with the circumstantial support of the administration's concentration on the macro-economic reform, a domain in which it availed of the main experts. It was helped also by the concentration of the ideological debate on the problems of the reform, which allowed it to select for key administrative positions cadres that shared its objectives and ideas. As regarded the administration, the financial technocracy did not trust in the members of the old administrations and it was right. That was one of the most important assets of the connection and cooperation between the enterprise technocracy and the administrative bureaucracy. The confrontation with them within the efforts to take over the control of the administration proved to be difficult, and the financial technocracy rapidly failed in its attempt to replace the incumbent bureaucrats with new ones, congenial too. The mainstays were three ministries – the Ministry of Industries, the Ministry of Agriculture and the Ministry of Finance. The administrative reforms that were operated twice a year in the period until the 1992 elections meant as many attacks against the administrative bureaucracy allied with the enterprise technocracy.

The first to be attacked were the industrial ministries and the Ministry of Agriculture. With the formation of the second Roman Government, in June 1990, the industrial ministries were dismantled and packed as departments in one huge ministry, the Ministry of Industries. That was a heavy blow dealt at the administrative bureaucracy tied to the industrial enterprises and it was followed by other ones, the dimantlement of the central industrial departments, the renunciation of the production balances and the abolition of the function of state minister for the economic ministries' coordination, which made it difficult to build a common front against the new economic bureaucracy promoted by the financial technocracy.

As regarded the agriculture, the battle was fought about the land reform and it was lost by the financial technocracy. The land reform as such might be considered as a victory of the financial technocracy, but it was incomplete, and the enterprise technocracy quickly compensated the loss. The dismantlement of the cooperative producer farms, the main effect of the restitution of the land to the owners, heavily affected an important component of the enterprise technocracy, the one created in agriculture, in form of the technical management and of the cooperative experts, on the one hand, and of the bureaucracy which administrated the agriculture, on the other hand. It affected even more powerfully the agriculture, as an economic branch, technologically pushing it one century back, but that side effect was less important. It has maintained the control of the State Agricultural Enterprises, of the specialized technical units – agricultural mechanization stations, collection and storage centers, vet centers, seeds production, etc., and, subsequently, it started reorganizing the agriculture through the farmers' associations. The financial technocracy could not capitalize on its initial advantage because it lost the next battle fought about the farmers' right to sell the regained land. Without turning the land into merchandise, meaning its equation with a certain amount of money, agriculture was left outside the sphere of influence of the financial technocracy. So, after a brief skirmish on the land law, the financial bureaucracy turned its back on agriculture and on land, except for the land inside localities, whose market exploded after the emergence of the official nouveaux riches. In the end, the technocracy in agriculture, excessively turned into bureaucracy in order to survive the land reform, became some kind of autonomous feud with whose affairs nobody would interfere, developing its own extensions both in the private sector – through trade and especially foreign trade in foodstuffs – as well as in the banking sector. It has built also its own political organization, its party – the Agrarian Democratic Party of Romania – pursuing its own objectives and proving to be an uncertain ally both for the NSF and for the DNSF.

But, the bureaucracy that resisted the best the financial technocracy's offensive has been that of the Finance Ministry. The reorganization of the Finance Ministry was tried in every possible way. To begin with, it was a Ministry. Subsequently, it was turned into a component of the Ministry of Economy and Finance – as the Ministry of Finance was replaced by a Ministry of Budget. That did not mean the economy's domination by the finance. On the contrary, it meant an attempt to reduce the role of the financiers. Moreover, an attempt was made to restructure the Ministry of Finance with the assistance of foreign experts, and the project of the new Finance Ministry had even started being applied when the elections came and the DNSF victory brought about the immediate desisting of the restructuring and a return to the old formula.

Falling in its attempt to undo the structure of that part of the administrative bureaucracy tied to the enterprise technocracy, the financial technocracy started developing its own bureaucracy inside the administration. The main method was to set up new governmental agencies and institutions, especially in domains directly associated with the economic reform. In those domains and for those institutions, the financial technocracy had no rival. All of them were set up to cover precisely its domains of activity and speciality, and for the occupation of the newly created posts it almost exhausted its reserve of cadres, its group of university staff, the scientific researchers and the former foreign trade staff who represented the intellectual wing of the financial technocracy. That strategy of having the hostile administrative bureaucracy overlapped by a congenial administrative bureaucracy which, with political and governmental support, would become prevalent, generated a fierce inter-department war inside the state administration. The heart and brain of the network of administrative institutions of this new financial bureaucracy obviously was the Council on Reform and Public Informa-

tion, whose head, Adrian Severin, was the main political and governmental leader of the financial technocracy. The network included reform institutions, such as the National Agency for Privatization, of foreign commercial and financial relations, from the Foreign Trade Department to the Romanian Agency for Development and other ones,
most of them having county and even non-governmental branches, such
as the Chambers of Commerce and Industry or the Foundation for Small
and Medium-Sized Enterprises (the main form of "business" which the
financial technocracy tried to oppose to the big state enterprises).

But, "the cream of the cake", the climax of that effort for building a
bureaucracy parallel to the extant one, congenial to the industrial technocracy, and for taking over the control of the economy had to be the
setting up of the State Property Fund and of the Private Property Funds.
Like I said, all the power of the industrial technocracy relied on the fact
that the technologies existed as equipment, installations and as technical restrictions of the economy, but they did not exist also in the form of
capital, consequently, they did not obey by its requirements and did not
respect its restrictions. The initial confrontations had proved that the
private sector was unable to grow enough to gradually substitute the
big state industrial enterprises, and, then, that they were immune to the
financial pressures, simply refusing to obey by the rules of the game.
Consequently, the strategic objective of the financial technocracy was
to simply take over the control of the enterprises' management, substituting by its own representatives the administrative bureaucracy's representatives in the enterprises' administration boards.

The opportunity offered for that was the privatization. There were
two main ways of privatization. One was the privatization implemented
by the administration, by administrative means, for a population selected by administrative criteria or uneconomic criteria in the best of
the cases, according to the model of the land reform. Such a privatization, that would disseminate the property in countless and minute components, impossible to coordinate, would only strengthen the positions
of the administration and of the enterprise technocracy, since they would
become indispensable for the coherence and coordination of the productive activities and the only decision center that would have survived
would have been the technological one.

The other way was the privatization by financial means, which would
have meant that all technologies and equipment would have signified
just an amount of money, nothing more, and the money was the special-

ity of the financial technocracy. Therefore, the privatization law, articulated with American technical assistance at a time when the financial technocracy politically controlled the reform, stipulated precisely these two things. First, the severing of the tie between the administrative bureaucracy and the enterprise bureaucracy through the setting up of five institutions that would control the whole economy – the State Property Fund and four Private Property Funds. Second, the turning of the enterprises simply into some financial asset (with which they had to be equated, irrespective of the method), and that asset had to be introduced into the financial circuit, through a token market of assets. Moreover, the sales of enterprises' shares were not even negotiated and decided by the enterprises' managers, but by the new institutions of the privatization, i.e. by the financial bureaucracy. That was the initial scheme, dating back to the period when the financial technocracy, although it had already lost the political battle in the 1992 elections, did not think it had lost the war as well. All it needed was the mechanism created for privatization to go on working. For that, the industrial technocracy did not need the government's control. It only needed the control of the economic reform, which it hoped to keep irrespective of what government would have been formed.

The opportunity was provided by the loose tie between the governments and the parties that won the elections and the central point on which that last attempt was focussed was, just like under the Roman Government, the Reform Council. By composition, leadership and ideas, the first Council on Economic Coordination, Strategy and Reform of the Vacaroiu Government was first of all an instrument of the financial technocracy. Its setting up concomitant with the Vacaroiu Government, a government which was in its essence one belonging to and acting for the enterprise technocracy, was prompted by a wider array of reasons, most important of which was the equilibrum that still obtained between the two groupings. But, as an instrument, the Reform Council was not efficient. The "reform strategy" articulated by it was never applied. Although presented as a government program and endorsed by the parties in the government coalition, it was buried in the same dusty shelves as the first project of the economic reform elaborated by the Institute of Economics in the spring of 1990. The fact that, although having the Parliament's formal political approval, the economic reform was ignored both by the administrative bureaucracy and by the enterprise technocracy, at least in the form given to it by the Reform Council, proves that they had no intention whatsoever to serve only as a political cover for a reform directed against their own interests. President Iliescu tried in vain to convince the public opinion, politicians and Western experts and especially the rulers that, irrespective of the government change, the economic reform continued the way it had been thought out. The only point about which he was right was that the economic reform did not depend on the incumbent government. For the rest, the reform, reconsidered according to the enterprise technocracy's interests was definitely different from the one projected by the financial technocracy right inside the Vacaroiu Government newly installed at the head of the administration.

The Enterprise Technocracy in Power

The counter-offensive launched by the enterprise technocracy after having eliminated the financial technocracy's political summit pursuant to the 1992 elections returns, proceeded on all planes. The first objective was the consolidation of the positions in the administration, of the ties between the administrative bureaucracy and enterprises and the elimination of the financial technocracy's influence on the government. The previous government's main objective of economic policy had been the macro-economic stabilization; as it appeared to be impossible without a restructuring at a micro-level of the industrial enterprises, especially of the big ones, they tried to press them to operate the required restructuring by themselves. The enterprises accepted the unemployment and production cuts, but did not restructure themselves. The enterprise technocracy's ideological reaction was to accuse the rulers of incompetence, as they ignored the technical conditions of production, and of ill-will, expressed in "the government's turning its back on the economy". The government formed after the 1992 elections was decided to radically change that state of affairs. Its central objective no longer was to implement an economic reform meant to change the type of prevailing economy in Romania, but to administrate the economy in such a way as to have it operate as well as could under the circumstances. The first thing the government did was to remake the ties between the central administration, on the one hand, and enterprises and local administration, on the other hand, which meant to a great extent to pre-revolution governing methods. But that did not bother the government. Its problem was rather that, because of the institutional changes come about after the revolution, it no longer availed of the levers the pre-revolution governments had, and the administration of the economy only and solely according to criteria of production was no longer possible. Therefore, the first effort of the enterprise technocracy was channelled toward regaining the control of the economy through the agency of the government bureaucracy.

Theoretically, the government was still directly running a big part of the industry, organized in form of national corporations. It was still controlling a part of the farm production, run by State Agricultural Enterprises, and it had the absolute monopoly of farm staples acquisition, storage and distribution on a wide scale. It also controlled the foods imports, as it was the only one that availed of the huge hard currency amounts required for that. The direct control by the Ministry of Trade of the retail sale had considerably diminished, but the distribution system was still under control, through the wholesalers and central warehouses. All these levers of the economy's centralized administration continued to exist but they did not function. The lower bureaucratic echelons had become autonomous to a great extent and were now tending to consider and handle the subordinated activities as a personal business and not as public activity. The government authority was rather theoretical and the only purpose for which it was still used was to legitimize and strengthen decisions made for purely personal interests. The new government started by a serious effort of resuming the administration of all these activities to the end of ensuring the administration of the economy and of the public for the period ahead. The government had been endorsed by the Parliament only in November, winter was coming, with demands for more expenditures and bigger supplies, nothing was prepared and according to forecasts a generalized chaos was drawing near, especially as a result of the administrative decomposition that had matched the elections and the transfer of the power from one government to another.

It did not happen that way, but there was no complete return to the control exercised by the new government either. The situation, that seemed to oscillate between chaos and a return to the centralized management of the economic life, got stabilized somewhere between the two extremes, with some sort of compromise among the various levels and components of the administration. First, if not a centralization, at least a minimal coordination was achieved of the actions and efforts among the components of the government administration, on the one hand, and between them and the economic enterprises, on the other hand. Second, the administration, the enterprises and private sector directly tied to the domains controlled by them were allowed room for manoeuvering for personal interests, illegal but considered as only "human".

The compromise thus constructed was neither the result of a project or of a decision, nor did it mean the application of any subtle strategy of the rulers. it simply resulted from a play of pressures and resistances. The pressure by the executive summit on the subordinated bureaucracy was high, in the cases in which the very destiny of the government might depend on the application of a certain measure, and far lower in the other cases. In turn, the ministerial and local bureaucracy offered far more resolute resistance when it was about its personal interests and about maintaining those ties that secured the participation in the profits of the private sector or of the enterprises, and it did not matter if that meant dissemination of corruption. The relations got stabilized when all participants – i.e. the various components of the administration – realized that they would gain from cooperation more than from confrontation.

The final result can be synthetized in three major consequences. First, the administration remade its ties to the state industry and developed a new series of ties with the private sector that thus started being integrated in the system. Second, the government delimited for itself a space of objectives and priorities with direct consequences on its survival, for which it obtained the administration's cooperation. Third, the administration too, obtained room for free and uncontrolled movement, equivalent to a participation in power, achieved mainly through the establishment of abuse and graft as an illegal, but inevitable rule of functioning of the state power.

The ensuring of the administrative bureaucracy's cooperation, parallel to its subordination, was only a component of the offensive on the administration. The other one was the gradual annulment of the parallel bureaucracy created by the financial technocracy. Its nucleus was the reform Council. As shown before, right after inaugural, the Vacaroiu Government saw itself forced to maintain, and even to reinforce in number, the Reform Council, consequent to the still powerful positions of the financial bureaucracy and to the internal and external pressures concentrated on the economic reform. The financial technocracy took advantage of that situation in order to consolidate even more its control of the Council which, right after the reorganization looked as if the DNSF had lost the elections instead of winning them. And so did the measures envisaged by it. And so happened that the beginnings of the enterprise technocracy's rule were characterized by paradoxic situations. Two of them are extremely illustrative of the complexity of the problems and their settlement: the Law of Foreign Investments and the negotiations with the IMF.

In 1990, under the first rule of the enterprise technocracy, the foreign investments problem was approached very cautiously. The enterprise technocracy needed capital, modern technologies and Western know-how, but it was not willing to pay for them by giving up its control of their own enterprises. For that reason, a first relevant regulation issued in that period was extremely cautious. For the financial technocracy it was just the opposite. It needed to attract as much foreign capital as could. First, because that would consolidate its position and make of it its main partner. Second, because that would weaken the enterprise technocracy's position. The first and most important consequence was the priority given to the financial conditions and to the business side of the industry, to the detriment of the technological one. Therefore, the enterprise technocracy worked in order to change the extant legislation regarding foreign investments in Romania, replacing it by a far more favorable one. The new Reform Council obviously supported that initiative, so the government could not put up open and efficient resistance to the articulation and promotion of the bill in the Parliament. The balance of forces in the Parliament changed again. The government coalition's MPs were against the bill articulated by the government, suspected of playing in their hands, so, after some amendments which convinced at least a part of the majority to vote for the bill, it passed, being voted also by the opposition.

The negotiations with the IMF illustrated the same dissensions extant inside the government and its unexpected political wavering, under the influence of the various pressure groups. Begun before the formation of the DNSF government, the negotiations had got in a final stage in the 1993 spring, when, because of contradictory positions of the negotiators' team – the National Bank, the Reform Council and the Finance Ministry –, they failed and had to be taken from the beginning.

Only in the autumn of 1993 did the government manage to reach a common position on its terms and to entrust a clear mandate to the Romanian party to the negotiations. Even more significant is that the mandate did not satisfy anyone, either the two Romanian camps, or the IMF, as it was most clear that although a compromise had been reached, it would not be respected and applied by any party.

The enterprise technocracy had no intention to bear more than strictly necessary a rebellious bureaucracy inside its own administration. A first step to counter the Reform Council was its transformation into a consultative body. By that, the Council's ability to play a real role in the governance was annulled. Its real function was to offer a positive image of the reform in Romania, both before the home public opinion and before the politicians of the opposition – who were thus confronted with a part of their own specialists –, and especially before the Western experts and authorities that, for the political change that was in sight, needed however a minimal justification. Its subsidiaries, like the National Agency for Privatization or the Romanian Agency for Development, gradually lost their importance and prerogatives.

The Council operated for a while as a theoretical body of the government, but its works, such as the above-mentioned "Strategy", had but little or no reverberation. The decisive battle for the Reform Council was fought in the summer of 1993 and it was lost by the financial technocracy. The Council's heads were changed and it was reorganized, so as to become functional in relation to the objectives of a rule for the benefit of the enterprise technocracy. And the battle was moved mostly to the economic and financial field.

That did not mean that the institutional battle was over. On the one hand, all that process of mutual probing, meant to find the end of the central administration's authority and the beginning of the sectorial or local autonomy continued and it still continues. On the other hand, although the enterprise technocracy had completely taken over in the autumn of 1993 the control over the executive and its mechanism, the power system was far from being completely at its disposal. Other two institutional networks continued to be autonomous and their control, as well as their way of employment continued to remain an essential problem of power sharing: the banking system and the Property Funds.

The banking system was itself the core of the financial technocracy. Without the banks' control, it would have soon become an elite of experts deprived of real power and would have repeated the story without glory of the research and design experts. Therefore, the battle for the banks' control was from the onset the toughest of all. At present, it is far from ended and, in spite of notable successes of the enterprise technocracy, that had to resort again to the tactics of the financial blockage, it is not very likely that it will end with a decisive victory of either camp. It is maybe precisely in this sector that the basis of a political and economic compromise will be laid, that should consecrate for good the politics of underdevelopment as the unquestionable policies of the next decade.

In turn, the banking system too, has a nucleus, consisting mainly of two banks – the National Bank and the Romanian Bank for Foreign Trade (BRCE). The National Bank is essential because, by its actions, it dictates the restrictive policy and terms of all the other banks' activity. Absolutely all banks borrow from the National Bank. Therefore, its interest rate policy is willy-nilly reproduced by the other banks. Then, the National Bank also controls the money supply in circulation, it sets norms and exercises control. As regards the BRCE, it is by far the most important foreign trade bank of Romania and the biggest holder of convertible currency after the National Bank.

The enterprise technocracy's main problem was that it could control only the state administration, which was ineffectual in relation to the banking system. On the other hand, although the Finance Ministry could be considered as one of its main institutional assets, the latter's connections with the banking system however prevented its use as the spearhead of its attack on the banking system. Such an attempt, right after the formation of a new government, was meant to give the administration the control over the hard currency existing in the banks. It would have been an almost decisive victory of the enterprise technocracy because it would have snatched the banks' most important weapon – the control of the foreign trade – and would have completely subordinated the private sector to the administration (the private sector relied mostly on the import-export activity), keeping it out of the financial technocracy's reach. On the other hand, it would have been able to use the thus obtained money mainly for the supply and operation of the industrial system that was traversing a severe crisis. The attempt was conceived almost as a commando action, kept absolutely secret, especially from the banks and the private sector. The Finance Ministry even drafted a resolution on taking over the hard currency supply from the commercial companies' accounts, but it was never applied, first of all for political reasons. The effect of the threat however was fast and lasting. The private sector rapidly transferred a part of the convertible currency abroad. So, paradoxically, Romania was in bad need of money, on the one hand, and it was exporting capital, on the other hand. The private sector lost its last shreds of confidence in the executive and it took more than a year to regain that confidence. And the executive learned that such adventuristic actions were as inefficient as they were expensive.

The clumsiness of that beginning of an offensive against the banking system was caused also by the euphoria born out of the political victory. The administrative representatives of the enterprise technocracy were sure that everything was possible. The failure of that first attempt was however telling and induced an important change of tactics. It was obvious that now, five years after the revolution, it was no longer possible to subordinate the banking activity to the executive and administration again. But there was another possibility – to control the banks by controlling their executives, instead of using regulations and relations of formal subordination. That solution, elementary at first sight, entailed both advantages and disadvantages. The most important advantage was that such a strategy allowed at long last for the use of the use of the political factor, the main domain in which the enterprise technocracy availed of absolute superiority over any of the real potential adversaries. Moreover, it even allowed for the consolidation of the links among three wings of the power – the technocracy proper, the administrative bureaucracy and the group of parliamentarians and party activists. The disadvantage too, was a double one – it increased the dependence on the otherwise embarrassing small allies, and shifted the weight center of the problem to the other big institutional problem of the executive – the Property Funds. In order to understand the unfolding of the battle and why it lasted more than two years without a decisive result, one should understand the control mechanism of these institutions.

Both the Property Funds and the banks with state capital are state institutions, public that is, but they are not subordinated to the executive. They are run by administration boards, appointed, in the case of the Funds, by the Parliament, government and president, and, in the case of the banks, by the State Property Fund and the Private Property

Funds, which appoint then the executive management of the institutions. In order to control the managements, the enterprise technocracy had to control the main political institutions, to set in motion all the slow and intricate procedure of changing the administration board and then to induce the boards to appoint the president and directors congenial to it. The amount of intrigue necessary in order to achieve such a result is tremendous for, as it is no longer about institutions and structures, but about real persons with their own inter-personal ties, friendships and enemities, the equations of change have a great many parameters. Besides, the process was delayed also by the process of transition of the main institutions – the SPF and PPF, which were only being organized when the new government was installed.

The attack for the domination of the banking system's leadership had started soon after the winning of the political battle, by building a negative image of the banks and of their executives. At first, it was concentrated on changing the National Bank's governor, but here too, the first attack was repelled. One and a half years passed before the executive and governmental politicians managed to change the banks' administration boards and to deal the first decisive blow – the replacement of the BRCE president. The signal issued to the bankers on that occasion was extremely clear and well perceived. The tension between the administration and the banking-financial elite was eased a little, with the latter becoming more careful and understanding with the government objectives, which were the objectives of the enterprise technocracy. However, a final victory over the banking system is no longer possible. The banking autonomy is supported right by the enterprise technocracy against the administrative bureaucracy. On the other hand, time worked here for the banks, allowing for the development and consolidation of a private banking sector. The result is that the banks and, with them, much of the financial technocracy, start leaving the camp opposed to the governance and become the most convenient ground for a compromise among the three main elites of the power – the enterprise technocracy, the administrative bureaucracy and the financial technocracy.

But not all offensives of the enterprise technocracy were fought through the administration and the executive. Actually, its most important victory was won not with the support of the administrative bureaucracy but against it. It was the taking over of the control of the State

Property Fund and the deviation of its functionality. The SPF was built precisely in order to introduce the industrial enterprises into another financial circuit that the one tied to payments (of raw and auxiliary materials, salaries, interests, etc.), that should allow for moving the center of decision about what is happening in the enterprise from the technical managers of the productive process to the holders of the capital based on which the enterprise was operating. Such a process was obviously directed against the enterprise technocracy. According to the law, the SPF held 70 per cent of the capital of the enterprises that were owned by the state and were not public corporations. Therefore, the SPF was vital for anyone who wanted to share the power in Romania. In broad lines, the SPF meant to transfer the state economy from the administrative bureaucracy's control to the control of whoever would come to control the SPF. In the beginning, the financial technocracy, that had advanced the project, had obviously reserved the SPF leadership for itself but, taking advantage of the political victory won, the enterprise technocracy took over its control and used it mainly for three things. First, in order to delay the privatization until it would manage to devise a form of privatization less destructive for itself. Second, in order to redistribute the capital gathered from all over the economy to the end of keeping the industry in function. Third, in order to counter the pressure tied to the micro-economic restructuring according to principles concerning the characteristics of production. About these purposes, it should be explained that the financial technocracy did not oppose the privatization or rendering the enterprises profitable, just as it was not against the economic reform in principle. It only opposed the forms of privatizing and rendering the enterprises profitable that would have led to a diminution of its own role in the economy and to the ascent of other categories, including the industrial technocracy.

A real battle was fought about the SPF among the various components of the industrial technocracy. Once the financial technocracy eliminated from the competition, the battle was mainly fought between the government bureaucracy, that courted for a long while the idea of having the SPF subordinated to the government, as it had courted the idea of having the National Bank subordinated to the government, and the enterprise technocracy, that saw in the SPF the opportunity no longer to depend on the administration for the industry's adjustment. Eventually, even the ruling party joined in the battle, since it saw the SPF control as the best guarantee of a permanent and unconditional political support given by the enterprise technocracy. The future of the SPF is still uncertain. But in the meanwhile, the enterprise technocracy tried to settle the problem of privatization. The solution endorsed mainly consisted of dissipating the property so that the owners should no longer make up centers of decision and control of the enterprise. The first method used to that end was MEBO. It was the more favored as the new owners, the enterprise's employees, were also directly subordinated to the technocracy through the productive process. The proposal then came of amending the privatization law so as to achieve some sort of generalized MEBO. Two purposes were pursued. One was to annul the advantage obtained by the financial technocracy that, after the issuance of the property vouchers, had promoted an intense trade in such vouchers and had accumulated impressive amounts itself. The other one was to narrow as much as could the access of the financial technocracy and of the private sector to the shares.

To employ the privatization legislation in order to get a decisive advantage in the competition among elites was not only the enterprise technocracy's idea. Some time before, the financial technocracy too, had tried the same thing. The proposal had been to amend the privatization law in such a way as to have the privatization proceed entirely through equities negotiated in the market or employed by investors. The model was an imitation of the Chechoslovak one – the privatization in the Czech Republic was considered a big success – and it was strongly supported by the international institutions' experts. A visit by the relevant Czech minister who outlined to the Romanian premier his country's experience, a documentary movie about privatization in the Czech Republic, shown on the national TV, and the promotion by the Romanian President's aides of that solution as a way to deblock the privatization in Romania, were as far as the project could advance. Obviously, it was not endorsed. But the financial technocracy's initiative, although supported by the government, did not seem to have more chances of success by the end of 1994, because of political complications. The privatization continued to be one of the enterprise technocracy's unsettled problems and as long as it remained unsettled it was a basis for the potential competitors to the power system.

The SPF was a stronghold of the enterprise technocracy not only because it secured its interests in the privatization process, but also because it helped controlling the enterprises' micro-economic restructuring. Obviously, the enterprises' restructuring is a necessity and a priority, but the big problem is how to do it. For, through restructuring one can radically change the balance of forces both inside the enterprise, between the economic bureaucracy and the technocracy tied to the productive process, and between the enterprise and the institutions that ensure its capital and its connections with the market. The launching of a vast restructuring drive was decided under the pressure of the international financial and political institutions, especially of the World Bank – that is releasing an important loan for restructuring – and of the IMF, that conditioned the stand-by loan agreement for the passage to micro-economic restructuring. The first problem was who should coordinate the action – the government or the SPF. It was the government that had concluded the agreement with the IMF and had committed itself to set up a government institution to run the restructuring – the Restructuring Agency. Here too, more problems emerged, because at least two ministries competed for the coordination of the restructuring – the Reform Council, because restructuring was a component of the economic reform, and the Industries Ministry, because after all it was about the restructuring of the industrial enterprises.

But, for the enterprise technocracy, the government was an institution far less secure than the SPF. The government was vulnerable as regarded the internal and external pressures. A government reshuffle might change not only the composition but also the policy of the government in some domains, and the restructuring was far too important to be left without a guidance. So, the SPF, which after all was the main owner of the whole industry – except for the public corporations -, refused to yield the control of the restructuring. The result was an as confusing as inefficient formula. The government set up a Restructuring Agency because it had formally committed itself to do so. In order to reconcile all parties at least at a government level, it was subordinated to the Reform Council, but it was placed in the Industries Ministry. For all its name, that Agency would not restructure anything. It only draws up restructuring surveys, probing the enterprises that will be restructured and advancing recommendations as to the changes that ought to be operated. The restructuring proper is still the territory of the SPF, which has set up its own restructuring department for which the Agency's schemes are not mandatory. They are taken as mere suggestions.

So, through the agency of the SPF, the enterprise technocracy controls the whole industry and more than that. The SPF is the main owner of the state enterprises and it makes all major decisions about privatization and restructuring. Its unrestricted management of the industrial enterprises, in close association with the union leaders where the unions are strong, and in disregard of the unions where they are feeble, and the close ties to the local and central administration secure its control of the population and the state's support. The financial technocracy is either defeated or cooperative, whereas in the relations with the private sector the cooperation is prevalent. The political support provided by the PSDR and its allies is secure and useful. Finally, the change in the international political strategies in the Balkans and East Europe is about to mend the only really feeble point of its power system – the lack of foreign support. By the end of 1993, the enterprise technocracy had conquered the power for good and started to govern Romania, bracing itself for the 1996 elections. The system was finally consolidated and it started to produce and to apply its own implicit policies – the policies of underdevelopment.

INDEX

DATE DUE

OC 07 '03			

Demco, Inc. 38-293